THE EVOLUTION OF
GREEN POLITICS

Development and Change within
European Green Parties

JON BURCHELL

Earthscan Publications Limited
London · Sterling, VA

First published in the UK and USA in 2002 by
Earthscan Publications Ltd

ISBN: 1 85383 752 0 paperback
       1 85383 751 2 hardback

Typesetting by JS Typesetting Ltd, Wellingborough, Northants
Printed and bound by Creative Print and Design (Wales), Ebbw Vale
Cover design by Yvonne Booth

For a full list of publications please contact:

Earthscan Publications Ltd
120 Pentonville Road
London, N1 9JN, UK
Tel: +44 (0)20 7278 0433
Fax: +44 (0)20 7278 1142
Email: earthinfo@earthscan.co.uk
http://www.earthscan.co.uk

A catalogue record for this book is available from the British Library
Library of Congress Cataloging-in-Publication Data

Burchell, Jon, 1970–.
    The evolution of green politics : development and change within European
    Green Parties / Jon Burchell.
        p. cm.
     ISBN 1-85383-752-0 (pbk.) – ISBN 1-85383-751-2 (hardback)
       1. Political parties–Europe. 2. Green movement–Europe. 3. Environmental
    policy–Europe. I. Title.

JN94.A979 B87 2002
324.24'087–dc21

                                                                2202012950

22883 Quicksilver Drive, Sterling, VA 20166–2012, USA

Earthscan is an editorially independent subsidiary of Kogan Page Ltd and
publishes in association with WWF-UK and the International Institute for
Environment and Development

Contents

List of Tables and Figures

TABLES

FIGURES

List of Acronyms and Abbreviations

BSE	bovine spongiform encephalopathy
CNIR	Conseil National Inter-Regional
EP	European Parliament
EU	European Union
FDP	Free Democrats
GE	*Génération Écologie*
GM	genetically modified
GNP	gross national product
MEI	*Mouvement Ecologistes Independent*
MEP	Member of the European Parliament
MfSS	'Manifesto for a Sustainable Society'
MP	Member of Parliament
NATO	North Atlantic Treaty Organization
POS	political opportunity structure
PS	*Parti Socialiste*
SPD	Social Democrats
UK	United Kingdom
US	United States

Acknowledgements

I would like to thank all those Green party activists and members in the UK, France and Sweden who took the time to talk to me and provided me with invaluable information without which this book would have been significantly weakened. In particular, I'd like to thank Niclas Malmberg for helping to arrange my interviews in Sweden, and the party members in Sweden and France who tolerated both my very poor French and complete ignorance of Swedish. Particular thanks go to Mike Kenny, for his guidance in the initial development of this research, and to Elizabeth Bomberg, Larry Wilde and Mark Williams for their help and advice.

My thanks also go to my family and friends who put up with my moaning and gave me a great deal of support. In particular Joe, Jarvis and Konker, without whom the whole experience would have been a whole lot harder, and Ann and Peter for their continued support. Thanks, also, to all of the politics staff at John Moores for letting me have time to work on this, and the students who have accepted my disorganization and distraction without too much complaint!

This book is dedicated to my grandmother, Joan Knott, and to Malcolm Vout, both of whom died before I finished this project.

Introduction

The emergence of Green parties throughout Europe during the 1980s marked the arrival of a 'new' form of political movement and a challenge to existing models of party activism and organization. The Greens were distinguished from other established party families by their ecologically oriented disposition, an anti-professional, participatory and decentralized attitude towards party organization, and a close link to the new social movements of the 1960s and 1970s. This challenge to conventional party politics was reflected within an emerging set of political science literature, examining the structural and institutional processes thought to underlie Green party development, the identification of distinguishing characteristics among the 'new' parties and an analysis of conflict and change within the Green parties themselves. The electoral successes of a number of these parties during the late 1980s took this challenge a stage further, as Greens broke electoral thresholds and gained parliamentary representation in countries such as Germany, Belgium and Sweden.

While the 1980s represented a period of breakthrough for the Greens, the 1990s presented an altogether different set of challenges. Green parties confronted serious difficulties in trying to solidify their electoral successes in the face of stiff opposition and the incorporation of Green issues by other long-standing political parties. The electoral successes of the late 1980s were replaced by electoral disappointments in the 1990s, accompanied by debilitating internal disputes. This process was most clearly documented in Germany where *Die Grünen*, having burst onto the political scene in a wave of publicity in the 1980s, found itself ravaged by internal disputes and factional conflict, and were rejected by the electorate in the first all-German federal elections in 1990.

Green parties in Europe have since undergone a significant process of reassessment resulting in substantial change: programmatic, organizational and strategic. This internal reassessment has been accompanied by an upturn in the Greens' electoral fortunes. In many cases, Green parties appear to be coming of age and are beginning to seek roles in government coalitions, such as in France, Germany and Finland. However, critics question at what price this transformation has occurred. In particular, it is argued that the process of development and change within the Greens, and their acceptance into coalition government marks the final institutionalization of the 'new politics' parties into the party establishment.

Despite the clear significance of this period for both the Green parties and for the future shape of European party systems, little analytical research has been devoted to providing a detailed understanding of this process of transformation within the European Greens. To date, no comparative studies have sought to analyse this period in depth and identify the challenges that face these parties in the coming years. Green party analysis has been successful in identifying the distinctive characteristics that initially shaped the development of the Greens. However, it has often viewed these parties in relative isolation from the wider political arena. In doing so, not enough attention has been paid to interpreting development and change in relation to the pressures placed upon any small political party struggling to gain a foothold within a competitive party environment. This book demonstrates that an improved understanding of the transformations in Green party politics and a clearer insight into their emerging political role can be gained through such a synthesis of existing approaches.

This book presents an in-depth, thematic, comparative approach to the analysis of Green party development and change, questioning whether the process of Green party evolution has resulted in the ideological dilution of Green ideals and objectives. Do Green parties still represent an alternative 'new politics' stance encapsulating the anti-party sentiments of the new social movements, or does Green party development represent the incorporation of the Green challenge within the established party systems of Western Europe? In tackling these questions, the book presents two primary innovations within the study of development and change among the European Green parties. Firstly, it demonstrates that a clearer understanding of the experiences of development and change can be gained by refining existing approaches to Green party analysis via a more effective incorporation of analytical tools utilized within political science research into more long-standing political parties. In particular, the research highlights the importance of viewing Green parties as subject to many of the same pressures and challenges facing other small parties active within the competitive party systems of Western Europe.

In focusing upon the 'party' dimension, the study incorporates the role of the 'external political environment' as a key factor in examining the pressures for change within Green parties. The analysis presents a picture of Green party development and change which balances internal pressures concerning the specific characteristics and style of the Greens, with external pressures emerging from the systemic context within which the parties are forced to compete. The study therefore incorporates both the distinctive dimensions of the Greens and the broader pressures and barriers facing political parties that influence their development and change.

The second innovative dimension lies with the comparative framework utilized within the book. Previous analysis of Green parties has primarily adopted two approaches. One approach has focused upon an analysis of individual case studies, a significant proportion of which has centred upon the German Green party, *Die Grünen*. The second approach involves the collation of a broad group of self-standing case studies which, while providing an expansive picture of Green party activity across Europe, has resulted in little detailed comparative analysis. Rather than presenting a group of self-standing case studies, this book focuses upon a thematic comparative discussion. The empirical chapters provide a comparative examination of Green party development within the spheres of party organization, policy and relationships with competitors.

The comparative analysis demonstrates the changing roles of the European Green parties and, in doing so, demonstrates the complexity, diversity and changing prioritization of party goals as the parties have evolved into their surroundings. Utilizing Harmel and Janda's (1994) definition of party goals as a guide, the analysis focuses upon an assessment of three primary goals. The first is the ability of the parties to gain votes and, subsequently, parliamentary representation. By definition, this is a key objective of any political party, distinguishing it from a pressure group. The second is the advocation of a specific set of interests or an ideology, in this case ecological issues. The final dimension is the implementation of party democracy, emphasizing the Greens' commitment to a new style of politics which challenges the conventional party political styles and structures, and emphasizes participation and direct democracy.

As already mentioned, the success of the German Greens resulted in an extensive analytical focus on the party, with *Die Grünen* becoming almost a model for Green party development. Change and division within the European Green parties has subsequently often been described and analysed on the basis of the German experience, as a dispute between moderate and fundamentalist factions, utilizing the 'realo–fundis' terminology adopted by *Die Grünen*. While this approach has provided a useful initial starting point for examining Green party development and, in particular, conflict and division within the parties, closer inspection reveals that this analysis has often served to obscure more than it reveals.

As this study demonstrates, the Greens are far from homogeneous, and the experiences of other parties highlights additional pressures sometimes neglected within the German Greens. For this reason, while the experiences of the German Greens are used as a guide, greater attention is devoted to the experiences of three other Green parties in this study. The analysis focuses upon the experiences of *Miljöpartiet de Gröna* in Sweden, *Les Verts* in France and the Green party in the UK.[1] The Green parties selected have developed under markedly different circumstances and have undergone significant transformations. These processes of reform have occurred under varying conditions and with fluctuating levels of internal debate. Within the context of traditional Green party analysis, these three parties represent useful case studies for examining whether traditional classifications remain a valid basis for Green party analysis.

With Green parties across Europe experiencing a significant upturn in support in recent years, the current period marks an important stage in the shaping of Green politics across Europe. In order to gain a clearer picture of the impact that the Green parties may have in the new millennium, one must understand the issues and themes that have shaped their re-emergence as a more mature political challenge. The process of transformation therefore represents a key milestone in the evolution of the European Green parties and highlights the pressures placed upon alternative parties by the confines and restraints of competitive European party systems.

The book begins by setting out the theoretical context to the comparative research, both in terms of 'Green' theory, Green party research and more traditional party analysis. Chapter 1 examines existing accounts of Green party ideology, conflict and change by tracing the development of Green party research during the 1980s and 1990s. The chapter identifies an important connection between Green party analysis and the theoretical roots upon which much of this research has been based. It argues that these theoretical foundations have been influential in shaping the manner in which analysts have attempted to explain both the characteristics of Green parties and their experiences of development and change. In particular, it is claimed that the analytical roots within new social movement literature and Green political thought have contributed to an over-emphasis upon internal binary distinctions as an explanation for party change and party factionalism. A broader analytical framework is suggested, which not only focuses upon the parties' specific internal 'Green' characteristics, but also recognizes their role as competitive political 'parties'.

Chapter 2 focuses upon the development of this broader analytical framework and the creation of a more comprehensive analytical approach to examining Green party development and change. Focusing upon analysis of traditional party systems and the functioning of parties within these systems, the chapter highlights the influential role that is attributed to the 'external political environment'. Of particular note here is the claim that party development is subject to a balance between internal and external pressures. The chapter examines previous comparative models for assessing party change, examining work on party factionalism, party adaptation and the competitive pressures facing small parties. The chapter discusses Harmel and Janda's analytical framework for assessing party change, which highlights both the balance between internal and external pressures and the importance of party goals in stimulating and influencing party change. An analytical approach for the comparative analysis of development and change within the European Green parties is proposed, based upon a synthesis of many of the ideas and themes combined within both Green party analysis and the analytical models highlighted above.

Chapter 3 provides a contextualized picture of the history and development of the four case studies. In particular, the chapter focuses upon two main themes. It identifies the central party system characteristics within the four countries, providing a comparative assessment of the structural barriers that these systems present to the Green parties. In doing so, the comparison highlights the classifications of the party systems, the electoral mechanisms through which the systems are maintained and also an assessment of the opportunities available to small parties such as the Greens, under these conditions. The chapter then focuses more directly upon the parties themselves, presenting a comparative overview of the emergence and electoral performances of the Green parties within their respective systemic contexts.

Chapter 4 focuses upon Green party relationships with other parties. In particular, it addresses the role of the Greens as 'anti-party' parties and the parties' emphasis upon 'autonomy'. The chapter assesses the possible aims of Green party strategy in the light of claims that they represent a direct challenge to more long-standing styles of party political activism. Also, it assesses Green party attitudes towards the traditional 'left–right' political cleavage and the development of a 'neither left, nor right' ideological stance. How has Green party strategy evolved in the light of opportunities for coalitions and alliances with other parties? The chapter examines changes to the Green parties' approaches to these issues and questions whether the changes identified represent a distinctive alteration to their ideological commitments.

Chapter 5 focuses upon the organizational structures of the Green parties and the reforms to these structures introduced over recent years. The prioritization of decentralist, participatory and 'anti-professionalist' organization has been identified as a core commitment within European Green parties. The study examines the initial organizational structures and their connection to these ideological commitments. It then assesses the processes of organizational reform undertaken within the Green parties, the level of internal conflicts and debates that surrounded these developments, and the nature of the organizational reforms introduced. Again, the analysis questions the extent to which the organizational reforms are representative of a distinctive shift away from the parties' commitments to the ideals of 'new politics'.

Chapter 6 focuses more directly upon the Green parties' attempts to influence policy direction and to represent (and, where possible, implement) Green ideas and commitments. The chapter begins by assessing Green party policy priorities during the 1980s, before analysing changes and developments during the 1990s. As well as emphasizing the difficulties in accurately assessing the 'true' policies of any political party, the chapter highlights the value of distinguishing between different aspects of party policy. In particular, it raises a distinction between the core values of a party and the policy issues and policy priorities that are emphasized within party manifestos and electoral programmes. The chapter focuses upon the distinction between 'social' and 'natural' environmental issues and the claim that policy development within the Green parties marks a process of ideological dilution. It assesses the validity of the 'social–natural' distinction as an accurate portrayal of differing approaches to Green party policy and asks whether these dimensions are not merely two sides of the same 'Green' coin.

Chapter 7 presents an overview of the patterns of development and change within the Green parties and summarizes the key issues raised through the thematic comparative analysis. In what ways has our understanding of Green parties been improved by such a detailed empirical study? Furthermore, how can this analysis help us to predict the future developments of not only the four case studies examined here, but also the broad range of European Green parties? The chapter assesses the contribution made by this analytical approach to a clearer understanding of Green party goals and the changing experiences of the 'new politics' parties as they evolve from their initial structures of the early 1980s. Does the pattern represent a weakening of ideological commitments to key Green principles, or is the process more reflective of a practical adaptation to the pressures of being a political party functioning within a competitive political environment? How should one perceive the continuing development of the European Green parties?

The empirical analysis in this study is based upon information gained from a broad range of sources. Access to the parties themselves provided an important resource and is reflected within much of the detailed discussion of both party development and change, and the context within which these changes took place. Interviews were conducted with national party activists; however, while these provided an interesting cross-section of attitudes towards the changes within the parties, there are obviously limitations to their use. The accuracy of personal recollection and activists' vested interests in proceedings must be considered when utilizing these sources. The information gained from these interviews has therefore been used to reflect and support issues raised during the study, rather than providing the primary source of empirical investigation.

Printed official documentation was also made available by the parties during this period, including newsletters, programmes, conference proceedings and strategy papers and debates.[2] Interviews were also conducted with party experts and academics. Again, these discussions provided invaluable contextual information, as well as aiding in the development of the theoretical approach adopted within this study.

In addition to direct contact, the emergence of the internet as a key resource cannot be overstated. All four Green parties maintain detailed party websites that provide party histories and outline party ideological beliefs and commitments, as well as detailed party policy. In addition, the development of numerous Green discussion forums provides access to debates within the individual parties, as well as wider debates across Europe. The remainder of the material has been collated from more traditional secondary sources.

Chapter 1

A 'New' Challenge to Party Politics? Analysing Green Party Development and Change

What makes Green parties so distinctive and why should the fact that they are changing represent a challenge to our understanding and perception of them? This chapter examines the development of Green party research in order to provide answers to these questions. In doing so, it will argue that while the ideological roots of the Green parties have played a significant role in our identification of them as a 'new' form of party politics, they have also influenced the parameters through which analysts have assessed their development. This can clearly be identified within attempts to classify the distinctiveness of Green parties and in theoretical attempts to explain their rapid emergence. However, more recent changes and conflicts within the Greens have forced us to re-evaluate our understanding of these parties. In so doing, our previous frames of reference only provide partial explanations, such as those provided by 'realo–fundis'-style factional divisions. Hence, it is argued that while there exists an accurate assessment of the emergence and classification of Green parties, analysis must be expanded further in order to understand the patterns of change witnessed throughout the 1990s, and the implications for future Green party development.

IDENTIFYING THE IDEOLOGICAL ROOTS OF THE EUROPEAN GREEN PARTIES

The Green parties' distinctiveness is clearly reflected in their ideological roots. These can be traced predominantly to two key processes.

The first is the emergence of the new social movements of the 1960s and 1970s and the 'unconventional' style of activism that surrounded these protests. The second is the expansion of eco-philosophy and the emergence of a new wave of green political thought. By briefly examining these two dimensions, one can identify key analytical themes and debates from within these spheres that have been influential in shaping the perception and interpretation of Green parties and Green party activity as a form of 'new politics'.

The New Social Movements

The new social movement activism of the 1960s and 1970s represented a radical and distinctive break from previous forms of political activism, and provided an initial home for many of the instigators of Green party development during the 1980s.[1] Many of the distinguishing features of Green parties are thought to reflect a commitment to the ideals and principles that emerged from within the new social movements. Theoretical explanations for the development and distinctiveness of these movements, therefore, provide an influential starting point in tracing analytical models of Green party formation and activity.

In the US, research into the social movement activism surrounding the civil rights campaigns and, later, the student and environmental movements of the 1960s and 1970s, focused upon the 'efficiency' of movement organizations. The basis of social movement activism, it was argued, lay not with the emergence of new conflicts and interests in society but the ability of movement organizations to mobilize resources.[2] Social movements could influence policy through the mobilization of a broader range of resources than those available to conventional political bodies, enabling them to pursue their goals through informal and unconventional methods, as well as through more traditional routes (Gladwin, 1994, p60). A movement's success, it was argued, reflected how well resources were utilized and the extent to which established institutions were aware of the importance of the movement's aims.

Critics of resource mobilization, however, argued that too much emphasis was placed upon the movement's organization, with little insight into why individuals sought to join or why these groups had suddenly risen to prominence. Gladwin, for example, criticizes resource mobilization approaches for:

> ...*normalizing the anti-institutional and anti-systemic aspects of social movements and under-theorizing those goals which relate to thoroughgoing social and cultural transformation* (Gladwin, 1994, p63).

The rationality of the resource mobilization approach is also identified as a contradiction to the specific and distinctive anti-systemic character of the social movements. Cohen (1985) argues that through its emphasis on the 'rational actor' it neglects other influences that are significant to the creation of these new movements:

> *It is necessary to analyse those aspects of experience that shape the interpretation of interests individual and collective, and affect the very capacity of actors to form groups and mobilize* (Cohen, 1985, p688).

A more European approach to new social movements, by contrast, focused upon the dimensions neglected within resource mobilization. Marcuse (1969), for example, identified a style of activism within these movements which, he claimed, entails something other than strategic or instrumental rationality (Cohen, 1985, p691).[3] Inglehart (1990) linked the development of new social movements to value priorities and socio-economic change, claiming that an adherence to 'post-materialist values' lay at the heart of these new movements (Inglehart, 1990, p45). In particular, he identified a shift away from the traditional concern with class conflict and material wealth and towards a greater concern for 'belonging, esteem and the realization of one's intellectual and aesthetic potential' (Inglehart, 1979, p308).[4] New values and new goals, he claimed, resulted in the adoption of different styles of political action.

Touraine (1985) links the development of new social movements to the search for alternative forms of social and cultural life, arguing that recent changes represent a reorganization of the relationship between society, state and the economy, with new movements the potential bearers of new social interests. Emphasizing the importance of their spontaneity of action and their anti-institutional characteristics, Touraine is sceptical of the value of movement organizations, fearing that they can destroy the creativity and vitality of a movement. Habermas also highlights a new focus for conflict based around issues such as cultural reproduction, social integration and socialization. He argues that it is no longer possible for these conflicts to be channelled through traditional parties and organizations as they are ill suited and often unprepared to tackle such issues. New social movements, therefore, provide an outlet for these conflicts and a defence against the encroachment of state and economy on society (Habermas, 1981, p35). In maintaining this position, Habermas argues, it is vital that the movements remain committed to the ideals of grassroots, horizontal control and the restriction of organizational growth.

Building upon these concepts, Melucci describes the movements as displaying a multidimensional character incorporating a 'plurality

of perspectives, meanings and relationships' (Melucci, 1989, p25).[5]
They function within a new 'political space' between state and society,
from which they can:

> *...make society hear their messages and translate these*
> *messages into political decision-making while the move-*
> *ments maintain their autonomy* (Melucci, 1985, p815).

This aspect is identified as an important element of what exactly is
'new' about these groups. New social movements seek to reveal
fundamental problems within a given area. As such, the social movements have an indirect effect, seeking influence over the central issues
and concerns of modern society. They develop grassroots, informal and
'hidden' forms of organization, and their strength lies in their ability
to stimulate radical questions about the ends of personal and social life.
Through their unique style of activism, Melucci argues, they are able
to 'announce to society that something "else" is possible' (Melucci,
1985, p812).

From this brief summary it is possible to identify some of the key
features that distinguish this 'new' form of social movement activism
from its more traditional predecessors: features that are reflected
within Green party analysis. Firstly, new social movements are seen to
represent a new social paradigm, contrasting with the dominant goal
structure of modern industrial society (Kuechler and Dalton, 1990,
p10). Emphasis is placed upon 'quality-of-life' issues rather than
personal wealth and material well-being, leading to a focus upon social
and collective values surrounding, among other things, issues such as
the environment and women's rights. While it is true to say that
feminist, ecological and peace movements all have a long history of
activism before the 1960s, what has changed is the value that society
places on these issues and the manner in which this has been channelled through the new social movements.

Organizational structure represents another defining characteristic
– in particular, the notion that form is as vital an element as substance.
Significant emphasis is placed upon moving away from traditional
structures in favour of more decentralized, open democratic organizations. A final key distinction is the identification of the role of conflict.
Whether viewed in terms of class conflict, 'old' versus 'new' values or
conflict between state intervention and society, new social movements
challenge the expansion of the modern state and highlight the contradictions that state interventions generate. This conflict helps to
explain the apolitical nature and non-institutional character of the
social movements.

The Influence of 'Ecologism'

The distinctiveness of Green parties, however, does not rest purely upon their representation of the new social movements. Green parties, by definition, represent a new political challenge that places issues of environmental protection at the top of the political agenda. The parties are, therefore, identified not only as vehicles for new social movement protest, but also as a voice for the newly emerging issues and debates surrounding both 'environmentalism' and 'ecologism'. This combination provides Green parties with an ideological basis that is clearly distinct from other political parties.

Although many of the ideas and concepts of ecologism, arguably, have quite a lengthy history, its ideological development is usually recognized as a relatively recent phenomenon. Dobson identifies it as:

> *...the accidental conjunction of circumstances, individuals and events in the 1970s which has provided a dynamic refocus for the ecological vocabulary* (Dobson, 1990, p215).

This recent wave of development is reflected in a surge of literature during the 1960s and 1970s concerning the nature of human development and its impact upon the environment.[6] At the heart of ecologism lies a critique of the nature and processes of modern industrial society. The cornerstones of this critique are the claims that modern society must reassess many of its core values and recognize the natural limits that exist to both economic and population growth. The continual emphasis upon growth within modern industrial society leads to the neglect of this limited capacity to the detriment of the environment.

The inability of modern society to recognize and react to this imbalance results from attitudes instilled within modern industrialism, which seeks to justify humans' present role as controlling and domineering nature. Continued emphasis upon the free market, it is argued, instils within society a strong commitment to the principles of competitiveness and individualism, while modern technological developments support the process of domination over nature. Green theory identifies significant dangers in accepting this paradigm of modern industrial society:

> *Growth-orientated economies cannot go on using finite resources. Technological innovations cannot solve the problems indefinitely, although appropriate small-scale technologies are seen as one aspect of the solution. Technological advances can only postpone the problems* (Vincent, 1992, p232).

The roots of ecologism, therefore, lie in a reaction against mechanistic science and what is seen as human attempts to dominate nature through technological development. It seeks a new relationship with nature based more upon cooperation and consideration, rather than domination. Achieving this new relationship necessarily entails a radical overhaul of modern industrial society and the ideologies and politics upon which this system is currently based.

One approach to this problem has been the concept of the 'sustainable society'. This model directly challenges the problems of continuous economic growth and provides for wider and more profound forms of fulfilment than those offered by modern society's focus upon the consumption of material objects (Dobson, 1990, p18). Sustainable living requires a re-education of society based upon consuming less and producing for basic needs on a self-sufficiency basis.[7] Ecological models also place great emphasis upon the importance of local organization, active participation and the development of self-governing communities – all of which, it is claimed, help to strengthen relationships and remove society's current emphasis on competitiveness and individualism. In addition, greater local autonomy arguably increases the likelihood of individuals becoming responsible agents within the social sphere.

While the discussion thus far implies a common core to Green political thought, these ideas represent key features of a very disparate literature, within which there are significant conflicts and debates. These debates primarily surround the identification of a central binary division between 'deep' ecology, centred upon the concept of ecocentrism, and a 'shallow' anthropocentric approach. The impact of this dichotomy has had far-reaching implications, not only for the development of Green political thought but also for the subsequent analysis of development and change within Green parties.

'Deep' ecology questions the assumption that places human welfare above that of all other species. Its focus is predominantly ecocentric, endowing all species of life on Earth with intrinsic value.[8] The principle of biospheric equality sees humans as being on an equal level with all other things, rather than being their masters. Naess (1973), for example, argues that humans' capacity for freedom depends upon this process of identification with external forces – in particular, the natural world. Merchant similarly argues that people must realize that they have a duty to maintain the integrity of the ecosphere (Merchant, 1992, p87).[9] Humans, therefore, represent merely one part of the wider ecosphere, dependent upon a balanced relationship with the rest of nature for continued survival.

In contrast, an alternative form of 'social' ecology can also be identified, based upon a 'light' or 'shallow' Green anthropocentrism.[10]

The distinction between ecocentrism and anthropocentrism is seen as less influential in this case. Humans' relationship with nature is identified as one where:

> *Humans may play the role of managers of natural pro-*
> *cesses as long as they act only to enable the natural and*
> *diverse evolution of organisms within the biospherical*
> *community* (Kenny, 1994, p240).

From this perspective, it is argued, there is a greater tendency to believe that the natural world only has value because humans themselves place a value upon it. This does not necessarily imply a lessening of the importance of nature. Rather, it highlights why preservation is so important for society. Vincent suggests that:

> *Nature can be an early warning system for us in terms of*
> *impending ecological disaster; it supports and nourishes*
> *us; we can do valuable experiments on it which can pro-*
> *long and improve the quality of our lives; we can exercise,*
> *admire, relax in ... and be aesthetically moved by its*
> *beauty* (Vincent, 1993, p255).

The identification of nature in terms of human values enables people to understand the significance that its maintenance holds for human society. While not extending the concept of 'value' as far as deep ecology, the recognition of the relationship between humans and nature clearly places this approach beyond more traditional anthropocentric perspectives that focus largely upon exploiting nature for human ends.

These distinctions are also evident among theorists who seek to provide a precise classification of what it means to be 'Green'. Hence, a similar dichotomy can be identified in theoretical distinctions between what is perceived to be a 'true' deep Green approach to environmental issues, in contrast to a weaker 'light' Green compromise. Dobson, for example, distinguishes between 'ecologism' and 'environmentalism', arguing that this distinction is necessary to provide a clearer understanding of Green political theory:

> *If we confuse Green politics (capital G) with either con-*
> *servationism or environmentalism (the latter being green*
> *with a small g) then we severely distort and misunder-*
> *stand the nature of the Green challenge* (Dobson, 1990,
> p4).

'Environmentalism' is thus identified as a managerial approach to environmental issues, whereas 'ecologism' seeks to radically alter the nature of our relationship with the natural world. Similar classifications and divisions are also evident in alternative dichotomous terminology such as 'dark' and 'light', 'deep' and 'shallow'.[11] At the heart of all these classifications, however, lies what Young described as 'the great divide' (Young, 1992, p14). The basis of this 'divide' rests with the assumption that authentic or 'true' Green politics is understood as 'deep' and must be based upon ecocentric motivations. All other Green activity, by definition, is classed as 'shallow' (Barry, 1994, p370).

GREEN PARTIES AS A 'NEW' FORM OF POLITICAL CHALLENGE

The ideological roots of the European Green parties have thus been closely related to both the actions and development of a new form of social movement protest since the 1960s, and the emergence of an ecological critique of modern industrial society, which highlights the environmental dangers posed by continuous growth. Both dimensions are part of a process resulting in a 'new' form of political activism. Social movement literature highlights a challenge to traditional, established political channels which involves not only the emergence of new issues and issue priorities, but also encompasses a new style of social protest based upon greater participation and alternative forms of organization and action. Ecologism, too, represents a radical challenge to the established principles and priorities of modern industrial society: one in which the need to change our relationship with nature results in a significant alteration in societal values and concerns.

Green parties have been identified as an emerging party political vehicle for many of these ideals and concepts. As such, analytical approaches to the study of Green parties have looked to both Green political theory and new social movement research for analytical tools. It is no surprise, therefore, to find that many of the ideas and concepts highlighted above are reflected in this analysis – both in terms of the central ideological commitments of these parties and the nature and style of party activism and organization.

Explaining the Formation and Development of Green Parties

Several theoretical approaches have attempted to examine and explain the process of Green party formation and the subsequent success or failure of Green parties as political organizations. A common thread throughout is the claim that Green parties mark the rise of a 'new' political cleavage. Kitschelt, for example, suggests that a combination of underlying structural change and 'favourable political opportunity structures' have resulted in the emergence of a new style of 'left-libertarian' political party (Kitschelt, 1988a, p197).[12] Such parties are most evident in countries with advanced welfare states, strong labour corporatism and regular participation of left-wing parties in government. New 'post-industrial' demands are constrained through established political channels, requiring the development of 'new political vehicles' to pursue these aims (Kitschelt, 1988a, p234).[13] In addition to these conditions, their emergence also requires the presence of rational actors in order to respond to the possibilities offered for the development of a new political party.[14]

Kitschelt claims that the motivating forces behind 'left-libertarian' parties reflect new social movement commitments and ideals.[15] The parties are thus critical of modern societal development and 'the institutions that underlie the post-war compromise between capital and labour in industrial societies' (Kitschelt, 1988a, p195). An ecological dimension is also evident, as 'left-libertarian' parties are seen to oppose the prioritization of economic growth over non-materialist concerns and attack patterns of policy-making that restrict democratic participation to 'elite bargaining among centralized interest groups and party leaders' (Kitschelt, 1988a, p195).

Müller-Rommel similarly identifies the 'perceived lack of responsiveness' from political institutions to the issues raised by new social movements as a major factor in the emergence of a new breed of political party (Müller-Rommel, 1990, p211). He also identifies 'new politics' parties as the political representatives of new social movements, but disagrees with Kitschelt that this signifies a change in the central political cleavage. Rather, the parties are 're-patterning' the traditional established party systems by 'adding a "new" conflict dimension to the "old" party system cleavage structure' (Müller-Rommel, 1990, p229).

Rüdig's (1990) research focuses more heavily upon the ecological dimension to Green party analysis. He again focuses upon changing cleavage structures as an explanation for Green party formation and development, but highlights an imbalance in other approaches:

Why is it that most social scientists analysing Green parties regard the 'ecological' identity of these parties as irrelevant, unimportant or, at best, as marginal? There seems to be a consensus that somehow they cannot be what they appear to be, that their appearance as ecological parties

*has to be a manifestation of some other social force which
is totally unconnected to the material content of their
demands* (Rüdig, 1990, p16).

While Rüdig accepts the connections between Green party formation,
the development of new social movements and the failure of established
political channels to incorporate new concerns, he argues that these
concepts do not fully explain why the new parties should define their
identity in terms of ecological problems (Rüdig, 1990, p29). Although
value change and social structure act as 'facilitators' for the development of new parties, Rüdig claims that the primary explanation for
their development has been the emergence of a specific 'ecological
cleavage'. Thus the 'emergence and politicization of environmental
problems' represents the key factor in accounting for the emergence
of these new parties (Rüdig, 1990, p31). Despite these differences,
however, explanations for the emergence of the Green parties clearly
have their roots located in the literature outlined earlier.

Green Party Classification

As with party formation, certain key characteristics have been attributed to Green parties, distinguishing them from their more traditional
counterparts. Kitschelt (1990, p185) identifies three such features:

- weak commitment mechanisms binding the activists to the parties,
  reflected in both limited levels of party membership and activism;
- a rejection of traditional, bureaucratic party organization in favour
  of a decentralized and horizontally coordinated mobilization of
  activists; and
- an emphasis upon collective decision-making and greater participation.[16]

Kitschelt also found that left-libertarian party activists display similar
social backgrounds – predominantly young intellectuals and profes-
sionals holding salaried positions in education, health care and cultural
services, or those being educated to fill jobs in these areas (Kitschelt,
1990, p186).

Müller-Rommel also recognizes the importance of decentralization
and participatory organizational structures within his classification.
He identifies a common ideology based around concerns for equal
rights, strong ecological thinking, solidarity with the developing world
and demands for unilateral disarmament.[17] He suggests that the parties
share a similar electorate with 'characteristics which differ from those
of established parties' (Müller-Rommel, 1990, p218). Again, this

electorate is identified as primarily young, highly educated, middle class, with white-collar occupations.

Poguntke's classification provides a more detailed picture, but again focuses upon three central dimensions. He cites sets of characteristics reflective of the two studies above. This includes a distinctive, unconventional political style emphasizing participation and grassroots democracy and a distinctive electoral profile (Poguntke, 1989, p185).[18] Reflecting Rudig's arguments, however, he also identifies programmatic features that display a 'new politics' orientation based around ecology, individualism, leftism, the developing world, unilateral disarmament and participatory, direct democracy extended to all areas of society (Poguntke, 1989, p180).

Poguntke's approach is important here, as he utilizes this classification to distinguish between true 'new politics' parties and those that merely appear to incorporate new politics issues.[19] In particular, he draws a line between conservative 'conservation groups' and the more radical progressive parties, including the majority of Green parties, for whom 'ecologism inspired by the new politics can be seen as part of a wider phenomenon which implies a new design of society' (Poguntke, 1987, p86). This distinction is the first example in which we can identify the divisions between 'dark' and 'light' forms of Green politics mentioned earlier, utilized within analyses of the Green parties. He develops this distinction further when examining the conflicts and changes within the Green parties as they have grown and evolved.

A CHANGING PICTURE: GREEN PARTY EVOLUTION AS A CHALLENGE TO 'NEW POLITICS' CLASSIFICATIONS

While the 'new politics' characteristics identified above have clearly been a key aspect in explaining both the impetus for the development of the Green parties and their initial distinctive structure and political style, more recent developments force us to re-evaluate our existing perceptions of the Greens and Green party analysis. Since the wave of Green political activity of the late 1980s, many Green parties have changed both organizationally and in their strategic outlook. Within a number of parties, this process of re-evaluation has been accompanied by crippling internal division and conflict.

Have these more recent developments resulted in a radical change within the European Greens? If so, what implications does this have for our perception of Green parties as a distinctive and 'new' form of political challenge? How can one explain both the changes that have been witnessed in recent years and the internal conflicts and debates that have often surrounded them? These questions have been at the heart of Green party research in recent years. In attempting to tackle these questions, analysis has again returned to the Greens' ideological and theoretical roots to help understand what has been happening to the 'new politics' parties, and to explain the divisions that have emerged.

Poguntke's analysis identifies two subgroups within the Greens: moderates and fundamentalists (Poguntke, 1989, p191). While they share common goals, he argues that they differ strongly over strategy. In particular:

> *Whereas the Moderates believe in the eventual success of piecemeal reform, the Fundamentalists fear the pacifying and demobilizing effects of this strategy* (Poguntke, 1989, p191).

Poguntke suggests that parties who have emerged from within new social movements often reflect 'a deeply rooted suspicion of the state and an erosion of trust in formalized political procedures', which clearly inclines the party to a more fundamentalist stance (Poguntke, 1989, p192). He also suggests that the chance of electoral success and the existence of 'Left–Socialist' or 'Communist' parties within the political system may also influence their stance. While Poguntke only provides the distinction between moderates and fundamentalists as a tentative theoretical model to differentiate between competing factions, similar distinctions form the basis for many of the explanations for Green party conflict and change.

Kitschelt takes these divisions a stage further in his analysis of the Belgian and German Green parties, distinguishing between three groups of party activists who have been central in shaping the parties' strategic direction. He classifies these activists as ideologues, lobbyists and pragmatists. The first and third of these categorizations form the principal divisions within the parties (Kitschelt, 1988b, p134).[20] Ideologues are defined as:

> *Activists who have a broad and radical vision of party objectives. . . They derive great satisfaction from a party organization which anticipates the participatory reforms they would like to implement in society* (Kitschelt, 1988b, p131).

Ideologues often have a history of political activism within other left-libertarian organizations, such as new social movement groups, before joining Green parties. In contrast, pragmatists have a much less radical view of the party's goals:

> *They are also concerned with comprehensive programmes for social change and selective policy gains but conceive of them more as guidelines for an incremental change of society. They put little emphasis on the party's peculiar organizational form and are more concerned with its electoral performance* (Kitschelt, 1988b, p131).

Kitschelt argues that left-libertarian parties face numerous difficulties in attempting to function within modern party political systems. Many of these reflect the problems of introducing a new type of political party, based around alternative styles and objectives, into a system rooted in tradition and structure. Parties such as the Greens, who place great emphasis on participation and decentralization, face significant constraints in coping with the traditional patterns of electoral competition. Unlike new social movements, parties express substantive political demands but must also accumulate a power resource in votes, competing with others in a unique competitive setting. Kitschelt argues that to have any sort of future, the new parties must find a method of rendering the ideology and aspirations of their core supporters compatible with gaining sufficient electoral support to influence policy-making (Kitschelt, 1990, p181).

Kitschelt defines this dilemma as a problem of combining a 'logic of constituency representation' with a 'logic of party competition' (Kitschelt, 1988b, p131). Tackling this dilemma draws the two sub-groups of 'ideologues' and 'pragmatists' into debate and conflict. Party strategy and development are therefore influenced by the internal balance of power between these two groups. Where ideologues are able to control the party's leadership and direction, it will largely follow a 'logic of constituency representation'. By contrast, when pragmatists gain the upper hand, the party is more likely to look towards a 'logic of party competition' (Kitschelt, 1988b, p131).

Kitschelt's analysis identifies a division within these parties that is influential in determining their strategic direction. Although his comparative empirical analysis may face criticism concerning the restricted nature of the study, his identification of competing groups within these parties and the focus of their conflict has proved to be an influential insight.[21] Again, one can identify clear links with the 'deep' and 'shallow' scenario highlighted earlier. Furthermore, one can distinguish a primary role for the dual dimensions of commitments to both new social movement forms and the emergent themes of ecologism. For Kitschelt, conflict is focused around two different approaches to party development. One path involves maintaining a commitment to new social movement principles of decentralization and openness by following a 'logic of constituency representation'. The other involves a level of acceptance regarding the need to function effectively within traditional European party systems, which requires an alternative course, based upon following a 'logic of party competition'.

'REALOS AND FUNDIS': THE GERMAN GREENS AS A MODEL FOR UNDERSTANDING PARTY DEVELOPMENT AND CHANGE

The groundbreaking success of the Green breakthrough in Germany has resulted in the German Green party *Die Grünen* (later *Bundnis'90/ Die Grünen*, following German unification) becoming the focal point for a large proportion of the analytical research into Green parties. The party experienced an initial period of development and success, followed by a period of internal debates and conflict caused by, and reflected in, a series of disappointing electoral performances. It is not surprising, therefore, to discover that much of our current understanding of Green party division and change has emerged from the analysis of the experiences within *Die Grünen* during the 1980s and early 1990s.

Central to the German case, and later transposed onto other Green parties, has been the identification of an internal factional conflict between two groups, reflecting the divisions highlighted by Kitschelt, which became known as 'realos' and 'fundis'. The conflicts within *Die Grünen* encompassed many important facets of Green party ideology and identity. In particular, conflict centred around how the party should move forward or, as Markovits describes it, 'defining *Die Grünen's* optimal strategy' (Markovits and Gorski, 1993, p119). How was social change to be achieved? What role did parliament play in this and what relationship should exist between parliamentary and extra-parliamentary activity? Also, what relationship, if any, should exist between *Die Grünen* and the Social Democrats (SPD)? (Hulsberg, 1988, p141). It is around these issues that the clearest picture of 'realo' and 'fundis' stances are presented.

Realos advocated a move away from a mass-movement focus and towards parliamentary politics, emphasizing the role of alliance and compromise within Green party policy. Coalition, it was argued, represented the only practical way to challenge the German right, as well as providing a pragmatic way to introduce Green policies into the political arena (Hulsberg, 1988, p146). For the realos, therefore, the role of the party can be identified as one of parliamentary mediator for minority social movements. Achieving these objectives, however, implied major changes to the nature and style of *Die Grünen's* organization, as Frankland highlights:

> *The realos rejected the 'warehouse catalogue' of demands approach to programmatic development; political priorities must be set and 'conscious compromise' must be a foundation for Green politics* (Frankland, 1992, p140).

The realos aimed for a parliamentary focus within the party, advocating the restructuring and 'professionalizing' of the party for a '*reform-politik*' that could be supported by a wider social base (Frankland, 1992, p114).

By contrast, fundis rejected any form of tactical orientation merely for the purposes of electoral gain. Any revision of style and objectives was viewed as betraying the original principles from which the party developed. The ideological objectives of *Die Grünen*, fundamentalists claimed, should not be open to compromise. As Greens no longer viewed left–right political distinctions as capable of solving the problems of modern industrial society, fundis argued that the party would not benefit from the development of left-wing coalitions. Parliamentary power could be utilized to greatest effect through tactical and logistical support of the social movements, such as public relations work, and financial and organizational support (Markovits and Gorski, 1993, p122). The stance of the fundis reflected a 'deep' Green conviction that only radical social change would provide lasting environmental solutions, reflected in Petra Kelly's claim that:

> *In certain questions, the Greens cannot enter into any compromises. There is not just a little bit of death, a little bit of annihilation, a little bit of cancer, a little bit of war or violence* (cited in Markovits and Gorski, 1993, p123).

The realos faction, as later chapters discuss, eventually gained the upper hand and instigated significant reforms within the party. However, the significance of these debates, and the eventual outcome, had important implications beyond merely organizational structures within the German Green party. Frankland identifies it as a defining moment in the development of Green party politics, during which:

> *. . .the anti-organizational allergies of the movement activists. . . collided with the pragmatic realos, who accepted the inevitabilities of parliamentarization, professionaliza-*

tion, and the role of the promis as political leaders (Frankland, 1992, p217).

Markovits and Gorski similarly identify the debates as reflecting a desire within the two groups for completely different types of political party, rather than merely an internal party struggle. Fundamentalists, they argue, sought the development of a radical, leftist, Socialist ecology party, reflecting the ideological and activist commitments of the new social movements.[22] The realos, in contrast, wanted to create a reformist party that would appeal to moderate middle-class voters and would provide a pragmatic approach to parliamentary electoral politics, developing an 'ecologically and socially informed restructuring of industrial society' (Markovits and Gorski, 1993, p216).

The nature of the conflict, therefore, appears to represent more than just an internal party struggle. To some it demonstrated that the principles of grassroots democracy were incompatible with the need for efficient political performance under the conditions of parliamentary democracy (Poguntke, 1993, p380). Others saw it as reproducing the structural tensions that had already existed between the new social movements and the newly formed party, although now at a higher political level (Markovits and Gorski, 1993, p216). The conflicts within *Die Grünen* clearly raised important question marks over the ability of the Green parties to maintain a commitment to new social movement principles, while also aiming to develop a solid and effective party platform from which to represent ecological concerns.

Issues and divisions such as those surrounding the 'realo–fundis' debates within the German Greens have also been transposed onto the patterns of development, change and conflict witnessed within other European Green parties. Here, again, analysis has focused upon the difficulties of marrying the parties' commitment to achieving ecological change with their commitments to the ideals and organizational style of the new social movements. The application of these themes to the European context has enabled Green party researchers to distinguish between 'light' and 'dark', 'electoralist' and 'decentralist', and 'realist' and 'fundamentalist' tendencies within Green parties, and to view change as the attempted resolution of factional disputes along these dimensions.[23] However, closer inspection begins to suggest that the experiences of these parties are actually far from homogeneous.

Within the British Green party, for example, Robinson identifies a 'realo–fundis' split between:

> *...those who resolutely seek to defend the purity of their 'Green' principles, and those who are willing selectively*

> *to forsake some of these in the interests of pragmatism*
> (Robinson, 1992, p211).

He identifies the fundamentalists as refusing to 'sell out' to the big power game of politics, while realists seek some level of political influence in the hope of achieving small, but tangible, environmental concessions (Robinson, 1992, p211). Although both groups are seen to share similar ideological beliefs, realists, it is claimed, are more prepared to compromise to achieve some level of political participation. Bennie et al's (1995) study, however, questions the ease with which we can utilize this dichotomy in the British case. Rather, they identify a far more complex pattern in which party activists were identified as 'realists' within particular spheres, such as party policy and strategy, but at an ideological level still viewed themselves as 'fundamentalists'. The study therefore raises questions regarding whether activist identification with such categorizations are largely issue specific rather than evidence of a completely distinctive ideological stance.

Realo–fundis classifications have also been utilized to examine changes and conflicts within the French Green party, *Les Verts,* and the Italian *Liste Verdi*. In France, debates over possible alliances with other parties have produced significant levels of internal factionalism and conflict within the party. These debates have been portrayed within the context of realo–fundis divisions, with Antoine Waechter's strategy of party autonomy being identified as a 'fundis' stance in contrast to Dominique Voynet's 'realo' position of favouring alliances with the left.[24] In a slightly different context, Rhodes's analysis of the Italian *Liste Verdi* identifies a split between those activists which he defines as 'pure Greens' and those activists within the organization who hold a new left commitment. Again, however, a primary factor in this division appears to be a strategic distinction between parliamentary and extra-parliamentary activity. He suggests that:

> *This split tends to mirror that between the supporters of*
> *demonstrations and grassroots activism (the piazza) and*
> *the advocates of national lobbying and parliamentary*
> *politics (the palazzo)* (Rhodes, 1995, p186).

Doherty (1992) extends the comparative application of the realo–fundis typology by examining the extent to which realo–fundis conflicts and divisions can be identified as a common factor within Western European Green parties. In doing so, he attempts to address the issue of whether these conflicts are necessarily an inherent result of the Greens' radical ideology and decentralized organization (Doherty,

1992, p95). His definition of the realo–fundis division again emphasizes the centrality of the two primary theoretical dimensions highlighted throughout this chapter. He describes fundamentalists as:

> *Those who are, in principle, critical of coalitions with other parties, opposed to centralization of the party organization and sceptical about achieving radical change by parliamentary means* (Doherty, 1992, p97).

By contrast, he claims that realists emphasize the importance of a solid parliamentary strategy, while not completely rejecting the importance of extra-parliamentary action. They seek changes to a number of the initial organizational principles of the parties, claiming that experience has demonstrated the weaknesses of these organizational structures when placed within the competitive system in which they seek representation and influence.

Doherty's analysis therefore focuses primarily upon the ambiguity in Green party ideas concerning political strategy. Within this context, the foundation for conflict and division rests with the balance struck between extra-parliamentary and parliamentary activity – in particular, between politics pursued outside existing channels of interest inter-mediation and 'a politics that accepts certain forms of institutionalization as inevitable' (Doherty, 1992, p97). He argues that these debates reflect many of the issues raised when the parties originally decided to move away from social movement activism and into the party political sphere. In attempting to remain true to their social movement origins, Green parties sought to create an organization and structure reflecting the ideals of these movements. It was only as these parties began to achieve electoral successes, and faced the organizational complexities of parliamentary representation at varying levels, that the original blueprint of party organization began to display cracks and deficiencies. Whereas diversity and debate regarding such issues represented a positive point for the social movements, it has proved more damaging to the Green parties as they attempt to represent many different opinions under a single coherent strategy.

Doherty's analysis suggests a common pattern of ambiguities within the European Green parties concerning the structure of the Green party and the parliamentary or extra-parliamentary focus for its activities, reflected within some form of realo–fundis dispute. Importantly, he also identifies a relationship between the specificities of internal conflict within Green parties, and the social and institutional conditions within which they function. Hence, controversy and conflict over strategy is often sparked by a relatively strong or weak competitive position. Either situation, Doherty argues, has the effect of polarizing the party between parliamentary and extra-parliamentary strategies (Doherty, 1992, p116).

To summarize, then, more recent Green party analysis has devoted significant attention to a conflicting division between realist and fundamentalist factions in Western Green parties that is largely reflective of the realo–fundi debates within *Die Grünen*. The factional division, as Doherty identifies, appears to focus upon ambiguities concerning Green party strategies towards parliamentary versus extra-parliamentary activism. The style of these conflicts, however, may also reflect specific national circumstances. The balance between realist and fundamentalist factions must therefore be viewed in relation to the party structure, the available political opportunities and the way in which Green party members respond to their own national and traditional contexts (Doherty, 1992, p117). Underlying this process we can clearly identify the continued ideological distinction between a 'true' or 'dark' Green perspective, focusing upon radical ecological commitments, and an alternative 'shallow' or 'light' Green perspective, which is more reactive to competitive party pressures and is prepared to compromise on key ideals and commitments. These splits are identified as being at the heart of the process of change witnessed within the European Green parties in recent years.

BEYOND REALOS AND FUNDIS: THE NEED FOR A BROADER UNDERSTANDING OF GREEN PARTY CHANGE

Binary distinctions such as those between 'realos' and 'fundis' represent an effective analytical tool for examining strategic positioning and change among the European Green parties. However, the breadth of change experienced within these parties demonstrates that strategic change is not the only focus for reform. Indeed, a brief inspection of recent developments within a number of European Green parties highlights the difficulties associated with adopting these approaches to Green party change, both structural and strategic. In particular, party change does not always result from the existence, and attempted resolution, of factional disputes within the parties based upon such dichotomous distinctions.

The Green parties in both Sweden and Austria experienced significant structural changes that cannot be fully understood purely in terms of internal realo–fundis divisions among activists. The Swedish Green party, *Miljöpartiet de Gröna*, as will be seen in later chapters, embarked upon a significant period of organizational change during 1991–1992, which was remarkably free of internal ideological division and conflict.

The implementation of structural change within the Austrian Green party, *Die Grüne Alternative,* during the same period, is also difficult to explain in terms of bitter intra-party squabbling along realo–fundis lines. Indeed, as Frankland points out, moves towards a more professionalized, pragmatic Green party 'did not lead to incriminations, resignations and splinters' (Frankland, 1996, p212).

An examination of strategic change within both the British and French Green parties also suggests that such change cannot be identified solely as the result of internal party feuding. Despite the deep divisions witnessed within the British Greens during the early 1990s, subsequent Green Party strategy has been shaped by both an 'anti-partyist' and 'pragmatic' stance.[25] Similarly, *Les Verts* have been embroiled in numerous strategic upheavals which, closer analysis suggests, have had more to do with the state of political competition than with internal ideological commitments and concerns.

Cases such as these begin to raise questions concerning the nature of Green party development that cannot be fully understood via factional conflicts over party strategy. For example, why should the Green party in Sweden be able to successfully restructure the party organization with relatively little sign of a strategic realo–fundis style conflict, especially when its roots can be traced clearly to the style of new social movement activism at the heart of fundamental Green party commitments? A similar question can be raised in the case of Austria. In contrast, why should the Green party in the UK be ravaged by internal party conflict over issues of party organizational structure, when the changes suggested were markedly less dramatic than those in the Swedish case? In addition, how can one explain the fact that although the party is now dominated by what would be identified as 'fundamentalists', it has maintained the organizational structures that were designed as a more pragmatic approach to party politics? Clearly, certain issues have proved more controversial in some Green parties than in others. All appear to have undergone a process of transformation, but have experienced this process in markedly different ways. Green party development and change thus appear more far-reaching than the previous picture of strategic division can identify.

One of the key difficulties within Green party analysis is the apparent gap between Green political theory and the practical experiences of the Green parties themselves. Bennie et al acknowledge this problem, claiming that:

> *There is . . . quite a substantial gap between 'green political theory' as developed and discussed in academic circles, and the ideas and beliefs of 'actual' Greens involved in practising 'Green politics'* (Bennie et al, 1995, p218).

Not only does this apparent 'gap' between theory and practice create problems in analysing Green party development, it has also been identified as having a direct effect on the parties themselves. Kenny, for example, suggests that the conflicts experienced within the European Green parties could be understood as resulting from a lack of ideological guidance due to 'the absence of a cogent and clear Green political theory' (Kenny, 1994, p222). Ecologism, as highlighted, offers a strong critique of modern industrial society and identifies the need for a change in humans' relationship with nature. However, the divergence within Green political thought and eco-philosophy leaves Green parties and environmental movements without a clear picture of the practical measures through which this change should be achieved. The nature and style of Green political theory, one might argue, does not adequately tackle the political realities facing the movements who are seeking to actively implement Green ideas.

Barry (1994) argues that it is important to attempt some level of integration between the philosophical aspect of Green political theory and the practical activism of the various Green movements, of which Green parties represent a case in point. He claims that the problems have arisen due to the separation of Green political theory into two distinct camps – namely, the shallow and the deep, long-range ecology movement, at the heart of which is 'an eco-philosophical dispute between anthropocentrism and ecocentrism' (Barry, 1994, p370). The emphasis currently placed upon deep Green philosophy has created a common perception whereby only ecocentrically motivated political action is identified as truly 'Green'. It is this distinction, Barry claims, that has resulted in inappropriate classifications of Green political activity. To gain a more accurate perception of Green political action, we must therefore move away from this focus upon 'deep' and 'shallow' Green politics. In practice, this involves questioning what is actually at the core of Green political thought and Green ideology. Barry's approach is to argue that:

> *The reconciliation of Green philosophy and politics depends on seeing that the normative basis of Green politics includes a concern with the human social world and its organization, as much as a moral concern with the non-human world* (Barry, 1994, p369).

The ecocentric standpoint, therefore, from which 'deep–shallow' dichotomies are produced, neglects a central aspect of Green party activism – namely, that at the heart of this activism is an inevitable concern with the human social world. By neglecting this factor and drawing a distinct line between 'dark' and 'light' Green, theorists are actually moving further away from providing an accurate picture of Green activism and widening the gap between thought and practice.

This theoretical 'gap' would appear to be central to the problems involved in providing an effective explanation of Green party development, change and conflict. In this case, analysis has focused predominantly upon the theoretical roots of the Green parties, emphasizing both the 'newness' of the political challenge and identifying what it means to be 'Green', along both ideological and philosophical dimensions. However, Green party research has yet to devote similar levels of attention to issues surrounding what it means to be a small, new political party struggling for recognition and attempting to represent and implement a distinctive and broad-ranging 'Green' ideology within established party systems. This may be one reason why, as Bennie et al note, one can identify a significant difference between the style and content of Green political theory and philosophy, on the one hand, and the empirical evidence that emerges from studies of Green party politics and activism, on the other (Bennie et al, 1995, p218).

The development of classifications, such as those between 'realos' and 'fundis', serve to provide an initial link between theory and practice within Green party analysis. However, closer inspection raises concerns that these approaches may tend to obscure more than they actually clarify. The strategic debates and changes that these classifications identify are often translated as a process of ideological dilution through a strategic shift away from broader ideological objectives. Hence, strategic change is connected with the pragmatic relaxing of party commitments to values identified as being at the heart of the ecological–new social movement framework. The identification of realo–fundis-style conflict has therefore taken on much broader ramifications regarding the 'professionalization' of the Green parties and, with it, the implication that recent developments have witnessed the increasing institutionalization of the 'new politics'.

UNDERSTANDING EUROPEAN GREEN PARTIES: A SUMMARY

This chapter has highlighted the importance of two central themes within Green party research: on one hand, the relationship of the parties to the ideology of ecologism and the perception of these parties as a vehicle for these values and ideals; and on the other, their relationship to the organizational structures of the new social movements. While these methodological foundations have proved insightful for initial investigations into both the formation and classification of the

European Green parties, in the context of Green party development and change, a broader framework is required.

The binary distinctions and conflicts identified within eco-philosophy and Green political thought have clearly influenced analytical attempts to interpret Green party conflict and change. However, they are likely to produce only a partial picture if, as Dobson claims, 'The politics of ecology does not follow the same ground rules as its philosophy' (Dobson, 1990, p69).[26]

Typologies such as those outlined in this chapter, while providing a useful insight into strategic patterns within Green parties, cannot necessarily explain the complex relationships between conflicting groups within parties. Neither do they necessarily help to explain the relationship between ideology and political action. Kenny suggests that we view the present stage in the development of ecologism as:

> *. . .a slow process of convergence in which disparate ideas, diffuse philosophical perspectives and various political preferences are gradually coalescing around a shared ideological agenda* (Kenny, 1994, p245).

The next stage of this process, he argues, is the development of a coherent body of political ideas – an aspect within which the evolution of the European Green parties plays a significant part. Within this context, a broader and more in-depth picture of Green party development and change represents a vital dimension in our understanding of the evolution of Green politics. Given this position, the issue that confronts any attempts to provide a comparative analysis of Green party change is how one can integrate the ideas and analytical concepts within Green theory, with the practical experiences of Green party activism.

It was suggested earlier that, although previous theoretical models provide a strong picture of what it means to be 'Green', along both ideological and philosophical dimensions, less detailed analytical attention has surrounded the Greens' role as political parties. While most analysts discussed here have undoubtedly recognized the influence of external political pressures upon Green parties, the primary focus has been upon their 'new politics' characteristics rather than the pressures and barriers facing a new form of political party struggling to gain recognition within long-established, traditional competitive party systems. This is a fundamental dilemma that Green parties themselves have been forced to face head on. The following chapter demonstrates how a more detailed emphasis upon the Greens' role as small political parties helps to provide a clearer framework for understanding their patterns of development and change.

Chapter 2

Placing Green Politics in a 'Party' Environment

While Green parties may represent an alternative approach to party politics, they nevertheless face many of the same pressures and constraints that have confronted the more established political parties across Western Europe. As such, invaluable insights into the processes of party evolution and change, and the implications of these changes, can be gained by examining broader research into the activities of political parties. In particular, highlighting the 'party' dimension within Green party research enhances the perception of the Greens as political actors who are integrated within the confines of competitive European party systems.

By examining development and change within political parties across different systemic contexts, this chapter highlights the important role accredited to the 'external political environment'. It demonstrates the importance of both 'internal' and 'external' pressures as factors influencing change and argues that an accurate understanding of party development must reflect this balance. These arguments provide the impetus for developing a theoretical framework for analysing Green party development and change, which recognizes the distinctive characteristics that have helped shape the Green parties. It also acknowledges the more general pressures that face a small party active within a competitive European party setting.

PARTIES, ORGANIZATIONS AND THE IMPACT OF THE 'EXTERNAL ENVIRONMENT'

In attempting to explain how parties work, change and adapt, theorists have focused predominantly upon their role as 'organizations'. Like other organizations, parties do not function in isolation but interact with their surroundings. To fully understand the process of evolution within political parties, therefore, one must consider:

> . . .not only the ways in which voters respond to a given set of political alternatives, but also the ways in which parties shape and respond to the strategic environment in which they operate (Wolinetz, 1988, p5).

Panebianco's analysis of party development and change follows a similar line, claiming that:

> . . .a party (like any organization) is a structure in motion which evolves over time, reacting to external changes and to the changing 'environments' in which it functions (Panebianco, 1988, p49).[1]

All political parties, therefore, are subject to two different but inter-related sets of pressures. On the one hand, they must deal with internal concerns stemming from within the party organization, while on the other they must also react to external changes in the larger political environment, of which the party is a part (Rose and Mackie, 1988, p534). If this is the case, analysis of development within political parties must incorporate both the key features of the 'external political environment', and the relationship between this environment and the process of party change.

Panebianco defines external 'environments' as interdependent arenas in which 'relations between parties and other organizations take place' (Panebianco, 1988, p207).[2] He claims that a party's position towards its environment will vary between the two extremes of either 'adaptation' or 'domination', depending upon the nature and strength of the environment and the nature of the different 'arenas' in which the party functions within the external environment (Panebianco, 1988, p12).[3] Similarly, Rose and Mackie argue that parties must be prepared to adapt to an ever-changing environment as 'a condition of electoral survival' (Rose and Mackie, 1988, p540). In doing so, this involves the parties striking an effective balance between 'introverted' and 'extroverted' goals. Conflict over these goals is identified as a key

factor in understanding the debates and processes surrounding development and change within political parties. Those who emphasize
internal goals, Rose and Mackie argue, seek to maintain the traditional
ideals and practices of the party, identifying change as a threat to its
cohesion. In contrast, others see refusal to adapt as a threat to the
electoral existence of the party. As such:

> *The big trade-off always facing leaders of parties is simply*
> *stated: how much weight should be given to external*
> *as against internal pressures* (Rose and Mackie, 1988,
> p 540)?[4]

External pressures undoubtedly play a crucial role in the development
and adaptation of political parties. While internal pressures reflect the
specific characteristics and ideological commitments of individual
parties, external pressures reflect the challenge posed by the nature
of the national party system within which a party operates. The
challenge for party analysts is to be able to incorporate both of these
dimensions and to provide an accurate picture of development and
change based upon the interaction of internal and external pressures.

This analytical balancing act represents an important consideration
for understanding Green party analysis past, present and future. While
studies of Green parties have so far successfully presented us with a
detailed picture of the specific internal characteristics and behaviour
of the Greens, little detailed analysis has been produced that effectively
presents party development and change in the light of both internal
and external pressures. In order to provide this form of analytical
synthesis, however, requires the consideration of three key questions
regarding research into political parties and party systems. Firstly, how
should one classify this 'external environment'? Secondly, what type
of impact has it had on development and change in other political
parties? And finally, how can its impact be analysed effectively?

CLASSIFYING THE EXTERNAL ENVIRONMENT: THE ROLE OF PARTY SYSTEMS

In gaining a clear perception of the external environment, party system
classifications provide an effective starting point for identifying the
various pressures, opportunities and barriers confronting political
parties across Western Europe. In particular, these classifications help
to identify the core features of the different party systems and, in some
cases, the possible styles of party activism likely to be adopted within

them. Although a wealth of alternative approaches to classification have emerged, analysis has often adopted either a numerical approach (Duverger, 1954; Dahl, 1966; Blondel, 1968; 1969) or has focused upon party relevance (Sartori, 1976).

Duverger (1954) provided an initial starting point for numerical classifications, distinguishing between 'two-party' and 'multiparty' systems. Two-party systems, he argued, represented traditional political structures in which choice was directed towards two distinct alternatives.[5] Multiparty systems represented a development from within the two-party model, resulting from a split within both conservative and radical parties, between moderates and extremists.[6] Dahl (1966), by contrast, identified two-party systems as the deviant cases and regarded multiparty systems as the 'natural way for government and oppositions to manage their conflicts' (in Mair 1990, p298). He provides a fourfold classification, founded upon the two-party and multiparty distinctions but also distinguishing between systems with high or low degrees of party unity.[7]

Blondel's (1968) study dissected these classifications further by noting that within two-party systems, the two main parties often only received between 75 and 80 per cent of the votes. Because of this, he argues, a number of political systems with three identifiable parties are not accurately accounted for by either the two-party or multiparty classifications. In addition, he notes that within these three-party systems, votes are rarely distributed evenly between all three parties. To accommodate these conditions, Blondel incorporates the relative strength of parties within a system and their positioning along the ideological spectrum as key factors in his numerical classification. This enables him to identify an alternative 'two-and-a-half-party' system, in which the two major parties are accompanied by either a small left-wing or centre party.[8] He also distinguishes between multiparty systems in which one party often obtained around 40 per cent of the vote and was relatively dominant within the system and those in which no party receives a markedly stronger percentage of the vote.[9] These additions result in a six-group classification still based around the two-party, multiparty distinctions.[10]

For critics of numerical approaches to classification, these models only demonstrate the level of fragmentation and dispersal of political power within a political system, rather than actually distinguishing between types of party system. It is not necessarily the number of parties within a system that matters but, rather, as Sartori suggests, the number of 'relevant' parties. This relevance he argues:

> *...is a function not only of the relative distribution of power – as is obvious – but also, and especially, of its*

> *position value, that is, of its positioning along the left–right*
> *dimension* (cited in Mair, 1990, p319).

Sartori measures a party's 'relevance' on the basis of possessing either 'blackmail potential' or 'coalition potential'. Some parties, he claims, are 'never needed or put to use for any feasible coalition majority'; therefore, they lack coalition potential (cited in Mair, 1990, p320). However, we cannot immediately discount all of these parties as 'irrelevant' because some parties, notably anti-systemic parties, do not necessarily seek roles within government. A party may be relevant to a system through its 'blackmail potential' whereby:

> *. . .its existence, or appearance, affects the tactics of party*
> *competition and particularly, when it alters the direction*
> *of the competition – by determining a switch from centri-*
> *petal to centrifugal competition either leftward, rightward*
> *or in both directions – of the governing-oriented parties*
> (cited in Mair, 1990, p321).

Identifying the relevance of political parties produces seven alternative types of party system, four of which are reflective of the European party systems examined here.[11]

Sartori supports Dahl's claim that the two-party system is not the natural polarization of a party system as it requires parties to be:

> *. . .aggregative agencies that maintain their competitive*
> *near-evenness by amalgamating as many groups, interests*
> *and demands as possible* (cited in Mair, 1990, p344).

Multiparty systems reflect the ideological distance between parties and are divided between 'moderate pluralism', 'polarized pluralism' and 'atomized pluralism'. Moderate pluralism defines those systems that have between three and five relevant parties, and where there is a relatively small ideological distance between them. These systems display a bipolar coalitional configuration and an emphasis on centri-petal competition, allowing little room for anti-systemic parties. In contrast, polarized pluralism defines those systems where differences between parties are based not only on policy alternatives but, more importantly, 'on principles and fundamentals' (cited in Mair, 1990, p332). Here there is a greater tendency towards centrifugal competi-tion, with parties moving away from the centre, providing opportuni-ties for anti-systemic parties. Generally, however, only those parties on the centre-left or centre-right have any real access to government. Sartori's analysis is valuable here as it demonstrates the influence of the systemic structure upon the strategies exhibited by the parties towards party competition. While two-party systems encourage parties to incorporate many different groups and issues, moderate pluralism emphasizes the opportunity to participate in coalition government, and polarized pluralism provides greater opportunities for anti-systemic parties within the system.

While party system classifications provide an initial picture of the different types of 'external environment' facing political parties, they do not provide an effective examination of the pressures and influences of these environments upon the individual parties themselves. They provide a context within which analysts have sought to assess and compare the activities of political parties.

THE INTERACTION BETWEEN PARTIES AND PARTY SYSTEMS

A brief glance at the literature regarding comparative party studies highlights the emphasis placed upon the influence of systemic barriers and constraints upon the activities and developments within all political parties. As Blondel explains:

> *No party exists in a vacuum. Even if only a single party exists in a given country, it must respond to environmental pressures. If two or more parties fight openly, as in Western countries, the fight has to follow rules which are often complex and have been elaborated over a long period. Both these rules and the environment come, with time, to affect the nature of each party. Thus, parties which exist in a given community tend to share common characteristics: they form, in the widest sense of the word, a system* (Blondel, 1978, p75).

It is likely, therefore, that certain barriers and constraints, such as the nature of the electoral system and the state financing of political parties, will impact upon all parties active within that party system, and as Mair (1994) suggests, can influence:

> *. . .how the party is organized, how its internal affairs are conducted, how it manages relations with its supporters and voters, and how it finances its activities* (Mair, 1994, p2).

These four criteria are clearly inter-linked. For example, the level of funding a party can obtain can have an influence on the options available for party organization and what that specific party can afford to do. Two brief examples highlight this interaction clearly. In France, changes to the electoral system under the Fifth Republic have strongly influenced the organization and internal mechanisms of French political parties. In contrast to the coalition governments of the Fourth Republic, the presidential system now emphasizes direct competition on a winner-takes-all level (Mair, 1994, p12). Cooperation and compromise have been removed from the political equation, and this is reflected in the centralized, election-orientated nature of the French parties.[12]

In the UK, a lack of state funding for political parties is identified as a key factor in the continued emphasis upon membership levels and political affiliations to finance party activity. Where state funding is available – as in Germany, for example, the pattern is noticeably different:

> . . .*if they can rely on funding from the state, the leaders of membership parties can afford to be more insulated from the influence of local branches. Members matter less and, as in the case of the West German Greens, there may be little incentive to recruit members* (Mair, 1994, p18).

Similarly, regulation controlling the level of expenditure on elections can influence the nature of party activity. Mair argues that such controls have been influential in preventing UK parties developing the more complex political organizations evident in Germany and Italy (Mair, 1994, p15). State funding based upon vote share can also represent a mechanism for protecting long-standing parties against competition from new parties, and can restrict the impact that small parties can have within the electoral sphere.

External pressures such as these may, therefore, produce common organizational results across all parties within a particular party system, regardless of their distinctive ideological nature. Poguntke (1994), for example, argues that the need to adapt to the 'constitutional parameters' of the German party system is a key factor in explaining the organizational similarity between the various political parties in Germany. Party organizations have an inclination towards maintaining 'stable and predictable' relationships with their environment, and are prepared to adapt in order to achieve this (Poguntke, 1994, p186). As a result, although at one time displaying different organizational forms, the process of adaptation to their environment has resulted in a general convergence towards a standardized party model.[13]

It would be wrong, however, to presume that all systemic barriers impact upon every political party within a party system. Indeed, some barriers are specifically imposed with the intention of maintaining the strength and status of established political parties and marginalizing, new challengers. Merkl and Lawson's (1988) study of why established long-standing parties 'fail' within some party systems, but survive within others, points at the failure of some parties to provide adequate representation for specific groups or issues, resulting in the development of new challengers. However, they argue that the variation in impact of this 'failure' is the result of a combination of factors, such as the number of parties within the party system, the adaptability of long-standing parties, and the 'protective mechanisms' within the political system safeguarding the positions of these parties. This relationship between the nature of the party system and the competition between established parties and new challengers obviously is significant for understanding the process of development within the European Greens.

Merkl argues that within two-party systems the failure of one, or both, of the major parties to tackle new issues can result in the development of a third party. However, this third party faces immense barriers to becoming a key force within the political system. Of particular importance here are the 'restrictive rules of the game, and well-established habits of mind on the part of the voters' (Merkl, 1988, p565).[14] In addition, the new party often loses support as the long-standing parties seek to adapt to new issues.[15] Using the German and Swedish party systems as examples, Merkl suggests that opportunities for alternative movements are increased within three- to five-party systems. In both cases, Green parties have had the chance to become 'hinge' parties within these party systems, gaining an influential role between parties on the left and right. Achieving this position relies, however, on the left- and right-party blocs being evenly matched and not able to control a parliamentary majority without the support of the hinge party.[16] By contrast, under different conditions such as within the French party system, the split between left and right remains the central priority within the political arena, blocking the growth of new issues and concerns and restricting opportunities for small parties:

> *While in Sweden and West Germany. . . the left–right polarization seemed to lose salience in the face of the environmentalists challenges, in France it clearly remained the most dramatic show at the centre of the political stage. The faltering of the right and. . . the triumphant surge of the left must have robbed the small oppositional fringe of much of its appeal for the time being* (Merkl, 1988, pp568–569).

As the number and range of political parties within a system increases, so the relationships become more complicated and the impact of new parties becomes more diffuse. The more open systems of proportional representation, with little or no thresholds to representation, do not provide long-standing parties with as much protection from new competitors. However, although political representation is often within reach of these new parties, it does not necessarily provide them with a position of influence.

It is clear from the discussion above that examining the systemic context within which parties function identifies barriers and constraints to both the style and nature of party activism. Party systems therefore represent a key factor in contextualizing the patterns of development and change within the political parties active within them. Some aspects of the party system may impact similarly on all parties within that system, regardless of the different ideological and organizational bases upon which these parties have developed. Other mechanisms, however, present specific barriers to new challengers. The identification of both of these sets of pressures and constraints is therefore necessary in developing a broader picture of the pattern of Green party development and change.

'SIMILAR BUT DIFFERENT': ANALYSING PARTY FAMILIES ACROSS DIFFERENT PARTY SYSTEMS

Further important insights can be identified, regarding the relationship between party and environment, through studies of development and change within 'party families' across different party systems. These studies bring together the two analytical dimensions identified so far – namely, the identification of specific characteristics, organizational and ideological, that distinguish a particular party family from other parties and the systemic contexts within which they operate. Often these studies focus upon specific aspects of party change, such as electoral performance or internal conflict, comparing the parties' experiences across different countries.

The examples selected here follow this pattern and reflect dimensions of party activity that, arguably, have been key features of development and change within the Green parties: party factionalism (Bell and Shaw, 1994), party adaptation (Waller and Fennema, 1988), the role of small parties (Pridham and Müller-Rommel, 1991) and electoral performance (Rootes and Richardson, 1995). These studies serve to briefly highlight a number of important themes and questions that Green party analysis must seek to address, and comparative tools which the current study will utilize.

One of the most important issues raised by comparative studies of parties across party systems is that party families should not be considered as homogeneous groups. Although it is possible to identify within these parties a specific set of characteristics that distinguish them as a member of that particular party family, this does not neces- sarily mean that party development and change will be a uniform process. Green parties, it appears, are not alone in experiencing vastly differing patterns of factionalism, adaptation and change. Significant differences exist both between, and within, parties within any party family. Although having a similar political culture and experiencing common organizational and ideological challenges, the parties differ markedly in that they face different political challenges relating to their respective party systems. Internal party characteristics alone, there- fore, while useful in distinguishing and classifying between different types of party, cannot suffice to explain the varying patterns of development and change witnessed within parties of the same party family.

This argument is reflected in Bell and Shaw's analysis of Social Democratic parties, in which they claim that the parties' experiences of factionalism are 'distinguishable by national characteristics' (Bell and Shaw, 1994, p1). Although all parties in the study display certain characteristics clearly defining them as 'social democratic' by nature, the authors note that:

> *The similarity of political family cannot disguise the differences of political situation...they all display a marked factionalism distinguishable by national characteristics* (Bell and Shaw, 1994, p1).

The dominance of one or other faction is, therefore, dependent not only on the interaction that exists between the various forces within the individual parties themselves, but also on the interaction of the party with its environment.[17] Hence, in Germany, the 'centripetal force' of the German party system is identified as a key factor in enforcing party discipline and constraining factionalism (Bell and Shaw, 1994, p2). By contrast, the Swedish Social Democrat's virtually continuous control of government is identified as a key factor in fostering party unity, at least in public, and avoiding 'the intense personal political factionalism' identified in other countries (Arter, 1994, p82). Factionalism has been a recurrent theme within the French Socialist party – a pattern that is linked to two key features of the French party system. Firstly, there is the existence of a large, strong Communist party, providing competition on the left. Secondly, there is the impact of presidentialism, which has resulted in the 'personalization' of politics and factional splits within the party around different potential presidential candidates.

A change in the political environment can often force parties to radically reassess their position and role within a party system, as is highlighted by Waller and Fennema's (1988) study of European Communist parties. In this instance, the parties faced a radically altered political landscape within which 'some parties have had greater success in adapting than others' (Waller and Fennema, 1988, p1). Again, external factors have proved influential in explaining the variation in success within these parties. In the UK, for example, the electoral system clearly restricted the opportunities available to the Communist party of the UK. In Ireland, the authors highlight the deep religious and political cleavages, which effectively blocked out the Communist party. The Communist parties in Sweden, Holland and Belgium, however, all appeared relatively successful in adapting to new issues and gained support from within the new social movements.[18] Only in Sweden, though, did the party find electoral space to enable it to transform support into electoral success. In both Belgium and Holland, the Communist parties found themselves competing with other radical left parties and were unable to fully capitalize on the new social movement support. Waller and Fennema's conclusion again returns to the impact of the political environment:

> *...success in this new orientation must depend particularly on the nature of the party system and the electoral system of the country concerned* (Waller and Fennema, 1988, p255).

In many ways, the Greens face a number of difficulties similar to those of the Communist parties highlighted in Waller and Fennema's study. Both are anti-systemic parties trying to adapt an organizational structure based upon ideological principles that is not necessarily suited to the party system within which it seeks to function. It is worthy of note, therefore, that for the Communist parties conflicts over adaptation and change appear to have varied in intensity, depending upon the level of support achieved and the relative flexibility of the party system.

Different types of party system present a diverse set of problems for all small parties who seek to make an impact, such as the Greens. Smith (1991) attempts to provide a broad overview of these challenges. As a general pattern, he claims that small parties have little or no influence within two-party systems. In two-and-a-half-party systems, however, small parties are occasionally able to play a 'hinge' role as a minor coalition partner, whereas within two-bloc systems small parties often develop roles within the respective coalitions. In a multiparty system where one party is dominant, the dominant party often relies upon small party support to gain a majority. However, in multiparty systems that lack this clear dominance, the coalition options are much wider and more flexible, and small parties often find their influence 'less pronounced than in dominant multiparty systems' (in Müller-Rommel, 1991, p8). Mair's analysis suggests a similar pattern, starting with the claim that in 'large party systems' small parties have no relevant impact. In 'small party systems', however, he argues that the vote for a 'small parties block' is more than 50 per cent and small parties have an important influence. Within 'intermediate systems' the small parties vote amounts to around 35 per cent; but small parties have slightly less influence within the system. Finally, in 'transitionary systems' there has been a change from a large to a small party system or vice versa (Mair, 1991, p47). [19]

Both of these studies are again largely one-dimensional, however – this time focusing predominantly upon external factors without recognizing the importance of the internal characteristics of the different parties. Recognizing this weakness, Pridham and Müller-Rommel (1991) redress this imbalance with a methodological approach to the study of small parties which attempts to tackle both internal and external factors. For each country, the study identifies both the type of small parties present and the nature of the party system under consideration. The role and performance of these small parties are then assessed with regard to three specific relationships.

The first relationship focuses upon the parties and 'the state'. This includes the pro- or anti-systemic nature of the party, its role in government, the nature of the electoral system, the level of state funding, and the level of representation in parliament. The second relationship examines the parties' links with 'other parties'. Within this category the authors include the political space and nature of competition, the relationship with the large parties within the system, and the nature of party strategies towards alliances and coalitions. The third relationship is that between the parties and 'society'. This relationship focuses upon issues concerning electoral strength, social cleavages, the parties' structure and organizational characteristics, and links with interest groups, movements and the media. The authors claim that:

> . . .by identifying a variety of key questions and themes under each relationship, the systemic approach allows for differentiation between the roles of small parties at different levels of the system, while acknowledging that there are obvious linkages between the three relationships (Müller-Rommel, 1991, p12).

As this study only briefly considers Green parties, its value here lies predominantly in its methodological approach.[20] The study undoubtedly tackles many of the key questions that must be considered if one is to develop a clearer understanding of development and change within the European Green parties. In particular, it highlights the interrelationship of a broad array of pressures and influences on the evolution of small parties such as the Greens – a consideration that is further highlighted by Rootes and Richardson's (1995) comparative study of the Greens' electoral challenge.

As with Pridham and Müller-Rommel, Richardson is quick to point out that:

> *...it is evident that no single factor can account for the differential development and varying electoral success of individual Green parties. Political ecologism has established itself in different ways, in different states, at different times, at different levels: theoretical, programmatic, electoral* (Richardson, 1995, p20).

Rather than identify any general theory for Green success, Rootes and Richardson seek to identify a set of key factors or criterion, the impact of which varies depending upon the party under consideration. While the authors largely restrict themselves to an assessment of Green electoral success and failure, the factors identified in this study clearly have a significant relevance for an assessment of broader patterns of development and change.

The first significant finding to note is that the comparative analysis found little direct correlation between the state of environmental consciousness in a country and the level of development or electoral fortunes of its Green party (Rootes, 1995, p232). Both Denmark and The Netherlands, for example, exhibit high levels of environmental consciousness; yet neither has a strong Green party (Rootes, 1995, p232).[21] Conversely, countries with a fairly low level of environmental consciousness have produced relatively successful Green parties, implying that other factors apart from environmental consciousness are required to explain the Green party phenomenon.

The study also challenges the assumption that Green parties are a natural development from the environmental movements, suggesting that 'Green parties exist alongside and in uneasy alliance with more organizationally diffuse Green movements' (Rootes, 1995, p237). Rootes claims that environmental movements often have long histories, producing other methods of contact with institutional bodies that do not include a role for Green parties. Institutional structures, therefore, play an important part in both the formation and levels of success of

Green parties. In Germany, for example, state funding of political parties encouraged the various disparate activist groups to develop an official party structure. Similarly, in the UK, the lack of costs and restrictions in creating a political party represented an influential factor in the formation of the UK Green party.

Rootes continues the institutional theme by demonstrating that different electoral systems have created markedly different opportunities for the European Green parties. As a general pattern he suggests that:

> *. . .in countries with federal constitutions and proportional representation electoral systems, the institutional matrix is much more favourable for the development and success of Green parties, and for the development of mutually beneficial relationships between Green parties and the environmental movement, than it is in centralized unitary states with majoritarian electoral systems* (Rootes, 1995, p241).

This is only a general pattern, however, and doesn't help to explain why some Green parties do well in relatively hostile environments, while others fail within systems that would appear to naturally favour Green party development. In order to tackle this dilemma, a third factor for comparative analysis is considered that is defined as the 'shifting balance of electoral competition'.

Rootes returns to the seemingly anomalous cases of Denmark and The Netherlands, where 'despite high levels of environmental consciousness, well-developed environmental movements and low-threshold electoral systems, Green parties have failed to flourish' (Rootes, 1995, p242). In both cases, he argues, fragmented party systems have led to mainstream left parties being more adaptable to environmental issues and, as such, accessible to the environmental movement.[22] In both systems, small parties can play a major role, resulting in intense competition for political space. In both cases, therefore, the Greens failed to develop any space within the party arena. Where Green parties have succeeded electorally, as in Germany and Belgium, they have been able to find electoral space either from the failure of long-standing parties to adapt to changing issues, or from the marginalization of other small parties.

Rootes and Richardson's study clearly highlights the value of analysis which incorporates both an understanding of features specific to Green parties as an individual phenomenon, and features which are common to certain types of political system. In summarizing, Rootes states that:

> *Even where citizens do accord highest priority to ecological*
> *issues, whether that priority is translated into activism in*
> *social movements, support for one or another established*
> *political party or votes for a Green party, [this] will be*
> *greatly influenced by the impact, actual and perceived, of*
> *the pattern of opportunities constituted by social and*
> *political institutional arrangements, and by the altogether*
> *more contingent balance of political competition* (Rootes,
> 1995, p249).

There is clearly much to learn from previous comparative analyses of
party families, such as those highlighted above, in shaping and defining
an effective comparative approach to understanding the developments
and changes within the European Greens. Firstly, the studies show that
it is vital that one avoids the pitfall of viewing Green parties as a
homogeneous group. While they may share a common ideological
starting point and face many similar challenges in seeking to 'Green'
party politics, the European Greens have had to undertake this challenge under markedly different circumstances, which will have had an
important impact on their evolution as a party.

Secondly, it is evident from the studies above that for any political
party the process of development and change reflects a complex interaction of multiple factors, both internal and external to the party. In
particular, an important interaction occurs between the specific internal
characteristics of that political party and the external opportunities,
barriers and constraints prevalent within the party system within
which it operates. This interaction results in vastly differing experiences and, hence, often different outcomes in the evolution of parties
within the same party family. At the same time, one can sometimes
identify similarities in parties across party families that are distinct to
a specific party system. Under these circumstances, comparison with
other parties operating within the same system may potentially prove
more enlightening than comparisons with other Green parties.

Unfortunately, the studies above have also shown that it is one
thing to identify an interaction between internal and external pressures, but an altogether more difficult task to provide a comprehensive
picture of exactly what these 'internal' and 'external' pressures are.
Bell and Shaw's study focused upon the nature of the party system as
influencing party discipline and factionalism, while also citing the
nature of the electoral system and party competition as other key
factors. Waller and Fennema's study similarly highlighted the influence
of the electoral system and political space, but identified the influence
of social cleavages and relationships with social movements as additional external factors.

Both Müller-Rommel and Rootes produce more general categorizations of external factors that provide greater scope for identifying specific national influences, but within a comparative perspective. A strong overlap is evident within these categorizations, with the result that Müller-Rommel's identification of 'relationships with the state' focuses upon similar themes to those identified within Rootes' category of 'opportunities and constraints imposed by institutional arrangements'. A similar comparison can be made between the category of 'relationships with society' and the themes identified by Rootes as reflecting the 'development of environmental consciousness'. Finally, a more direct comparison can be made between the 'relationships with other parties' offered by Müller-Rommel and the 'shifting balance of political competition' identified by Rootes.

These studies also highlight some important methodological questions regarding the style and focus of comparative party analysis. These relate to both the breadth of party change being examined and the detail of the comparative analysis presented. Regarding the breadth of analysis, it was noted earlier that comparative studies have often focused upon particular aspects of party development and change – for example, party factionalism, party adaptation or electoral performance. While identifying key patterns within each of these spheres, it is surely impossible to consider them in isolation from one another. Hence, while Rootes and Richardson focus upon the changing electoral performance of the Green parties, this cannot be understood outside of the context of changes in organizational structure, the internal conflicts and pressures within the parties and, also, divisions between different party levels. All of these factors have been important aspects in the development of the Greens and have subsequently had a strong bearing on the electoral performances of these parties. It is therefore important to take a broader perspective, in line with Pridham and Müller-Rommel's analysis, and examine party change as a more fluid process influencing different parties in different ways.

Although Pridham and Müller-Rommel's analysis provides this broader perspective, the study itself doesn't actually give a detailed comparative examination along the thematic dimensions identified.[23] As with many other studies, the themes are examined within a series of self-standing, individual case studies. A more thematic comparison would enable an assessment of both the ways in which the key relationships identified for small parties have changed in different party systems and, also, the factors influencing this process. Arguably, the adoption of this approach within a comparative study represents a methodological choice between providing either a broad and inclusive range of case studies covering numerous countries or focusing upon a more detailed, thematic comparison of fewer cases. In developing a more detailed examination of Green party development and change, this study focuses upon the latter, seeking to substitute analytical breadth, in terms of the number of case studies under examination, for comparative detail and a broader perception of party change.

ANALYSING DEVELOPMENT AND CHANGE WITHIN THE EUROPEAN GREEN PARTIES

Although identifying the key themes and perspectives which need to be considered in interpreting party development and change, the studies discussed above still fall some way short of providing an effective method for operationalizing this type of detailed comparative analysis. The analysis must not only be able to provide a framework for identifying both internal and external pressures, but must also be able to examine the relative influence of these factors upon the processes of party change among the different Green parties. Again, guidance in these issues can be found by looking beyond the analytical realm of Green politics and turning towards broader analyses of political parties – in particular, Harmel and Janda's (1994) model of party change. Harmel and Janda's work focuses upon 'why parties change their political strategies, organizational characteristics and issue positions' (Harmel and Janda, 1994, p259).[24] In doing so, the study focuses upon similar parameters to those at the centre of this current investigation – namely, the internal and external pressures facing political parties and their relative influence on patterns of party change.

Through the development of a quantitative comparative study, Harmel and Janda identify three independent variables that impact upon the process of party change. They argue that:

> *Far from assuming that party changes 'just happen' or 'must happen', we suggest that party change is normally a result of leadership change, a change of dominant faction within the party and/or an external stimulus for change* (Harmel and Janda, 1994, p262).

It is the relationship between these three variables that explains the patterns of party change across a number of different areas of party activity: organization, strategy and issue stance (Harmel and Janda, 1994, p266). While, in some cases, change results purely from internal pressures, in others 'external stimuli may act as an important catalyst for the process that ultimately results in change' (Harmel and Janda, 1994, p265).

While the categories of leadership and factional change are relatively self-explanatory, the concept of 'external stimuli' requires some clarification. The external 'shocks' or 'stimuli' referred to are defined as 'those which cause a party to re-evaluate its effectiveness in meeting its primary goal' (Harmel and Janda, 1994, p265). A party's primary goal can be classified along four dimensions: winning votes; advocating issues/ideology; implementing party democracy; or gaining executive office. Depending upon the primary goal, the authors suggest that it is possible to identify appropriate external stimuli for change. Examples of such stimuli include exceptionally good or bad electoral performances for parties whose primary goal is gaining votes; change in party size for parties whose goal is responding to members wishes; or, alternatively, loss of a central policy issue for those parties whose main goal is policy or ideologically oriented.

While Harmel and Janda's approach provides the clearest model so far for comparing party development and change, some adaptations are required in order for this framework to be effective for the comparative analysis of Green parties sought in this study. Firstly, Harmel and Janda claim that it is important to isolate a party's 'primary goal' in order to identify the type of external stimuli likely to provoke change. However, as Lucardie notes, identifying the 'primary goal' of a Green party can be problematic. In their study, Harmel and Janda isolate the goal of 'implementing party democracy' as a primary goal for 'new politics' parties, focusing upon the German Greens as a particular example. However, a closer examination of their classification of party goals reveals that, in fact, all four could feasibly be identified as a Green party's 'primary' goal. Indeed, identification of this primary goal might be seen to differ, not only *between* but also *within* Green parties.

For a broad quantitative study such as Harmel and Janda's, restricting analysis to a single primary goal represents a practical necessity. However, the framework of this much narrower comparative study allows for greater flexibility. To overcome this problem, therefore, this study focuses upon three of the primary goals identified by Harmel and Janda that are central to Green parties. These are 'winning votes' (by definition, a principal goal of any political party), 'advocating interests/ ideology' and 'implementing party democracy' (Harmel and Janda, 1994, p273). This approach enables the comparative analysis to focus upon the identification of a broad range of influential factors along different dimensions. In addition, it reflects changing priorities and goals within, and between, respective Green parties. The fourth primary goal – 'gaining executive office' – can now also be identified as a realistic Green party goal, given the recent successes in countries such as Germany and France. However, these aspects arguably require more time before the goal's impact can be incorporated into this comparative model fully. Therefore, while not fully incorporated into this model, the impact of this goal will be highlighted where appropriate.

Adapting Harmel and Janda's model addresses many of the key issues raised throughout this chapter regarding effective comparative analysis of party development and change. It enables the comparative analysis in this study to focus upon the identification of a broad range of influential factors along different dimensions. In addition, this approach also reflects changing priorities and goals within, and between, respective Green parties. Thus, it is possible to develop a picture of fluctuating priorities both within individual Green parties and within a comparative perspective.

A final consideration concerns the operationalizing of Harmel and Janda's model and, in particular, the identification and representation of these internal and external pressures. Wolfgang Müller's (1997) analysis of change within the Austrian Social Democrats provides a useful guide in this respect. Müller incorporates Harmel and Janda's model within a single case study, identifying key internal party developments and external stimuli confronting the Austrian Social Democrats. Placing these events on a time line, he is then able to compare the timing of these factors with the experiences of significant party change.

The time lines provide an effective diagrammatic tool with which to examine key factors influencing party change. While they may not prove direct causality between party change and the factors identified, the time lines indicate the context within which party change takes place. In presenting a comparative, case study-oriented piece of research, the identification of groups of factors is often more relevant than attempting to identify one key factor as direct cause.[25] The use of time lines therefore provides a diagrammatic examination of the wider context within which change takes place. It is then possible to examine the relationship between the pressures identified upon the time lines and the process of party change.[26]

COMBINING 'GREEN' AND 'PARTY' DIMENSIONS WITHIN A COMPARATIVE ANALYSIS OF GREEN PARTY DEVELOPMENT AND CHANGE

By focusing upon lessons from other party literature, this chapter has identified a comparative framework for analysing Green party development and change, which expands upon the patterns of Green party analysis highlighted in Chapter 1. The analytical framework therefore represents a synthesis of both specific aspects of Green party analysis, and the incorporation of ideas and models identified from within the comparative analysis of other political parties.

By recognizing a party's relationship with other types of organizations, it has been noted that political parties face two distinct sets of pressures. On the one hand, 'internal' issues exist regarding the specific characteristics of a particular party and, on the other, 'external' dimensions exist concerning the systemic context within which that party operates. Transposed onto Green party analysis, this means that one must look beyond merely the distinctive 'Green' characteristics that have traditionally been the focal point for distinguishing these parties as an alternative form of 'new' politics. One must also attempt to contextualize development and change within the Greens in relation to the pressures of the external political environments within which the parties function. Harmel and Janda's model of party change provides a foundation for achieving this. They highlight that party change in the areas of political strategy, organizational characteristics or issue positions results from the influence of three key factors: leadership change, change in the dominant factions, and the impact of external 'stimuli' that occur as the result of a direct challenge to a party's primary goal.

The selection of both the case studies and the thematic focus also reflects the importance of both 'Green' and 'party' dimensions within this study. Parties were selected which reflected key characteristics of 'new politics' parties and which had experienced significant processes of development and change. In addition, the cases selected function within different types of party system. Following the classifications discussed earlier in this chapter, we can identify the UK as a 'two-party' or 'large party' system, while Germany represents a 'two-and-a half-party' system. Sweden represents a 'multiparty' or 'small party' system, while France provides an example of a 'transitional' system, where the relatively recent systemic overhaul within the Fifth Republic has presented new challenges for all political parties.

The thematic focus also reflects this balance of 'Green' and 'party' criterion, seeking to reflect the distinctive characteristics of the Green parties while also acknowledging the other party categorizations discussed earlier. These categorizations include the 'three relationships' identified by Pridham and Müller-Rommel, the three dimensions highlighted by Rootes and Richardson, and the primary areas of party change outlined by Harmel and Janda. The comparative analysis therefore focuses upon three aspects of Green party activity that incorporate the above criteria: Green party strategy towards other political parties and issues of party positioning; the development of Green party organizational structures; and, finally, development and change within party policies and party programmes.

The following chapters present a comparative analysis of development, conflict and change within four European Green parties. For each area, the experiences of the German Green party will provide an initial frame of reference. This pattern of development and change will then be compared with the processes of reform and conflict experienced by the Green party in the UK, *Les Verts* in France and *Miljö-partiet de Gröna* in Sweden. By undertaking this form of detailed thematic comparative analysis, this book seeks to identify an overriding explanation for organizational change within Europe's Green parties and a more comprehensive interpretation of transition among the Greens.

To achieve this it will address the following questions. Firstly, what factors were influential in instigating change within the Green parties and are these factors common among the four different case studies? Secondly, does the process of development and change represent a significant move away from the 'new politics' commitments traditionally attributed to the Green parties? Thirdly, is this pattern of change a response to external pressures to conform to the exigencies of the party political system, or does it reflect internal issues regarding the nature of Green parties and Green party goals? By examining and understanding these processes of development and change, it will be possible to consider the implications of this process for the future evolution of Europe's Green parties and for the Greens' role as the parliamentary representatives of the 'new politics'.

Chapter 3

Seeking Space and Opportunity: The Emergence of Green Parties in Germany, France, Sweden and the UK

To contextualize the process of Green party development and change, this chapter focuses upon the formation and electoral performance of the four parties in this study. Concentrating initially upon the emergence of *Die Grünen*, it identifies the opportunities and constraints that helped to shape the impact of the Greens upon the German party system. Transposing these factors onto the other three case studies allows for a comparison of the systemic pressures facing the parties, and their relative influence upon the specific nature of Green party development. The constraints of the system, it is argued, impact upon the political opportunities available to each of the parties, the roles which they may potentially adopt within the system and, subsequently, their perceptions of 'success' and 'failure'.

CHALLENGING THE SYSTEM: THE EMERGENCE OF *DIE GRÜNEN* IN GERMANY

The transition of a 'motley crew of ecological romantics, naive peaceniks and unruly populists' (Schoonmaker, 1989, p41) into an established party actively involved in coalition government in Germany represents, for many, the strongest example of the impact of Green politics on Western European political systems, and a model for other Green parties to live up to and to be measured against. However, the evolution of the German Green party was far from uneventful, and its successes and failures cannot only be attributed to the actions of the Greens themselves.

As outlined in Chapter 1, the history of Green party development is closely connected to the rise of new social movement protests during the 1960s and 1970s. In Germany, this was reflected in the growth of new-left student movements, citizen action groups and campaigns against nuclear power that were a constant aspect of the German political arena during the 1970s. By 1977, there were approximately 50,000 civic initiative groups in West Germany. Approximately 1000 of these were members of the Federal Association for Civic Action in Protecting the Environment, which could boast a combined membership of over 300,000 (Schoonmaker, 1989, p47). Many activists felt disillusioned with the established political parties and their failure to confront these new issues and concerns. Disillusionment was also felt by left-wing activists disappointed by the Social Democrats' (SPD's) moves towards the centre ground and the party's support of both nuclear power and the deployment of nuclear weapons in Germany. By the late 1970s, therefore, the opportunity existed to pull together 'the energy and experience of a relatively large pool of unattached young educated activists' (Frankland, 1995, p26).

The Green challenge within the electoral process began in isolated campaigns at the local level. In particular, the emergence of a small environmentalist party in Lower Saxony provided the incentive for a more unified process of electoral campaigning by these disparate movement groups at both local and *Land* level. These party lists were able to gain reimbursement of campaign expenses. The expansion of this process to a Green electoral list to contest the European parliament elections in 1979 further highlighted the value of an electoral strategy. Despite continued reservations regarding the value of a unified party organization, *Die Grünen* was formed in 1980 with the aim of campaigning as 'the aspiring parliamentary arm of both the anti-nuclear movement and the peace movement and of the new social movements, in general' (Frankland, 1995, p27).

Despite a poor performance at federal level in 1980, where the party only gained 1.5 per cent of the vote, the newly formed party continued to gain seats at both local and *Land* level. At both levels, the party began to gain influential roles, developing its reputation as a new political voice in German politics. A breakthrough at federal level was also achieved with relative speed. In October 1983 the party gained 5.6 per cent of the vote, resulting in the election of 27 Green deputies. This was strengthened in 1987 when they gained 8.2 per cent of the vote and 42 seats. In European parliamentary elections, the party polled approximately 8 per cent of the vote in 1984 and 1989. By the end of the 1980s, therefore, the party had federal representatives,

European representatives and held seats in 8 of the 11 *Landtage* (Frankland, 1995, p29).

The political experiences of the early 1990s, however, served to demonstrate to the Greens the precarious nature of their position at this time. The party became embroiled in a number of internal debates and conflicts that threatened its continuation as a national political actor. Increasing influence at *Land* level raised the possibility of potential coalition agreements, mainly with the SPD. This subsequently raised important questions regarding the core objectives of the Greens and was a major factor in the factional realo–fundis split within the party, outlined in Chapter 1.

Internal pressures were further compounded by a rapidly changing external political environment. German reunification meant that the Greens faced not only internal disagreements, but a new political landscape within which to compete – one that they did not tackle effectively. As well as adopting a very cautious and pessimistic attitude towards reunification, the Greens decided not to form a coalition with the East German Greens for the first all-German elections in 1990 (contrary to the other major political parties). The two parties chose to campaign independently and to discuss a possible merger after the election. Combined with the internal conflicts within the party, the election proved disastrous. *Die Grünen* only gained 4.8 per cent of the vote in the West, failing to break the parliamentary threshold. The East German Greens, *Bundnis '90*, did, however, gain 6.1 per cent, which meant a Green representation of only 8 seats. Had the two parties merged before the election, however, the result would have produced 26 Green seats.

The electoral failure in 1990 proved to be the catalyst for the realos to gain control within the party. The party undertook a process of organizational and strategic reform (discussed further in later chapters), which attempted to regain the political impetus that the party had achieved during the 1980s. In particular, the party concentrated upon establishing itself as a natural coalition partner for the SPD and, on rare occasions, for the Christian Democrats.

The reform process, while resulting in resignations within the party and criticisms that the Greens were losing their radical edge, served to stabilize the party. The new direction was accompanied by improving electoral performances, which subsequently engaged the Greens in numerous coalitions at *Land* level. The issue of Green unification was also finalized in 1993, when the two parties agreed to merge under the title *Bundnis '90/Die Grünen*. 1994 represented a major test for the party, with both European and federal elections. Both signified the resurgence of the Greens as they gained 10.1 per cent and 7.3 per cent respectively. The federal result was particularly significant, as the Greens became the first party in Germany to regain representation at federal level. It also established the Greens as the third major political party in the German political system. The Greens had already begun to displace the Free Democrats (FDP) as the major coalition partner at *Land* level, and now the same process was in evidence at federal level.

Further successes at *Land* level gave the Greens coalition roles in North Rhine-Westphalia (1995), Schleswig-Holstein (1996) and Hamburg (1997). The federal elections in 1998 finally broke the remaining obstacle for the Greens. With 6.69 per cent of the vote, the German Greens gained 46 seats and became the SPD's coalition partner. Joschka Fischer became minister of foreign affairs, Andrea Fischer became minister of health and Jürgen Trittin became minister of the environment.

While the 1998 election clearly represents a landmark in the German Greens evolution, the party found the coalition far from easy. The Greens found it hard to implement many of the initiatives that they sought when entering government and have had to make numerous compromises that have, at times, angered party supporters. One of the most notable examples of this was the debates concerning Germany's participation in North Atlantic Treaty Organization (NATO) actions in Kosovo. For a party with a strong pacifist commitment, being seen to condone a military campaign challenged core values and raised questions about how much compromise the party should make to its principles for the sake of government participation. In addition, Andrea Fischer resigned from her post as health minister during the BSE crisis in February 2001.

Recent years have witnessed a downturn in electoral support for the German Greens. Although gaining 6.4 per cent at the 1999 European parliament election and 7 Members of the European Parliament (MEPs), the general pattern has been one of decline. In every regional election since early 1998, the Greens have been losing votes. This has resulted in the defeat of the Red–Green coalition in Hesse and a weakening of the remaining coalitions in North Rhine-Westphalia, Schleswig-Holstein and Hamburg.[1]

CHARACTERIZING THE POLITICAL ENVIRONMENT: IDENTIFYING OPPORTUNITIES AND CONSTRAINTS

Undoubtedly, *Die Grünen's*, historical development was influenced by the political environment in which the activists found themselves and the reaction of the established political actors to the new Green challenge. The German example highlights two important themes in this respect. Firstly, there was the manner in which the established system tackled and reflected the 'new' issues surrounding the Green agenda. In particular, how strong was support and protest around these issues and what opportunities existed for these issues to be institutionalized within the system? Secondly, there was the nature of the electoral challenge facing a newly formed Green party. What barriers existed to the formation of a new party and, subsequently, to the new party achieving an electoral impact? While, in the case of the German Greens, the political environment encouraged the evolution of a 'new politics' party, to what extent can the same be said for the political opportunities in Sweden, France and the UK?

The German case highlights the close links between Green party development and social movement activism, discussed in Chapter 1, and the reaction of established state structures in responding to these new issues and concerns. In Germany, the closed structures of the established political institutions encouraged a radical form of new social movement protest exemplified by the student movement, citizen action groups and anti-nuclear campaigners. Lack of access to the political system and little response from established actors to the new issues and concerns raised by these groups forced them to seek alternative channels of activism which eventually provided the impetus for the creation and emergence of the Green party.

Kitschelt (1986) defines this relationship in terms of 'political opportunity', consisting of the:

> *. . .specific configurations of resources, institutional arrangements and historical precedents for social mobilization, which facilitate the development of protest movements in some instances and constrain them in others* (Kitschelt, 1986, p58). [2]

Kitschelt identifies within this concept both the relative 'openness' of political systems to societal demands and also the strength of these systems' capacity to implement policies (Kitschelt, 1986, p64).[3] These dimensions, he claims, influence the opportunities available to new forms of political activism. Where political systems are 'open' and 'weak', movements can focus their activities upon established institutions. However, where systems are 'closed' and display 'considerable capacities to ward off threats to the implementation of policies', movements are more likely to be forced to adopt 'confrontational, disruptive strategies orchestrated outside established policy channels' in order to influence political decisions (Kitschelt, 1986, p66).

As well as a formal setting, however, informal processes also influence the levels of access available within a political system. Kriesi et al classify these informal procedures and strategies towards challengers as being either '*exclusive* (repressive, confrontative, polarizing) or *integrative* (facilitative, cooperative, assimilative)' (Kriesi et al, 1992, p222). By combining both the formal and the informal structural settings, they identify a range of different contexts within which political mobilization takes place.

However, classifications such as these only go so far in explaining the pattern of political opportunities facing new challengers to established systems. Rootes (1997), for example, argues that political systems represent a much more fluid process than these types of classification allow for. Informal procedures can often have strikingly diverse impacts upon different groups within a political system. At one level, states and state institutions may vary in their treatment of different social movements and movement organizations across policy areas. Hence, a system that is informally inclusive for one group may remain exclusive to another. Alternatively, the openness of a political system may also reflect the ability of groups to respond to the political opportunities available to them:

> *For those taking collective action, it is not simply a question of whether a political system is objectively open or closed, but also whether (and how) it is perceived as open or closed. Even the perceived existence of opportunities and constraints does not mean that they will automatically be seized or accepted: collective actors do not simply shape their action to fit pre-existing contours of the political landscape* (Rootes, 1997, p14).

Clearly, therefore, many contingent factors have to be considered within the context of the political environment, which are not necessarily reflected within structural classifications such as those provided by Kitschelt or Kriesi et al. This analysis, therefore, utilizes these classifications merely as a comparative starting point, before looking more closely at the specific experiences of new social movements within different party systems.

As well as gaining a picture of the opportunities available for movement activism, further comparative criteria are also required to assess the opportunities available for transforming this into a party-political context. Party system classifications, such as those outlined in Chapter 2, provide a starting point by both distinguishing between multiparty and two-party systems of different varieties and, also, in line with Sartori's classification, assessing whether parties possess either 'blackmail' or 'coalition' potential.[4] Mair's classification of the opportunities available to small parties within different types of party system can also be applied to the Greens in this context.[5] Again, referring back to the discussion of the German Greens above, the existence of state subsidies to support campaign expenses, and the relatively low 5 per cent threshold to parliamentary representation, encouraged activists to view the electoral path as a viable option. Indeed, Frankland even suggests that the low threshold was 'a vital ingredient of the glue holding the Greens' heterogeneous activists together' (Frankland, 1995, p26). At both federal and *Land* level, the Greens could potentially develop both blackmail and coalition potential, which gave them a strong position from which to develop.

How does this compare with the situation facing the emerging Greens in Sweden, the UK and France? Table 3.1 provides a comparative guide to the political environments facing the Greens in these three countries. The first two categories use political opportunity structure (POS) classifications to identify the formal and informal patterns of access available for the representation of new issues and concerns within the state structures. Since Green parties are clearly identified as the political arm of the 'new politics' protest, the level of accommodation to such concerns within state structures is clearly an important factor. The remaining categories look more specifically at the party systems and the opportunities available for small parties to gain a role within them. The categories focus upon defining the type of party system, identifying the nature of the electoral system and, finally, outlining the opportunities available to small parties within these systems.

Table 3.1 identifies all three countries as having strong, centralized state structures that are relatively autonomous from their environments, especially from newly emerging pressures such as 'new politics' issues. Few 'formal' opportunities exist for access to the state. However, closer examination of these systems reveals some important differences. Indeed, opportunities for the representation of new issues vary markedly between the three countries, despite the suggested closure of the state structures to new forms of protest.

Both the British and Swedish systems are classified as reflecting a pattern of 'informal inclusion', in which, although formally appearing closed to new issues and challenges, various 'informal strategies exist, which make the state more accessible than one might have expected at first' (Kriesi et al, 1995, p37). In the UK, for example:

> *...there may be Schumpeterian competition for 'control' of the executive in a winner-takes-all electoral system – but outside this there has been, since the early 19th century, a wealth of informal activity and influence by non-governmental groups on particular 'new' issues* (Grove-White, 1991, p8).

Table 3.1 *Party System Structures in the UK, France and Sweden*

Country	Formal State Structures	Overall Structural Settings	Classification of Party System	Electoral System	Opportunities for Small Parties
UK	Strong; centralized	Informal inclusion	'Large party system'; two-party; moderate left–right cleavage	Single-member constituency (first past the post)	Weak; lack blackmail or coalition potential; main opportunities at local level
France	Strong; centralized	Selective exclusion	'Transitionary system'; multiparty (two block); strong left–right cleavage	Double-ballot majority	Weak unless part of a coalition; possible coalition or blackmail potential; local level offers greater opportunities
Sweden	Strong; centralized	Informal inclusion	'Small party system'; multiparty (left dominant); moderate left–right cleavage	Proportional representation (4% threshold)	Strong on passing 4% threshold; good possibilities of coalition or blackmail potential; local level offers chances to hold balance of power

These informal channels are not open to all groups, however, and are accessible at a price – namely, to 'conform to, and operate within, the court-like culture of the capital and its dominant interests' (Grove-White, 1991, p8). The UK system therefore encourages groups to seek to work within the confines of the political system and to seek a level of pragmatic accommodation within it. Arguably, this process of informal accommodation may be an influential factor in the mobilization of more radical environmental protest groups in the UK during the past decade, critical of the perceived 'institutionalization' of more established groups such as Friends of the Earth.

The Swedish system, by contrast, displays a different set of dynamics. It primarily revolves around the close relationship between the political parties and the state, reflecting a more elitist model with 'a clear emphasis on policy leadership on the part of the political parties' (Pierre and Widfeldt, 1994, p334). This is exemplified by the early parliamentary recognition of environmental issues and, in particular, nuclear debates, and the relative weakness of the environmental movement. Hence:

> *What in other countries was largely left to movement organizations and only slowly, if ever, brought into the parliamentary arena was, in Sweden, the central focus of a national election* (Jamison, Eyerman and Cramer, 1990, p42).

The early parliamentary recognition of environmental issues forced the environmental movement in Sweden to direct its activities towards established political channels rather than developing a 'new politics' identity outside of the established system. Jamison, Eyerman and Cramer go so far as to suggest that it has become so integrated within the parliamentary framework that 'the very notion of an environmental movement has faded, to some extent, from common usage' (Jamison, Eyerman and Cramer, 1990, p59).

The French system displays a pattern of 'selective exclusion', combining both a strong state with an exclusive dominant strategy. New social movement mobilization, as a consequence, is concentrated more within unconventional forms of protest. A strong tradition of protest has, however, influenced the impact of 'new politics' protest. Environmental protest groups who represented a radical alternative in countries such as Germany had to share the political stage in France with many other protest movements. Even where environmental protest movements, such as the anti-nuclear movement, were successful in mobilizing protest, the state has largely been successful in dealing with it. A 'feather-quilt strategy' (Berger, 1972) was often adopted whereby established parties merely made small, cosmetic changes and waited for the protest groups to self-destruct through internal divisions, knowing that they lacked the political strength to continue for a prolonged period without access to state or political representation. The French political system offers few positive avenues for environmental campaigners beyond the confines of the established political parties. Social movement activism in France has, therefore, focused more upon attempting to influence the main political parties rather than seeking the creation of new parties and protest groups.

Clear distinctions are also evident within Table 3.1 regarding the nature of the electoral opportunities and barriers confronting the respective Green parties. In France, although classified as a multiparty system, the four major parties within the Fifth Republic are divided into coalitions of left and right, producing a system more akin to a two-party system, both practically and ideologically. In contrast to many of the other European countries where the left–right cleavage is perceived to be weakening in defining individuals' political allegiances, this dichotomy has remained at the heart of contemporary French politics, largely due to the left's exclusion from government between 1958–1981.[6] Although new issues such as the environment were evident within French political debates, these issues continued to be internalized within left–right dimensions, rather than challenging them. This has proved electorally problematic for small parties since voters have tended to be disinclined to transfer their allegiance from the traditional parties to support a new minor party 'even if it represented ethnic nationalist or ecological interests with which the voters sympathized' (Wilson, 1988, p521).

The double-ballot majority voting system further strengthens the position of the established political parties, placing significant barriers in the way of small parties. While national parliamentary representation is identified as a mark of political credibility, the electoral system firmly restricts access to this representation.[7] For small parties to succeed electorally, therefore, they must usually seek alliances, largely by positioning themselves on either the left or the right of the political spectrum. As Cole and Doherty summarize:

> *The French party system places a high value on parties able to construct alliances, but penalizes those that through choice or necessity remain without allies* (Cole and Doherty, 1995, p54).

Without this support, small parties in recent years have faced life on the margins of French politics.

The UK party system is classified as a 'large party system' dominated by two major parties. The only 'two-party system' within this comparative analysis, it is characterized by a high degree of internal party unity and a predominant emphasis upon national-level political activity. As in France, national parliamentary representation and influence play a strong part in shaping a party's political credibility in the eyes of the public.[8] Webb (1994) describes it as almost a 'party cartel', with established parties maintaining the first-past-the-post electoral system in order to solidify their positions of strength, monopolize state resources and almost completely eliminate small parties from access to the media.

Although the rules for creating a political party in the UK are relatively relaxed, the harsh political environment severely limits a new party's potential impact. For small parties with support relatively evenly distributed throughout the country, electoral support is rarely translated into parliamentary seats under the 'first-past-the-post' majoritarian electoral system. Even if they surmount this hurdle, the tendency towards single-party majority governments means that representation is unlikely to translate into any significant national political influence as they generally lack either 'blackmail' or 'coalition' potential. The European level, via direct European elections, has, until recently, also been closed to small parties. However, a change from the majoritarian electoral system to a more proportional 'alternative vote' method in 1999 has provided an interesting new opportunity for political influence.

In contrast to the party systems discussed above, Sweden is classified as a 'small party system' in which small parties often account for more than 50 per cent of the overall vote. For much of the past century, the Swedish party system represented a stable five-party system dominated by the left-wing Social Democrats. The arrival into parliament of *Miljöpartiet de Gröna* actually broke a 70-year stranglehold on representation by the established parties. The dominance of the Social Democrats in Sweden provides a striking contrast to both the UK and French political systems in which a left government has been the exception rather than the rule. Unlike many other multiparty systems, the Social Democrats have largely dominated the right-wing opposition, but have often sought 'broad legislative coalitions rather than narrow majorities, to pass major reforms' (Einhorn and Logue, 1988, p193). This tendency to seek a broad cross-party consensus for key policies is seen as a distinctive feature of Scandinavian party systems.

The close relationship between the Swedish political parties and the formal state structures has resulted in the emergence of parties that are often more geared towards functioning within the state than they are towards functioning as social representatives. The dominant position of the political parties has been identified as a key factor in determining their marked organizational similarities and their emphasis upon centralized organizational structures. Media focus upon key personalities and national issues has further strengthened this centralizing process.

Also contributing to the centralization of party control has been the high level of state subventions to political parties, which have replaced subscriptions and donations as the parties' major source of finance, and removed their reliance upon membership. The level of state funding received by a political party is related to the level of representation in parliament, which, as in Germany, is dependent upon breaking an electoral threshold (4 per cent). Although the financial remuneration is generous on passing this threshold, until this is achieved small parties find it hard to compete both in terms of resources and media attention. Electoral results therefore play an important role in influencing the future strategy and financial status of a party as 'the economic incentive is clearly to win votes rather than to gain or keep members' (Pierre and Widfeldt, 1994, p346).

Although this suggests little opportunity for new political parties to gain any real influence, new challengers have, at times, been able to benefit from the close relationship between the parties and the state. As the established parties have become more isolated from both their membership and society, it is argued that they became insensitive to newly developing concerns and issues such as the environmental problem, thus weakening their credibility and leading to the emergence of new challengers (Pierre and Widfeldt, 1994, p333).

SYSTEMIC CONSTRAINTS: A COMPARATIVE SUMMARY

The discussion above clearly indicates the many differences within the political environments that face the newly emerging Green parties, many of which differ quite markedly from the conditions confronting the German Greens in their battle for political space and opportunity. The state structures, both 'formal' and 'informal', provided diverse settings for the emergence of new social movement activism. As in Germany, new social movement activism reflected a notable challenge to established political protest in both Sweden and the UK. However, in Sweden this protest gravitated towards the party sphere, while in the UK, environmental movements were able to develop informal channels of access and influence if they were prepared to adopt more conventional tactics. By complete contrast, the emergence of new social movements in France represented merely another dimension within a long tradition of protest activity directed against an 'exclusive' state structure.

If the environment for social movement activism displays an interesting variety, a similar diversity is evident when comparing the opportunities for Green party development. In each case, achieving a national electoral breakthrough represents an important step in a party's potential development. However, the respective systems provide differing barriers to achieving this outcome. In Sweden, as in

Germany, electoral breakthrough leads to considerable financial resources once the electoral threshold is breached. In both France and the UK, the main importance of national representation lies in the political credibility that such representation provides. However, in both of these cases the electoral systems offer little encouragement for small parties, such as the Greens, to gain this credibility.

Given the broad disparity in political opportunity, context and setting, it is no surprise to discover that Green party evolution and electoral fortune follows different patterns from country to country. In particular, there are noticeable differences between the experiences of the three parties outlined below and that of *Die Grünen,* outlined earlier.

FRANCE: *LES VERTS*

Although an official party structure did not emerge until 1984, *Les Verts'* roots lie firmly within the social movement activism of the late 1960s and early 1970s. Environmental organization in France focused primarily around conservation and anti-nuclear groups.[9] Despite being able to mobilize large numbers of protesters, however, the anti-nuclear campaigns achieved little in terms of tangible success. National elect-oral campaigning began in 1974 when René Dumont was selected to stand as a presidential candidate, although notions of a unified party organization were disregarded at this time.[10] Instead, electoral cam-paigns were loosely coordinated with groups organizing campaigns together but disbanding any formal unified organization after the election.

This pattern continued during much of the 1970s, with electoral participation representing a strategy for focusing people's attention upon the ideas of alternative living and campaigning rather than an expectation of gaining parliamentary representation (Faucher, 1996, p1).[11] The double-ballot electoral system enabled voters to express a preference for small groups in the first round of voting without feeling that their votes would be wasted overall. However, continued participa-tion in elections inevitably led to calls for a more permanent form of organization.

The electoral success of the *Parti Socialiste* (PS) in 1981, and its failure to champion Green issues, provided further impetus for a new political party. When the PS opted to continue the French nuclear programme, environmental movements who had hoped for a new attitude from a left-wing government realized they must now seek an alternative Green voice. Consequently, despite continued reticence among many movement activists, a national organization was created in 1984 under the title *Les Verts – Confédération Écologiste/Parti Écologiste*. However, as Faucher suggests:

> *. . .despite their proclaimed unity, the ecology movement was still divided into several groups.* Les Verts *could pretend to be the sole Green voice in politics but many Green societies and groups remained active at the margin of the political scene* (Faucher, 1996, p2).[12]

Initial electoral performances for the newly formed party were encouraging, achieving 3.4 per cent of the vote in the 1984 European parliament elections, and gaining its first three regional councillors in 1986. These results gave *Les Verts* an additional level of legitimation within the system and justified an electoral strategy.

Following the successes of 1986, the party developed its identity under the *de facto* leadership of Antoine Waechter.[13] Waechter emphasized the importance of electoral success to the party, stating that it would 'never be efficient until we have overcome the electoral threshold of credibility' (cited in Prendiville, 1994, p45). The party's electoral performances improved steadily during the late 1980s, reflecting both national and international environmental concern. Waechter gained 3.8 per cent of the first round votes in the 1988 presidential elections, further establishing himself at the forefront of the party. In 1989 the party gained 1369 seats in municipal elections, with support rising to 10–15 per cent in many large towns and breaking the representative threshold in the European parliament elections (Prendiville, 1994, p45).[14]

While placing the environment firmly on the political agenda, electoral success also created its own controversies. In 1990, Brice Lalonde created a direct rival to *Les Verts* with a new party, *Génération Écologie*.[15] *Génération Écologie* largely represented a vehicle for Lalonde's personal political ambitions, containing none of the organizational or structural characteristics of other European Green parties and adopting a more pragmatic stance upon key issues such as nuclear power. While *Les Verts* quickly disassociated themselves from any form of cooperation with *Génération Écologie*, the exigencies of the French political system soon highlighted the implausibility of this stance.

Initially the two parties competed directly against one another, resulting in a direct split in the Green vote. In the 1992 regional elections, *Les Verts* received 6.8 per cent and *Génération Écologie* 7.1 per cent (Cole and Doherty, 1995, p45). Although the combined environmental vote of nearly 14 per cent represented a strong overall Green performance, *Les Verts* activists were disappointed to find that having struggled for nearly ten years for a level of electoral respectability, their thunder had been stolen by Lalonde's ability to attract significant levels of support. Despite this, the regional election results still contained successes – most notably, Marie-Christine Blandin becoming both the first ecologist, and the first woman, to be elected leader of a regional council in Nord Pas de Calais (Holliday, 1994, p65).[16]

The election results clearly demonstrated that regardless of the party's attitudes towards Brice Lalonde and *Génération Écologie*, while the environmental vote remained split, *Les Verts* would be unlikely to gain national representation. In 1992, therefore, after significant internal debate, *Les Verts* and *Génération Écologie* signed the *Entente Ecologiste,* agreeing to act as a single campaigning unit for the 1993 national elections. With opinion polls estimating support for the alliance at around 15 to 20 per cent, it seemed that national representation was within reach. However, the *Entente* lacked cohesion, with the two parties often openly contradicting one another. In addition, voters were keen to position the Greens within left- or right-party parameters, encouraged by the PS, who openly declared their intention to stand down in favour of better-placed environmental candidates in the second round. The Greens found themselves allied to the left in the public's eyes, despite having no commitment to such a position.[17] The final results reflected these difficulties, with the *Entente* only gaining 7.7 per cent of the vote. [18]

Failure to break the parliamentary barrier provoked bitter recriminations from the two parties. Within *Les Verts,* internal division focused upon strategic direction that became personalized around Antoine Waechter and Dominique Voynet during candidate selection for the presidential election. At the 1993 party conference, Voynet gained the upper hand as activists voted against a continuation of the 'autonomous' stance and in favour of closer links with the alternative left.[19] The early 1990s were a disappointing period for *Les Verts.* The party lost its European representatives and although the number of Green councillors rose, few were elected on purely Green lists (Faucher, 1996, p12). The presidential election proved no more successful, with Voynet only gaining 3.35 per cent of the vote.

A dramatic and largely unexpected change in fortunes occurred during 1996–1997 as Voynet's left-leaning strategy culminated in an electoral agreement with the PS as part of a broad left alliance. President Chirac's decision to call parliamentary elections a year early resulted in a surprise win for the left coalition. While *Les Verts* still only gained an average of 5.12 per cent in the first round of voting, their position within the alliance ensured that eight candidates were elected after the second ballot and resulted in the installation of Dominique Voynet as environment minister. *Les Verts* had therefore, somewhat paradoxically, finally succeeded in breaking the national parliamentary threshold, while gaining a smaller share of the vote than in previous national elections. The role in the governing coalition has served to increase the visibility and impact of the Greens. While being subject to the pressures of compromise, as in Germany, *Les Verts* have been able to highlight government successes such as the stopping of the *Superphénix* and *Le Carnet* nuclear plants and a continuing role in the climate change negotiations surrounding the Kyoto protocol.

This position has also enhanced the Greens' electoral profile. The party continues to have to face rivals for the Green vote, in the form of *Génération Ecologie* and a new party led by Antoine Waechter, *Mouvement Ecologistes Independent* (MEI); but it has overcome this, gaining 70 regional council seats in 1998 and consolidating its support with 9.8 per cent of the vote and 9 MEPs at European level the following year. In contrast to the downturn in support in Germany, surveys in France indicate a strong level of support and approval for the Greens as a coalition partner, and municipal elections served to confirm the importance of the Greens for the continued electoral success of the left coalition.

THE UK: THE GREEN PARTY

In the UK, the emergence of the British Green party was not primarily the result of the integration of new social movement groups within a party organization. In fact, party development was never a prime concern for new social movement activists in the UK. As Wall (1994) describes, the Green party's creation was actually a rather ad hoc affair:

> *Finding to their surprise that there were no legal require-ments necessary to establish a party, they simply placed an advertisement in* the Coventry Evening Telegraph *on 31 January 1973 proclaiming the existence of PEOPLE and asking for members willing to stand as candidates* (Wall, 1994, p16).

Although the political system presented few barriers to party forma-tion, it was not as forthcoming in nurturing its development. During the 1970s, the party developed small regional groups to stand candi-dates in elections, but had difficulty gaining media exposure or increasing membership.[20] The 1980s reflected a change of direction as the party gained a more left-wing, 'new politics' identity, becoming a more decentralized, community-based, 'anti-party' organization in line with other emergent Green parties. Funding difficulties continually restricted the party's electoral strategy; while a good campaign might increase public awareness, it could also result in financial collapse with the loss of electoral deposits. Electoral activity, therefore, remained minimal and focused primarily upon local and parish council elections.[21]

Nationally, the party stood its first by-election candidate in 1975 and stood 53 candidates at the 1979 general election, gaining the right to a television election broadcast. The environmentalist Jonathon Porritt emphasized the importance of this strategy, claiming:

> *The whole future of the Ecology party is at stake on this issue. . . . A campaign of 50, and the resulting media coverage will totally transform the nature of the Ecology party, in terms of its national credibility, its overall strength, the calibre of its membership, its range of influence and its whole future* (cited in Wall, 1994, p36).[22]

The electoral strategy focused almost exclusively upon heightening the party's profile rather than any real consideration of gaining parliamentary representation. An increase in party membership to 5000 by 1980 in this context, therefore, represented a more significant outcome than the 40,000 votes that the candidates received at the polls (Wall, 1994, p38).

The new influx of members continued the transition to a more alternative party, utilizing political strategies such as community action, Non-Violent Direct Action campaigns, and the development of a closer attachment to the environmental movements.[23] However, the more centralist members argued that the party needed to focus more upon its electoral activities, marking the beginning of a long-term factional split within the Green party similar to that within *Die Grünen*. While some activists identified poor electoral results as evidence against prioritizing an electoral strategy, others interpreted these results as an indication of the need to accept the rules of the game within the party political arena.

The Green party's biggest electoral success came during the 1989 European elections. As in France, external forces played a key role in influencing these developments. As well as international environmental issues, more localized events, including seal deaths along the UK coastline and the discovery of poisonous algae in the North Sea, made the environment a central issue of the European campaign. In addition, the major parties in the UK were in a state of flux, placing the Greens in an unusually strong position.[24] Nevertheless, even given such favourable circumstances, the 14.9 per cent of the vote that the party received surpassed even their highest expectations.[25]

This result represented the first evidence that the public identified the Green party as a credible political force, and led to unrealistically high expectations within the party for the forthcoming general election. A mood of optimism prevailed, often in the face of contradictory facts. A more realistic perception of the situation would have recognized that the established parties would be far more competitive in a national campaign and that convincing the electorate to vote Green at a general election would be a far tougher task. In addition, the Green party's European performance had resulted in intense media scrutiny and a dramatic influx of members.[26]

Attempting to build upon the electoral breakthrough of 1989, the party sought to reorganize itself via the Green 2000 initiative. Unfortunately, Green 2000 proved to be the battleground for control of the Green party, acting as a spark igniting tensions between those members who saw party politics as the best way forward and those who wanted a much broader frame of activism. Factional conflicts, accompanied by a changing political climate, were detrimental to the party's 1992 general election campaign. Although standing more candidates than in any previous general election, the party received on average only 1.3 per cent of the vote. The reaction to the electoral disappointment provoked deeper internal factionalism and a dramatic fall in membership. In combination with the large financial cost accrued during the election campaign, the party found itself verging on bankruptcy.

From this low point, the Green party has, in recent years, concentrated upon rebuilding itself (Burchell, 2000). A new strategy plan, 'Basis For Renewal', was introduced in 1993, aimed at reconciling the factional tensions within the party. The party's electoral focus was transferred to the local level, where representation was clearly more attainable. The strategy did not ignore national elections, but saw them more as an opportunity to challenge the major parties on policies, raise the party's profile and highlight the undemocratic nature of the UK electoral system. Although not as dramatic as the 1989 election results, the strategy has proved relatively successful. In 1993, the Greens gained a seat on Oxford County Council, which was followed by other successes in the local elections in 1995 and 1996. A similar approach was adopted for the 1997 general election, with campaigning focused upon areas in which Green party support was strongest.[27]

1999 and 2000 brought some small breakthroughs for the Greens and gave a suggestion of what might be possible under a different electoral system. Changes to the electoral system for the European parliament elections resulted in the Greens facing a national-level election under a proportional system for the first time. Proportional systems had also been utilized earlier in the year for the elections to the devolved assemblies in Wales and Scotland. Although failing to make a breakthrough in Wales, the Scottish Green party gained one representative in the new parliament. This limited success was followed by the election of two MEPs in the European elections, giving the Greens a voice within the Green group in the European parliament for the first time. In May 2000, the Greens also gained 11 per cent of the votes for members of the new London assembly, giving them 3 of the 25 seats (Burchell, 2000). However, the extent of this breakthrough was again put into perspective by a continued pattern of marginalization in the 2001 general election. The results provided little prospect for a Green party breakthrough at national level.

SWEDEN: *MILJÖPARTIET DE GRÖNA*

Miljöpartiet de Gröna's emergence shares some similarities with *Die Grünen* in that it reflects the failure of the long-standing political parties to effectively incorporate the newly emerging issues and debates of the 1960s and 1970s into their political programmes. In many respects, this is surprising, as Sweden has often displayed a progressive attitude towards environmental issues.[28] Within the party sphere, environmental issues were duly represented, with both the centre party and the left party adopting an environmental stance and championing the anti-nuclear cause. Nuclear power lay at the heart of Swedish environmental protest and played a key role in the Social Democrats' first electoral defeat for almost 70 years in 1976. However, while anti-nuclear campaigners looked to the centre party to instigate reform, it chose to compromise on the anti-nuclear stance in order to gain concessions from its centre–right coalition partners in other policy areas.

The nuclear issue returned to the forefront of the political agenda following the Three Mile Island accident in 1979; faced with mounting pressure, the Social Democrats proposed a national referendum on the nuclear power issue. Although the referendum once again ended in defeat for the anti-nuclear campaigners, the campaign united previously localized and disparate groups under a single umbrella organization, the People's Campaign Against Nuclear Power, which would later provide the foundations for *Miljöpartiet de Gröna*. The referendum itself further damaged the reputation of the main political parties and the party system in the eyes of many activists, leaving few potential channels for action:[29]

> ...*the environmentalists had attempted to phase out nuclear power through the mechanism of ordinary parliamentary elections and through the extraordinary mechan-*

ism of referendum. Both had failed. The most promising remaining option was to form a party (Vedung, 1991, p271).

Miljöpartiet de Gröna emerged in the wake of these events during 1981. The strong feeling over the anti-nuclear issue and the growing distrust of the long-standing political parties helped to provide a solid base from which to build support for the party. The party programme pronounced:

> *More and more people are experiencing political homelessness. The old parties are too tied up with traditions and prestige. Thus, they cannot press for the essential change of course with enough will and strength* (*Miljöpartiet de Gröna*, 1985, p6).

Miljöpartiet twice fell short of surpassing the 4 per cent threshold required to gain national representation, gaining 1.7 per cent in 1982 (Ruin, 1983, p7) and 1.5 per cent in 1985 (Lindstrom, 1986, p77). The system of state funding severely limited the resources available to *Miljöpartiet de Gröna* in comparison to the other parties, while lack of national representation also restricted access to the media and excluded the party from specific election programmes (Vedung, 1988, p95). In addition, opinion polls placed the Greens under 'other parties' rather than giving them an individual listing. As voters could not accurately calculate whether or not the party had enough support to break the threshold, they were prey to false claims that votes for the Greens would be 'wasted'.

Although the national level proved inaccessible, the party was able to make notable inroads at the municipal level. No representational threshold meant that the party gained 124 seats on 96 of the 284 councils in 1982 (Ruin, 1983, p70), and improved on this in 1985, averaging 3 per cent of the vote and gaining 260 seats on 160 councils (Lindstrom, 1986). These results provided the party with an important breakthrough in terms of political credibility.

As with the other Green parties, both national and international environmental problems played an important role in strengthening the party's position during the late 1980s. By 1988, environmental issues and political corruption were at the top of the campaign agenda in Sweden, with Green issues dominating to such an extent that analysts described the 1988 national election as 'the environment election' (Bennulf and Holmberg, 1990).[30] The party received 5.5 per cent of the national vote, gaining 20 seats and breaking the parliamentary stranglehold of the major parties.

Although this represented a vital breakthrough, the party failed to gain the balance of power between the two major 'blocs', leaving it relatively marginalized.[31] However, *Miljöpartiet* had managed to turn support into national representation, negating the claims of 'wasted' Green votes, and the additional resources gained through parliamentary representation allowed it to compete on a more even footing. The party also made considerable gains at municipal level, gaining 698 seats on 260 municipal councils and holding the balance of power on 40 of them. In addition, they gained 101 seats and representation on all 25 county councils.[32] Again, increased electoral support led to greater media attention, a rise in party membership and competition from other parties for the environmental vote. The party also faced pressure from supporters who wanted to see Green party members active within parliament. Here, again, the expectations of what the party could achieve far outweighed the practicalities of the political situation that it faced.

By 1991, *Miljöpartiet's* electoral position had weakened. With the environment replaced by national economic issues, the Greens found their support slipping. Internally, *Miljöpartiet* also faced difficulties, running a poorly organized campaign with party spokespersons at times openly contradicting one another. In addition, the party was forced into 'left–right' political debates despite claiming these divisions to be irrelevant. The party's refusal to work with a government headed by Conservative Carl Bildt automatically placed them on the left and lost them votes from the centre, where they had traditionally gained substantial support. *Miljöpartiet* also failed to show their competence in other fields when environmental issues were no longer at the top of the agenda. The impact of these pressures proved crucial, with the party failing to maintain its parliamentary representation and gaining only 3.4 per cent of the vote (Bennulf, 1995).

Electoral failure forced the Greens to re-evaluate their position. In contrast to the conflict evident in the other case studies, however, party activists, convinced that they could regain national representation, united to restructure the party organization and tackle the problems that had emerged during the party's first parliamentary term. Although national representation may have been lost, the party maintained a key role on a number of municipal councils. In Gothenburg, for example, it was seen as a credible political partner by both left and right. However, loss of state funding forced the party to reduce its national activities and facilities, further highlighting the importance of national representation.

The 1994 election was significant, not just because *Miljöpartiet* regained national representation (becoming the first party in Sweden ever to do so), but also because of the nature of the campaign. In contrast to 1988, the 1994 election was described as 'grey', with spending at the top of the agenda and a campaign billed as a 'Swedish competition in who can save the most' (Bennulf, 1995, p142). *Miljöpartiet's* campaign focused upon what could be described as a 'non-Green' issue – namely, opposition to Swedish membership of the European Union (EU). In addition, the party displayed a much more 'professional' approach to the electoral contest, presenting a well-coordinated and organized message and appearing as a more 'conventional' political party. The party gained 5 per cent of the vote and 18 seats in the Riksdag, but once again narrowly missed gaining the balance of power.[33]

If the 1991 election highlighted the frailty of the Greens' support when the environment was not top of the political agenda, 1994 demonstrated the value of highlighting alternative issues in order to achieve success on a long-term basis. The EU issue proved to be a powerful campaign tool, not only in 1994 but also in the 1995 European parliament elections. Increasing animosity towards the EU among the Swedish electorate following membership, and the opportunity for a protest vote in a 'secondary' election, resulted in an unprecedented level of support. The party received the highest vote for any Green party in a national election, gaining 17 per cent of the vote and four seats in the European parliament.[34] Interestingly, however, experience had taught the Greens to cautiously play down the impact of this result.

The party has continued to be threatened by the prospect of losing national parliamentary representation due to the instability of its support. As such, one of its primary aims has been to develop a stable electoral base that can provide at least the 4 per cent of the vote required to break the threshold. This difficulty was in evidence again at the 1998 national elections when estimates of support for the Greens ranged from approximately 3 per cent to 8 per cent. Despite the uncertainty, however, *Miljöpartiet* gained 4.5 per cent and maintained a national presence of 16 seats in the Riksdag. More significantly, the election results proved to be the worst for the Social Democrats for 70 years, and forced them to rely upon the support of the Greens and the Left Party to form a government. Rather than a formal coalition, however, the Greens agreed to a 'toleration' agreement whereby the party supported the minority government on certain issues in return for concessions to the Greens. While the 1999 European election results were always bound to prove a disappointment in comparison to the result in 1995, the party was still pleased to gain 9.5 per cent and 2 MEPs, maintaining a relatively solid base of support.

Linking Party History with Political Context

While primarily providing a useful contextual background for many of the issues and conflicts discussed in more depth in the following chapters, the discussion above demonstrates the varying challenges facing the Green parties. All of the Green parties have been influenced by the growth of the new social movements and the significance of international environmental concerns during the late 1980s; however, the impact of these factors has varied in line with national specificities and structural constraints.

All three parties differ from the German model regarding party formation. In both France and Sweden, movement activists were initially reluctant to move towards the development of a formal party organization. However, systemic barriers restricted the opportunities for the movements to gain any form of political voice either through informal channels or through existing party structures. It was clearly these pressures that forced both sets of activists to consider the formation of a new political party. In France, for example, the creation of *Les Verts* is identified as:

> *. . .a compromise on the part of ecologist activists who, no doubt unconsciously, transformed a somewhat diffuse 'social movement' into a political party with the consequence of precipitating a loss of radicality and an increase in institutional representation* (Prendiville, 1989, p87).

Similarly, in Sweden the failure of traditional parties to provide an effective voice for the anti-nuclear campaign pushed these groups towards the creation of a new political party to represent their views. The Green party in the UK, by contrast, appears something of a rarity in that its formation had very little to do with the experiences of the new social movements at all, often being regarded as a hindrance rather than as a necessary development. Hence, while movement activism, as in Germany, was influential in shaping the Swedish and French Green parties' anti-party, 'new politics' commitments, the UK party's roots lie much closer to a less radical form of conservationism, with the 'new politics' dimension only emerging during the early 1980s.

The broad growth in environmental awareness throughout Europe during the late 1980s provided all of the parties with increased recognition and electoral support, allowing them to take advantage of a more high-profile position. However, the extent of electoral success enjoyed by these other parties often failed to match that experienced by *Die*

Grünen. A common dilemma for the parties was that increased success was accompanied by greater media attention, on the one hand, and increased expectations from party activists and supporters, on the other. The political salience of Green issues also brought an instant reaction from established political parties in all cases, as they attempted to react to these new concerns.

Die Grünen were not the only Green party to suffer electoral set backs during the early 1990s. With the environment no longer taking centre stage, Green parties were forced to compete under much less favourable conditions. Electoral disappointments were accompanied by internal post-mortems, which involved reassessing party strategies and procedures. Again, the French and Swedish cases are similar to the German example in that internal party change was followed by electoral success. However, in the UK the Green party again spent much of the decade marginalized within the political system, with success emerging only via a change of systemic rules.

Despite clear similarities in the historic pattern of Green party development, it is evident that the different electoral systems have placed a diverse pattern of constraints on the Greens gaining representation at a national level. While these barriers have been breached in all four cases, the extent to which this has been achieved has varied significantly. In the UK and France, the electoral barriers are severe, with both parties facing majoritarian systems that drastically restrict the opportunities for small parties. The Green party in the UK has continually failed to break this barrier effectively at the national level. *Les Verts* also failed to break the majoritarian electoral system independently, gaining representation via an alliance with the left. Electoral barriers in Sweden and Germany provide less of an obstacle, with the main barrier being an electoral threshold. While, in both cases, the parties took some time to breach these thresholds, remaining above them has proved a more significant challenge. Defeats in the 1990s highlight the volatility of Green party support and raise questions over the parties' abilities to maintain a solid base of support.

While gaining electoral support may represent a significant achievement, translating this into effective parliamentary representation proves far harder. All of the parties recognized an important connection between national representation and political credibility. Gaining national representation in each case was seen as vital to the process of raising awareness of Green issues and, subsequently, support for the parties. Although all of the Green parties experienced a dramatic increase in support during the late 1980s, only *Die Grünen* and *Miljöpartiet* in Sweden were able to turn this support into national representation.

Gaining representation undoubtedly provided an impetus for Green supporters and activists and suggested to voters that a Green vote could be influential. Failure to achieve this, however, often resulted in the opposite effect. As a result, the Green party's success in the 1989 European elections can be regarded as a double-edged sword. While it identified a substantial level of support for the party, the result demonstrated that even with 15 per cent of the vote, it could not gain representation under the majoritarian electoral system. While this encouraged calls for a change in the electoral system, the more immediate response was to imply that Green votes were wasted votes. Despite gaining public support, without representation the Green party remained a negligible political force. By contrast, *Miljöpartiet* gained credibility at both local and national levels via electoral success, although failure to gain a 'hinge' position restricted the influence that the party could achieve while in parliament. Finally, in France the importance of breaking the national barriers to representation were clearly influential in pushing the party towards electoral agreements with both *Génération Écologie* and the PS.

State subsidies also appear to play a crucial role in shaping a party's development. In Sweden, breaking the 4 per cent threshold resulted in significant financial remuneration for the Greens. Conversely, failure to maintain this level of support and the loss of the subsidy both have important repercussions. This undoubtedly provides added incentive to the prioritization of a national electoral strategy. In stark contrast, the complete absence of state subsidies in the UK has made electoral campaigning a very different strategic and financial issue. Financial considerations affected both the number of seats in which the Green party could stand candidates and the level of campaigning available to support this. Added to the deposit costs for standing candidates, funding is as much of a barrier in the UK as the electoral system itself. Party membership, as the central source of funding, becomes another crucial issue for the Green party, a pressure that is removed from both the Swedish and German Greens. In terms of resources, the UK Green party lies far behind the other parties that it seeks to challenge, as well as many of the other European Green parties.

One of the most direct impacts of these structural pressures is reflected in the differing perceptions among the parties themselves of Green party 'success' or 'failure'. While the most direct measure of success ultimately rests with the level of support a party gains at elections, as has been demonstrated, the impact of the results achieved by the four Green parties reflects the context in which these results were attained. In Sweden and Germany, the Green parties measured success or failure in terms of breaking the electoral threshold and the ability to maintain this position. By contrast, in both France and the

UK, 4 or 5 per cent of the national vote doesn't reflect the same level of success because it rarely results in any form of representation. In France, gaining 'success' through national parliamentary representation involved the development of strategic alliances more than increasing vote share. Thus, the 1997 election was perceived as a success as the party achieved this goal, even though it managed to gain fewer votes than at previous national elections.

For similar reasons, the Green party in the UK translates the 'success' or 'failure' of electoral campaigns quite differently. The stark electoral opportunities offered by the UK system means that failure to gain national representation is not identified as a significant failure for the party. Instead, the party has increasingly focused upon gaining slow success at local level and greater recognition from the public. However, the change in the electoral system for both the devolved assembly election and the European elections placed a different slant on results. Although the party still received a level of support that would provide no success at national elections, the election of Green representatives represented a vital breakthrough for the party.

Clearly, therefore, significant ambiguity exists in defining the Greens' electoral development in terms of success or failure. We cannot simply assess the success or failure of the different European Green parties purely in terms of the number of votes gained at elections. As these four cases demonstrate, similar levels of support can have vastly different repercussions, depending upon the opportunities and constraints provided by the respective party systems. Under such circumstances, it is very difficult to directly compare the electoral histories of the four Green parties. External conditions can be a major factor in shaping a party's perceptions of success or failure. Indeed, it is the perceptions of what the parties must do to 'succeed' within these vastly differing contexts that have shaped many of the internal developments and conflicts within the European Green parties. This will be demonstrated in the following chapters.

Chapter 4

Awkward Partners: Changing Strategies towards Other Parties

Whereas the conditions for the emergence of left-libertarian parties were not chosen by, but imposed on, the parties' future activists, the maintenance and growth of such parties, once initially established, is to a considerable extent a matter of activists' own calculations and choices, in interaction with those of their competitors (Kitschelt, 1993, p103).

The Green challenge concerns not only the political issues that the parties seek to represent, but is also reflected in their approaches towards political activism. The emphasis upon the inapplicability of established political processes to the 'new politics' has contributed to their identification as 'anti-party' parties and to the claim that the Greens 'advocate a set of alternative values that differ from those of the established larger parties' (Müller-Rommel, 1989, p217).[1]

The Greens' challenge to the established concepts of party political activism and their refusal to place themselves within 'left–right' parameters have, on many occasions, resulted in antagonism regarding working with other parties. Environmental solutions are not possible through the traditional ideological constructs of either left or right, it is argued; therefore, any relationships with established parties whose foundation lies within this traditional axis will inevitably prove unsatisfactory. Any links with other parties inevitably involves a connection with the political system that Green parties seek to change: they would merely be attempting to work with parties who themselves represented a significant part of the problem. An autonomous stance, therefore, represents both a critique of the established political system and an important aspect of distinguishing between 'green' and 'grey' political style and content.

As Chapter 3 demonstrated, however, Green parties have been unable to avoid at least some level of interaction with other political parties. In fact, as the Green parties have emerged as a more potent political force, this interaction has increased. While Green parties gained electoral success during the 1980s and 1990s, the 'autonomous' strategy was placed under increasing pressure as opportunities arose for some of the parties to contribute to government decision-making.

Green parties faced the difficult task of balancing the maintenance of fundamental principles that distinguish the new parties from their more long-standing counterparts, on the one hand, with the potential to develop alliances and coalitions, on the other. While coalitions could strengthen and improve the parties' development and influence, they could also result in the dilution of party principles. As Kitschelt summarizes, while a radical 'fundamentalist' Green stance could result in the party being 'abandoned by all but a hard core of committed voters', moderating their aims and working with others could mean that they become 'virtually indistinguishable from conventional leftist competitors with slight libertarian concessions in their own pro-grammes' (Kitschelt, 1993, p103).

For many, changes in Green party strategies towards other parties reflect a process of adaptation and institutionalization within estab-lished party systems.[2] Accepting to work in coalition signified not merely a change in strategic direction but, more significantly, a general acceptance of the established structures and practices of traditional competitive party politics. The more moderate a Green party becomes, the more open it will be to alliances and coalitions.

These debates certainly played a major role in the evolution of the German Greens as the party transformed its coalition strategy from one of complete hostility to one of national coalition with the Social Democrats (SPD). Conflict over this transition was also at the heart of the 'realo–fundis' disputes that ravaged the German Green party.[3] In its formative years, the Greens largely favoured a strategy of 'funda-mental opposition' (Frankland, 1995, p32). The primary aspect of this strategy was a refusal to compromise the core principles of the party merely for a share in government office. However, as Chapter 3 out-lined, electoral success has brought with it opportunities to participate in government. The German Greens have therefore had to confront this commitment to 'fundamental opposition' in the face of numerous opportunities for coalition roles at both *Land* and federal level.

The coalition process began in Hesse in 1984 and has since involved 13 regional coalitions across 9 of the 16 *Lander*. In Hesse, Greens agreed to support a minority SPD government in 1984. This followed a long process of debate and consultation regarding the suitability of a coalition strategy, and criticism of the process from the federal level of the party. Greens had already worked in local council coalitions in Hesse and this encouraged the *Land* party congress members to support the process. It also encouraged similar negotiations between the Greens and the SPD in Berlin in 1989 and Lower Saxony in 1990. The coalition process subsequently went further, with 'traffic-light' coalitions between the Greens, the SPD and the Free Democrats (FDP) in Brandenburg and Bremen. However, these early attempts often proved not only controversial but also difficult to maintain. In Hesse, the coalition lasted only 14 months and ended when Joschka Fischer resigned as environment minister over the granting of a licence for a nuclear power station. In Berlin, conflicts over issues such as German reunification and a strike by kindergarten teachers also contributed to the eventual downfall of this coalition. As Frankland suggests: 'The Greens learned how constrained a junior partner can be in enacting its radical-reformist programme' (Frankland, 1998, p13).

Coalition activities at regional level also served to heighten tensions and debates within party factions at federal level. Fundamentalists within the party pointed to the concessions that the regional parties were having to provide in order to participate in coalitions, and claimed that the very identity of the party as a radical challenge to conventional party politics was being placed in danger for few tangible gains.

The realos, by contrast, claimed that the experience and influence gained at *Land* level should be capitalized upon and expanded into further coalitions with the SPD. The party must not only win the battle over ideas and policy, they argued, but must also demonstrate to voters that they had the ability to implement these ideas. As Markovits and Gorski summarize:

> *The realos believed that it was indispensable for the Greens to issue clear-cut, unambiguous coalition offers to the SPD, especially in states with progressive SPD leaders. . . . The more Red–Green coalitions were established, so the realists hoped, the more the position of the SPD left and Green realos would be strengthened in their respective parties. Public anxieties and mistrust vis-à-vis the Greens would be stilled* (Markovits and Gorski, 1993, p216).

As the party's electoral performances waxed and waned at the end of the 1980s and early 1990s, the factional divisions became stronger and focused predominantly around the coalition issue. Fundis argued that the realos had focused far too heavily upon the relationship with the SPD and had begun to forget what the party really stood for. Meanwhile, the realos blamed the fundamentalists for seeking to almost marginalize the party when opportunities clearly existed for it to gain greater influence.

The shock of the poor electoral performance in 1990 gave the realo faction the upper hand in the party and signalled a transition in the party's strategy towards active engagement in coalitions with the SPD. These were reflected in *Land* coalitions and an overall agreement before the 1994 federal election that an SPD–Green alliance might represent the best possible way to stop the rightward trend that had dominated German politics for more than a decade. The party chose to commit itself to sharing governmental responsibility if the opportunity arose. The party programme for the 1994 election stated that the party was ready for 'a coalition of "serious" reform politics with the SPD' (Frankland, 1996, p89). Interestingly, however, the party's Mannheim conference produced a far more radical programme than this coalition strategy might have suggested. Indeed, Frankland identifies a confusing paradox emerging from this process:

> *The Mannheim conference resulted in a consensus to participate in federal government and a programme whose policies included some that (if adhered to) could block governmental participation* (Frankland, 1996, p90).

While a right-wing election victory put pay to any form of coalition in 1994, the failure of the SPD and the continuing weakness of the FDP in comparison to the Greens made the prospect of a federal Red–Green coalition a stronger possibility as the 1990s progressed. By the time of the 1998 federal elections, there was a strong level of support for the coalition policy from within the party, with 79 per cent of party supporters declaring themselves in favour of an alliance with the SPD (Hoffman, 1999, p140). However, this enthusiasm for coalition was not matched by the electorate, 63 per cent of whom stated that they did not think the Greens would make a reliable coalition partner (Roberts, 1999, p151).

The performance of the German Greens in coalition at both federal and *Land* level has, without doubt, proved to be a mixed bag, with some reaching a second and third term, while others collapsed in animosity within a relatively short space of time. However, the transition into a party of national government marked a significant step in the evolution of the German Greens, and in many ways must be attributed to the skills, knowledge and experience gained through not only the regional coalitions but also the debates and conflicts which surrounded them. The Greens were therefore able to enter into a federal coalition with a much more mature attitude regarding what they could achieve.

Clearly, therefore, within *Bundnis '90/Die Grünen,* the accept-ance of alliances and coalitions with established political parties represented a key factor in the debates and conflicts regarding the nature and direction of the party. Furthermore, it not only altered the picture within the German Greens but also altered the perception of the party externally, while also radically reshaping the political role of the party from critical outsider to partner in a governing coalition.

The German Greens have not been alone in facing this transition, however. During the 1990s, other Green parties have also had to confront the question of Green 'autonomy' and the potential of coali-tion head on. In many cases, the Green parties are no longer being viewed as radical outsiders but as potential coalition partners. In assessing the impact of changes in party strategy towards other parties, the following discussion will consider the different strategic approa-ches adopted by the Greens in Sweden, France and the UK. In partic-ular, it will question whether there is a common pattern of change evident among the Greens and assess the impact that these changes have had upon internal conflicts and debates.

GREEN PARTY STRATEGIES TOWARDS OTHER PARTIES DURING THE 1980S

Before assessing the pattern of strategic change within the Greens, it is important to consider whether the perception of Green parties as autonomous 'anti-party' parties during the 1980s is an accurate one. Also, one must also question whether this strategy was actually the result of internal party choice or forced due to the practicalities of the Greens electoral position.

Practical barriers certainly appear to be heavily influential in the UK case, as the Green party focused predominantly upon raising awareness of Green issues among the public. The environmentalist Jonathon Porritt claimed that:

> *Even as a political party, we have no illusions about the fact that our primary function is still an educative one, the spreading of Green politics to as wide an electorate as possible* (Porritt, 1984, p9).

The Green party has, however, continually distanced itself from the mainstream, even refusing to endorse other parties' candidates as being 'Green' or 'Greener'. The party justified its stance by claiming that 'the necessary radical transformation of the economy and of society is only likely with the election of Green party MPs' (Green party, 1989). The Green party's strategic emphasis therefore focused upon developing an identity as a unique party with a distinctive message concerning 'green' rather than 'grey' politics. Although links with Liberal Democrat and Labour party activists were discussed, these primarily focused upon the Green party providing an alternative home for disillusioned activists, rather than suggesting any direct links between the parties themselves.[4]

The political climate in Sweden offered more choices for *Miljö-partiet de Gröna* during the 1980s. Small parties such as the Greens could gain 'hinge' positions at both national and local levels, where their support would be required by either left- or right-party blocs, in order to gain a parliamentary majority.[5] As in the UK, however, *Miljö-partiet* sought to distance itself from traditional left–right dimensions:

> . . .*bloc politics is no longer applicable in Sweden. The new political issues of achieving a sustainable society demand other and more comprehensive solutions than the traditional ones of more growth and changed distribution of wealth (Miljöpartiet de Gröna, 1988).*

While failure to gain a hinge position at national level meant that the party remained relatively marginalized in the Riksdag, at local level *Miljöpartiet's* strategy was challenged following the 1985 elections, when they were offered a coalition role within Gothenburg City Council. Although the party agreed to a 'limited toleration agreement', it achieved little influence and made no substantial policy gains.[6] Although sharing similar attitudes towards the value of left–right distinctions as the UK Green party, the Swedish Greens appeared more ambiguous in their attitudes towards their political competitors.

Party strategy towards other parties has constantly been at the heart of debates within *Les Verts*. As outlined in Chapter 3, the French electoral system encourages small parties to seek alliances in order to gain representation and influence and discourages parties who stand in isolation. As such, it forces the party to constantly assess its relationship with other parties, with parties advising supporters on how to vote in the decisive second round of voting. It is maybe surprising, therefore, that *Les Verts'* strategic approach in the 1980s also focused upon autonomy from other parties, under the leadership of Antoine Waechter. Waechter declared that *Les Verts* should not merely be perceived as one part of a wider left movement and that the need to prioritize ecological concerns must necessarily direct the party towards an autonomous political stance. The party emphasized that 'ecology is not available for marriage', with the result that 'Green autonomy

became the defining creed of the majority current within *Les Verts*'
(Cole and Doherty, 1995, p54).

ALLIANCES, COALITIONS AND AGREEMENTS: CHANGING RELATIONSHIPS DURING THE 1990s

It would appear, therefore, that the dominant focus among the Green
parties during the 1980s rested with maintaining a distinctive Green
stance and the raising of largely neglected environmental issues and
concerns onto the political agenda. However, while the issue of
autonomy may be clearly highlighted, the prioritization of such a
strategy also reflected the limited influence and opportunities available
to the Greens at this time. In each case, lack of substantive electoral
support during this period arguably resulted in little interest from the
other political parties. By contrast, however, the late 1980s and early
1990s witnessed a dramatic rise in concern over environmental issues
and a substantial growth in support for the Green parties, raising many
more strategic questions and debates regarding interaction with other
political parties.

The Green Party: Searching for a Parliamentary Voice

Despite the rapid expansion of environmental awareness and increases
in electoral support during the late 1980s, the Green party remained
isolated within the UK party system. The major political parties sought
to incorporate environmental issues into their political agendas, rather
than developing any form of direct relationship with the Greens. Most
notable examples of this sudden convergence included Mrs Thatcher's
environment speech to the Royal Society in 1988 and the introduction
of a White Paper entitled *Our Common Inheritance* in 1989, which
it was claimed would 'set the environmental agenda until the end of
the century' (Robinson, 1992, p223).[7] During the 1990s, therefore, the
Green party was forced to accept that it was no longer the only party
discussing policies for environmental protection. By successfully
forcing environmental issues onto the political agenda, the party had
partially contributed towards its own marginalization.

Despite this, the Green party has still had to consider its attitudes
towards working with other parties during this period. Given the
difficulties of gaining a directly elected Green representative, the
Green party has sought alternative methods of gaining a parliamentary
voice. One such opportunity involved the *Plaid Cymru* MP Cynog

Dafis, who worked with the Green party on a number of environmental initiatives and whom the Green party had actively supported
during the 1992 general election. The relationship provided the basis
for a Green party-inspired private members bill concerning household
energy conservation and potentially represented an important development in the party's fight against political marginalization.

However, not all party members were comfortable with this relationship and the debate was heightened when the Cerediggion Greens
agreed to support Dafis as a joint *Plaid*/Green party candidate prior
to the 1997 general election. Critics claimed that the Green party
should not share a platform with a party that exhibited significantly
'non-Green' attitudes towards issues such as nationalism, nuclear
power and live animal exports. After lengthy debate, the national
executive concluded in April 1995 that the Green party should withdraw from the alliance due to ideological differences. As well as
resulting in the resignation of a number of Welsh party members, the
debate had broader ramifications. The issue tested the relative strength
of the national executive and, in this case, local party autonomy came
a clear second to national party strategy. The party has not entirely
broken its links with Cynog Dafis, however, resulting in a relatively
ambiguous strategy in Cerediggion at the 1997 general election.[8]

The Green party has also gained support from among the Liberal
Democrats, although this relationship appears to have benefited the
Liberal Democrats more than the Greens. The most significant example
of this was the Road Traffic Reduction Bill, introduced to parliament
by Liberal Democrat MP Don Foster and successfully passed in March
1997. The Green party's role, however, was largely ignored, leaving
many activists feeling that an important party initiative had been
hijacked by another political party, with the Greens gaining very little
from the process.[9]

The few attempts made by the Green party to develop relationships
with other parties have therefore proven relatively unsuccessful; little
has been achieved, while the process has often provoked internal party
conflict. However, for a party at the fringes of the party political arena,
it is argued, such relationships may represent the best route to gaining
influence at national level. One activist claimed:

> *Can we really believe that we are able to go it alone? Every
> other European Green party that's made it into any type
> of parliament or even onto councils has found that it
> hasn't got the power on its own. What makes us think that
> we are going to be any different? If we are going to have
> to make coalitions in the future, what's wrong with making
> coalitions now?* (Interview, 30 March 1996).

However, while the Green party can arguably claim credit for raising the profile of environmental issues and initiatives, wider recognition of its role has not been forthcoming. The problems experienced have clearly influenced the development of Green party coalition strategy, as can be seen in the following extracts from the party's 1996 strategy papers. In highlighting the dangers of such policies for the party, it stated that:

> *The Green party must preserve our own identity. Whilst appealing across the political spectrum our message should not be diluted* (Green party, 1996, p6).

It ends with a warning that 'Green party endorsements of other organizations can be dangerous for our image' (Green party, 1996, p6).

How then can one explain these strategic debates within the Green party? Figure 4.1 attempts to identify the key pressures surrounding the debates outlined above, using Harmel and Janda's criteria of 'change in dominant faction', 'leadership change' and 'external stimuli' (change which challenges the party's 'electoral', 'policy' or 'party democracy' goals).[10]

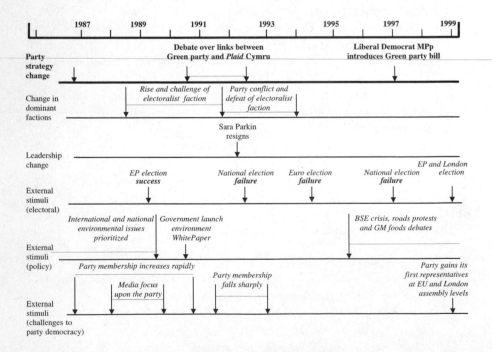

Figure 4.1 *Potential Sources of Strategy Change: The Green Party*

Figure 4.1 indicates that the party has been able to maintain a position of relative autonomy from other political parties, partly because it has not experienced any significant external stimuli challenging it to reconsider its position. A significant external stimuli may be required before the Green party is likely to be faced with important questions regarding relationships with other political parties within the UK system. The use of more proportional electoral systems in the Scottish parliament and Welsh assembly elections, and in the European parliament elections, may provide such a stimuli, but this has not been evident thus far.

Figure 4.1 highlights the links with *Plaid Cymru*, and the Liberal Democrats, although it is debatable whether these represent direct formal relationships with other parties or, rather, links with specific individuals with strong environmental commitments. The figure does suggest a rationale for the decision not to pursue the relationship with *Plaid Cymru*. The initial relationship between the Greens and *Plaid* in Cerediggion coincides with the party's period of commitment towards a national electoral strategy. Under such circumstances, support and active campaigning on behalf of Cynog Dafis clearly reflected the party's commitment to 'electoral' goals.

By contrast, the decision to end these links was taken under markedly different circumstances. Figure 4.1 indicates a change in factional dominance within the party away from the electoralist group. With the party moving away from a committed national electoral policy, concerns were expressed regarding the relationship with *Plaid Cymru* and its challenge to other party goals. In particular, the relationship with *Plaid Cymru* represented a challenge to the party's commitment to the goal of maintaining a pure policy stance. This prioritization of the 'policy' goal could also explain party conflict surrounding the relative merits of utilizing MPs from other parties to implement Green policy initiatives. While some activists questioned whether the strategy was worth the level of commitment merely for the sake of getting a diluted and often relatively weak bit of legislation onto the statute book, supporters claimed that given the unlikely imminence of an electoral breakthrough for the Green party, it represented the best alternative for achieving at least some policy goals.

Miljöpartiet de Gröna: The Unwanted Coalition Partner in Sweden

The failure to gain the hinge position in 1988 was crucial in shaping the opportunities and options available to the Greens. Affigne (1992) highlights the significance of this for the party, claiming that had the Social Democrats won three fewer seats:

> *The 20 Green deputies would have represented the critical*
> *swing bloc between the two major formations, with the*
> *power to help form – or obstruct – either a socialist or a*
> *bourgeois government, and to veto subsequent legislation*
> *proposed by either bloc* (Affigne, 1992, p7).

In contrast, both left and right blocs could largely avoid any direct relationship with *Miljöpartiet*. Overall, the established parties focused more upon regaining the 'Green vote' and removing the new party from parliament, rather than seeking areas for possible agreement or coalition. However, during the party's first parliamentary term, one opportunity did arise for the Greens to gain a greater national role and produced significant internal debate.

An opportunity to develop a working relationship with the Social Democrats arose in 1990 when changes to the government's economic policy left them with insufficient support in parliament.[11] The Social Democrats were forced to look towards the support of *Miljöpartiet's* deputies to pass the measures and opened negotiations with the Greens to this effect (Affigne, 1992, p6). Despite what appeared an important political opportunity for *Miljöpartiet*, attitudes within the party were divided. Those in favour argued that an agreement would display to voters that the Greens could be a significant and influential political force. However, critics claimed that political influence should not be gained at the expense of ideological commitments, as the economic policies proposed by the Social Democrats represented a direct contradiction to many of *Miljöpartiet's* own policy ideals and objectives.

Fears were also expressed that an agreement would threaten the party's independence and tie the Greens too closely to the left. One leading party activist, explained that:

> *I didn't think that we really wanted to do this because it*
> *seems that the parties who go too deeply into the arms of*
> *the Social Democrats, they lose at the next election. I think*
> *this is a problem, because you have to be part of a lot of*
> *decisions that you don't really like* (Interview, 21 September
> 1995).

The issue exacerbated emerging tensions between the new parliamentary group, who strongly favoured some form of agreement, and the rest of the party. This division was not kept purely within the confines of the party either, with both groups releasing different messages to the media and to the Social Democrats regarding the negotiations.

The talks between the two parties eventually collapsed and *Miljö-partiet* voted against the economic proposals. Although the Social Democrats were able to pass an alternative economic programme soon after, the experience had long-term implications concerning the Social Democrats' perception of the Greens as potential coalition partners.[12] There were also internal repercussions for *Miljöpartiet*: the debates raised questions regarding organizational coherence and authority within the party, and highlighted the emerging conflict between the attitudes within the parliamentary party and those of the broader national party membership.

Miljöpartiet de Gröna found it increasingly difficult to portray effectively, to both the media and the electorate, the rationale behind its commitment to a 'neither left, nor right' stance. External percep-tions of this strategy, however, often placed the party along these dimensions despite itself. In 1991, for example, the party's criticism of Conservative party leader Carl Bildt automatically gave the percep-tion of leaning to the left. Although not actually representing a change in policy, this 'perception' of a move to the left has been identified as a significant factor in the party's electoral failure in 1991, and undoubt-edly heightened its awareness of the volatility of Green support and the importance of attempting to maintain a centrist stance.[13]

As mentioned earlier, the party's experiences in Gothenburg provide an interesting example of the significance of the changing attitudes towards coalitions among Green activists at municipal level. The lessons of the poor agreement in 1985 enabled the Gothenburg Greens to be more prepared for the pressures and challenges of alliance discussions when similar opportunities arose in 1988, 1991 and 1994. Although failing to reach agreement in 1988, the local party caused a major controversy by agreeing to a 'sophisticated toleration agreement' with the three 'bourgeois' parties in 1991. Parkin argues that the experience of the Gothenburg Greens in 1985 and 1988 helped to explain the rationale behind the controversial stance in 1991:

> *Experience taught the Swedish Greens that the further you are from a coalition, the less power you have. If you want power, then you have to take responsibility* (Parkin, 1996, p20).

Actively taking a role within government in Gothenburg, it was argued, would demonstrate the Greens' ability to become serious political partners rather than merely a 'single-issue' environmental pressure group. Being in the government allowed the party to take direct credit for 'Green' initiatives. In addition, the toleration agreement also enabled the party to disassociate itself from those policies that it could not condone. The party could demonstrate a commitment to participation, in contrast to previous occasions when it had often been portrayed as adopting an unrealistic and unworkable stance.

This experience served the party well in producing a similar agreement in Gothenburg in 1994. The party again displayed flexibility and political aptitude in that, on this occasion, the resulting coalition was with the Social Democrats and the Left Party (Parkin, 1996, p21). For the Greens, this represented a true reflection of the 'neither left, nor right' strategy. The experience of local activists in Gothenburg, and elsewhere, has been significant in redefining the party's strategy towards other parties. Political experience and expediency gained from local negotiations has undoubtedly fed into a changing attitude within the party at the national level. As one parliamentary representative explained:

> *Over the years we have had a lot of people working in communities where they have formed alliances with other parties. So we now have a lot of people who know how to work in these political situations, which we didn't have earlier. They were more used to it, and they gained a lot of results when they cooperated. We now accept that you can go forward in small steps. Earlier people wanted to go forward in great leaps, which, of course, is something that people want to do. But if you are small, then, of course, you can't* (Interview, 22 September 1995).

Loss of national parliamentary representation in 1991 reflected the failure of the party to demonstrate its effectiveness as a national political actor, and resulted in a significant process of restructuring, both organizationally and tactically. The party's failure to make the most of the few opportunities that emerged, it was argued, contributed to the portrayal of the Greens by their opponents as an ineffective political force whose focus lay with obstruction rather than constructive policy proposals. Gaiter's (1991) study of *Miljöpartiet's* activities during the 1988–1991 parliamentary term reflects this difficulty in portraying itself as an influential and effective national political actor. Although it is evident that the party was active within Riksdag debates and votes, few substantive policies were implemented that it could claim direct credit for when again facing the electorate in 1991.

Local party activities, by contrast, demonstrated the impact that could be achieved by working with other parties. Throughout the 1990s, *Miljöpartiet* representatives were active in government at local level and continued to work with parties of both left and right. Hence, when *Miljöpartiet* re-entered parliament in 1994, the party focused upon ensuring that it was seen to make a political impact beyond merely gaining parliamentary representation. Both the 1994 and 1998 elections have enabled the Greens to adopt an influential position between the two traditional blocs. As a result, the party has avoided the dangers of direct coalition witnessed within other European examples; but it gained a position of active involvement in policy-making. This pragmatic stance was reflected in interviews with leading party activists following the 1994 election. One leading activist admitted:

> *We have changed. Earlier we said we would never work with the others and the others wouldn't work with us. However, today we have been negotiating with the govern-ment, and we have given them something and they have given us something. So there is more political reality if you like. The party wants to change things and if we don't cooperate we will never change things. We will just bang our heads against a brick wall. It doesn't get you anywhere* (Interview, 21 September 1995).

Prior to the 1998 national election, the party held a debate to decide whether or not it should provide direct support for the Social Democrats in the hope of gaining a governmental role. The outcome was that the party would not provide direct support but would, instead, outline key policy areas where it could potentially vote with the Social Democrats. Today, *Miljöpartiet* holds 16 seats in the Riksdag that provides the party with a relatively effective bargaining position. It has utilized this position to some effect, both in supporting the government and also in linking with the opposition parties to defeat government plans. Adopting this approach has also allayed fears that the Greens might find themselves acting as merely a 'Green satellite' for the Social Democrats.

Figure 4.2 identifies the pattern of change in *Miljöpartiet de Gröna* in line with the model identified by Harmel and Janda.

One might have expected that the 'electoral' stimuli of gaining national parliamentary representation, or the 'policy' stimuli of other parties incorporating Green issues, would have resulted in a change in party strategy towards other parties. However, this appears not to have been the case, due largely to the party's failure to achieve a 'hinge' position. In the Swedish context, therefore, electoral stimuli for change would be more likely when electoral performance resulted in such a 'hinge' position. This would certainly help to explain the changes to party strategy at local and municipal level where such electoral stimuli have offered the Greens a chance to gain public office.

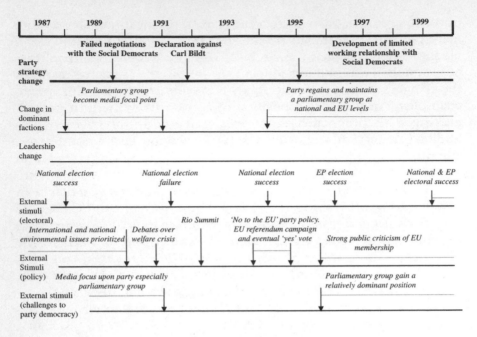

Figure 4.2 *Potential Sources of Strategy Change:*
Miljöpartiet de Gröna

This pattern doesn't, however, explain why, when the party had the opportunity for national influence, *Miljöpartiet* rejected the alliance with the Social Democrats at the national level. As with the UK example, explanations may lie in an examination of the balance between 'electoral' and 'policy' goals. On this occasion, it appears that the party's commitments to policy goals proved more influential than the merit of entering into an agreement with the Social Democrats for electoral goals. As such, this opportunity did not represent a strong enough stimuli to force an emphasis upon electoral goals and thus a change in party strategy. The prioritization of 'policy' goals in this context may also help to explain why the Greens chose to work with the Social Democrats on certain policy issues, rather than seeking a full coalition role.

Les Verts: Alliances with Green and Red

More in keeping with the experiences of *Die Grünen,* strategic positioning has often dominated *Les Verts'* party conferences and has led to numerous conflicts. These debates have centred around two attempts at coalition: firstly, with *Génération Écologie* and, secondly, with the *Parti Socialiste* (PS).

Electoral results and the obvious failings of a split Green vote provided the primary motivation behind the entente with *Génération Écologie*. However, many *Les Verts* activists were sceptical of this relationship because both the organizational style and political focus of *Génération Écologie* were markedly different from that of *Les Verts*. As with the UK Green party's relationship with *Plaid Cymru,* although *Génération Écologie* displayed a general commitment to environmental concerns, the party's 'Green' credentials were questionable. Indeed, its moderate form of environmentalism was far removed from the ideological commitments of *Les Verts*. The entente brought into question *Les Verts'* commitment to party autonomy, which had been a cornerstone of party ideology and the basis upon which Antoine Waechter had developed his position as de facto leader. Combined with a deep distrust of the motives of Brice Lalonde, opponents saw the relationship as 'a sell out of identity and soul' (cited in Faucher, 1996). What emerged, therefore, was primarily a relationship largely built upon distrust, animosity, but – most significantly – necessity.

Despite these reservations, the entente reflected members' readiness to overcome initial scepticism in the hope of gaining national electoral success.[14] One party activist described the decision as follows:

> *At the general assembly we voted for the alliance 72 per cent. It's a great score, 72 per cent, but we can consider that perhaps half of these people voted contrary to their hearts. But they voted for the possibility to save political ecology in France. In fact, it proved to be the opposite* (Interview, 28 September 1995).

Once the entente failed to break the parliamentary barrier, however, the ideological differences between the parties were exacerbated. *Les Verts* activists no longer viewed the entente as a valuable or acceptable compromise, thus hastening its demise:

> *Some people felt that we should have stayed in the alliance with* Génération Écologie *until after the European elections [1994] and get representatives there. But for the majority of people within* Les Verts, *our point of view was different. We wanted to appear different from* Génération Écologie (Interview, 28 September 1995).

For many, the collapse of the entente marked an overall failure to create an effective, independent Green alliance within the French party system: a challenge to the established party allegiances of left and right. Inevitably, the party began to question its commitment to the 'autonomous' Green strategy, suggesting that it was time to seek wider accommodation within the party system and, in particular, with the parties of the left. Many activists argued that faced with an electorate who viewed the party political process in left and right terms, the Green commitment to an autonomous *'ni droite, ni gauche'* approach merely confused voters. The Greens had been perceived by many as a party of the left and linked with the Socialists, regardless of its own statements to the contrary.[15] The new strategy proposals, championed by Dominique Voynet, called for greater links with the alternative left and a change in policy focus towards 'social' rather than predominantly 'natural' environmental concerns.

The redirection in party strategy did little to unify the wider Green movement in France, and resulted in the resignation of a number of prominent figures within *Les Verts.* That said, Voynet's strategy paper gained a significant level of support from party members within *Les Verts,* and encouraged negotiations to forge a Red–Green alliance that eventually produced a direct cooperation agreement with the PS in 1996.[16] Voynet justified this agreement by arguing that there was no other way for the party to move forward than by 'allying with the forces of the left to obtain stronger parliamentary representation' (*Les Verts*, 1 September 1996).

Under the Red–Green Accord, *Les Verts* and the PS agreed to a process of electoral cooperation in 100 constituencies. *Les Verts* agreed to support Socialist candidates in 70 of these constituencies, in return for the PS's commitment not to stand candidates in the remaining 30 constituencies where *Les Verts* had strong levels of support. This transfer of support provided the Greens with a tangible opportunity to overcome the double-ballot electoral system and break through the parliamentary threshold.[17] Many members felt that considering the party's weak political situation, the agreement represented a good opportunity for the party. Critics, however, were concerned about the level of influence the agreement gave the Socialists and the potential danger of transforming *Les Verts* into a 'Green satellite' for the PS, leaving it little room for independent manoeuvre. *Les Verts* activist Jacques Caplat argued that: 'We are on the way to accepting to be marginalized, as the Greens of the left; the environmental specialists of the PS' (*Vert Contact*, 1997).

The surprise decision to call early elections in 1998 tested the Red–Green accord earlier than anticipated, and produced a result far in excess of what *Les Verts* had anticipated. Not only had the party gained parliamentary representation, but it was now also an active member of the government. Initial developments within the coalition suggested that the Greens would be able to exert at least some influence over the Socialists. Most notable actions included the cancellation of the Rhine-

Rhone canal project and the closure of the *Superphénix* nuclear reactor. However, as with the experiences of the German Greens, *Les Verts* have found themselves party to certain government decisions that have directly challenged their ideological credentials. In 1997, the government authorized the cultivation of genetically modified maize, which led to active campaigns by environmental groups. In addition, debates also ensued regarding the underground storage of nuclear waste, the continued production of Mox (a plutonium-based nuclear fuel) and the government's road-building policy. Many of these pressures directly challenged the credibility of Dominique Voynet as a 'Green' environment minister and have raised awareness among the Greens regarding the pressures of government participation.[18]

Despite this, however, the overall picture suggests that the coalition experience has been a relatively positive one for the Greens. Indeed, the party has outlined its intention to seek a stronger and more detailed commitment from the Socialists for a continuation of the coalition process. Electorally, as well, the party has gained in credibility and support since being in coalition, suggesting that a continuation of this policy is the most viable path for Green party development.

Figure 4.3 identifies the pattern of strategy change in *Les Verts* in line with the model identified by Harmel and Janda.

Les Verts have clearly undergone much broader change in this area than the other case studies and appear to have faced many of the same

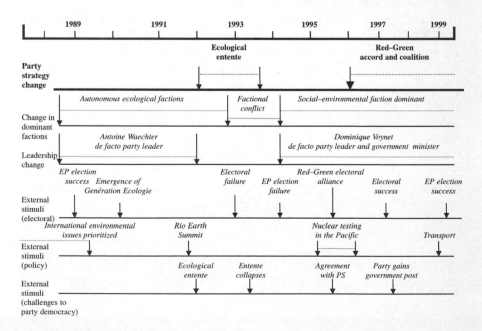

Figure 4.3 *Potential Sources of Strategy Change:* Les Verts

debates and problems witnessed within the German Greens. Figure 4.3 highlights a number of factors influencing the changing pattern of relationships. The entente represented the culmination of electoral disappointments during the period of 'autonomy' and the emergence of *Génération Écologie* as a direct Green challenger to *Les Verts*. Clearly, the emergence of *Génération Écologie* provides, in itself, a direct external stimulus that challenges the Greens' 'electoral' and 'policy' goals. Arguably, the entente implied a prioritizing of electoral goals within *Les Verts*. Consequently, its electoral failure ultimately forced a challenge to this strategy. Factional conflict and a focus upon electoral goals appear the primary motives for the party's move towards a coalition with the left. This process followed the demise of the entente, a change in factional dominance within the party, and the rise to prominence of Dominique Voynet. As in the German case, factional conflict focused directly upon issues of electoral strategy and alliances.

It is important also to note that the party's electoral goals were more clearly defined than merely aiming to gain more votes. Under the majoritarian electoral system, an increase in votes didn't necessarily equate to parliamentary representation and influence. The party's electoral goals, in this case, specifically prioritized the development of a strategy focused upon gaining national parliamentary representation. Hence, although *Les Verts* actually gained less votes in 1997, the results were perceived as the party's most successful because *Les Verts* were able to gain parliamentary seats.

The experience of coalition government also highlights the increasing prioritization of electoral goals for the Greens. As outlined above, the party has been associated with a number of awkward decisions that represent direct challenges to party policy commitments; but it has chosen to compromise on these issues for the sake of maintaining the coalition agreement. This represents a significant transition from the 'ecology is not for sale' attitude of the party under Waechter. It also suggests a growing significance of the fourth possible goal of 'maintaining public office' for *Les Verts*, since government influence has undoubtedly increased the party's image as an influential political actor in France, and has provided evidence of direct 'Green' influence on policy to put before the electorate.

CHANGING RELATIONSHIPS: A COMPARATIVE SUMMARY OF THE THREE CASE STUDIES

All of the Greens have confronted the issue of working with other parties. In doing so, they have encountered a dilemma concerning

Table 4.1 *Changing Green Party Strategies*

Party	Opportunities for alliances/coalitions	Strategy of established parties to the Greens	Green party links with other parties	Primary aim of links with other parties	Resultant party strategy
UK Green party	Party system makes opportunities for alliances or coalitions at both national and local levels negligible.	Main parties sought adaptation of Green issues to political agendas. Little or no contact with Green party.	Coalition links with *Plaid Cymru* in single constituency, although collapsed after 1992. Links with Social Democrats over policy implementation.	Links with *Plaid* focused upon gaining elected representative and raising key issues. Links with Social Democrats focused upon raising key issues. Raise public profile.	Party focuses upon maintaining a distinctive independent Green stance. Seek to raise awareness of Green issues.
Miljöpartiet de Gröna	Opportunities available for coalitions at both national and local level. Green party needs to hold balance of power between left–right blocs.	Main parties seek links with Greens at local and national level when Greens hold balance of power. Otherwise, focus is upon adaptation of Green issues.	Coalitions with parties of left and right at local government level. Failed discussions with Social Democrats at national level.	Gain role within government at both national and local levels. Implement Green policies. Raise public perception of party's effectiveness.	Coalitions, where acceptable, at local level. Support the 'Greenest' government at national level. Maintain independent stance. Implement Green policies.
Les Verts	Party system encourages coalitions both at local and national level. Marginalizes small independent parties.	Socialists seek direct links with Greens at national and local level. *Génération Écologie* (GE) also sought links with *Les Verts*.	*Entente Ecologiste* with GE, collapsed in 1993. Electoral agreement with PS, leading to government coalition in 1997. Coalitions with left parties at local level.	Gain national parliamentary seats. Role in government. Implement Green policies at local and national level. Raise public profile.	Coalition with left at national and local levels. Gain influence in government. Implement Green policies.

whether it is more important to maintain an autonomous and independent Green position, or whether the significance of being perceived as an effective political actor outweighs the potential compromises to Green identity. As in Germany, relationships with other parties have been identified as a primary means of gaining political influence. As Table 4.1 demonstrates, however, the impact of this development in party strategy has varied significantly.

The explanations for these differences undoubtedly reflect the contrasting contexts and opportunities confronting the Green parties. While not providing a clear explanation for the changes in strategy, Harmel and Janda's framework does raise some interesting questions regarding party goals and objectives. In all three cases, identifying stimuli that challenged the party goal of 'winning votes' did not tell the whole story. For both the UK and French Green parties, gaining more votes did not necessarily result in gaining parliamentary representation. In the Swedish case, while gaining votes does translate into representation, it does not necessarily result in the party gaining any notable political influence. Given this, it is clear that to instigate change within the parties' attitudes to other parties, the stimuli must influence their abilities to achieve more specific goals – namely, achieving parliamentary representation in the UK and France, and gaining a position of political influence in Sweden and Germany.

While, on one level, the question of Green autonomy may be considered an ideological one, it must also be viewed in the context of the systemic opportunities and constraints facing the Greens and a perception among party activists of how best to push forward Green policies and environmental awareness. In France, as in Germany, political opportunities placed the issue of alliances and potential coalition strategies at the heart of party debates and conflicts. *Les Verts* have struggled to find a niche within a party system that rewards alliances and coalitions and where political credibility is gauged through parliamentary representation and political influence. As one activist argued:

> *When persons are elected and are in charge of real problems, they tackle these issues to make visible their work – to make visible their party – and it gives credence and solidarity to the party. When persons aren't in charge of problems these things don't take up most of their time. They are then free to make struggles, internal party struggles* (Interview, 29 September 1995).

Les Verts have been forced to reassess their stance towards other parties since alliances represented one of the only possible chances of an electoral breakthrough within a discriminatory electoral system. The failure of the entente, following the failure to break through under an autonomous stance, ultimately led to the party negotiating with the left. Since recent electoral results indicate that the party would have remained marginalized had they not undertaken this strategy, the electoral agreement with the PS represents a key phase in the party's search for an effective political role.

The UK majoritarian system provides even fewer opportunities for the Green party. Relationships with other parties have not provided opportunities for direct Green parliamentary representation, but have focused upon gaining influence via more indirect channels. This lack of opportunity helps to explain why the party should be less dominated by strategic debates over relationships with other parties. The Green party has, instead, focused upon maintaining a distinctive Green image and has looked towards issue-based strategies, rather than concentrating upon alliances and coalitions. Where debates over relationships with other parties have emerged, they have been closely linked to strategies concerning policy issues. Both links with *Plaid Cymru* and the Liberal Democrats have been seen less in terms of developing direct relationships between the two parties; rather, these links are about gaining access to parliament for Green policy initiatives.

In Sweden, *Miljöpartiet* succeeded in breaking the electoral threshold without having to form any relationship with other political parties. The challenge, in this case, however, has been to develop a stable position that enables the party to maintain its parliamentary status and secure the benefits accruing from this. Access to decision-making has regularly eluded the party, though, and threatens its ability to prove itself as an effective political actor. The party faces the danger of remaining relatively marginalized unless it can gain a more influential position. In some ways, the Swedish case mirrors that of the UK, in that weak coalition potential at national level has resulted in the party focusing less upon alliances and coalitions in favour of an issue-based strategy. Electoral success has often relied upon the party's ability to raise key issues such as the environment in 1988 and the European Union (EU) since 1994. Subsequently, where *Miljöpartiet* has cooperated with other parties at the national level, the focus has been upon individual issues rather than detailed, long-term alliances or coalitions.

Undoubtedly, the parties' attitudes towards alliances and coalitions reflect the opportunities that are available to achieve political influence. The greater the opportunities, the more likely each party is to accept compromise for the sake of alliance. Hence, *Les Verts* chose, on two occasions, to accept compromise for the opportunity of gaining national parliamentary representation. The party experienced internal division over the suitability of both potential coalition partners; however, the differences between the parties were not enough for the Greens to withdraw from electoral agreements. By contrast, both the Green party and *Miljöpartiet de Gröna* have proven more reluctant to work with other parties so directly at national level. In these cases a distinctive Green identity has generally been prioritized above the potential gains to be made from agreements with *Plaid Cymru* and the Social Democrats respectively.

However, national strategy is not the only important factor in these developments. In all four parties, many of the strategies and debates have emerged from the experiences gained from working with other parties at a sub-national level. National party policy has often been slower to accept the concept of cooperation and alliance, partly because opportunities first arose at local rather than national level. These agreements have raised not only the same concerns over the levels of compromise by the Greens, but have also, on many occasions, brought conflict between national and local parties. In the UK, the decision to work with *Plaid Cymru* was chiefly a local one. The intervention of the national party executive was viewed as a direct attack on the local party's constitutional right to organize local strategy independently. Similar patterns are evident in Sweden, where the actions of the Gothenburg Greens brought them into direct conflict with national party policy.

In both the French and Swedish cases, the persistence of local parties has often been a key factor in changing national party strategy. One French party activist suggested that local alliances were necessary to 'show the ignorant and the sceptical the real possibilities of Green politics' (Interview, 29 September 1995). Undoubtedly, the French and German Greens' successful experiences of coalition at regional and local levels were influential factors in shaping the national parties' acceptance of links with the left. As local parties and party activists continue to gain practical experience of political decision-making, they have become more aware of both the value and the dangers of coalition strategies. These experiences may help to explain why in France, Sweden and Germany, where the Green parties have been actively involved in local coalitions, there is greater acceptance of the need to work with other parties. In the UK, by contrast, where local parties have not been able to develop these relationships, the Green party is still divided and often hostile towards working with other parties.

THE PERILS OF BEING 'NEITHER LEFT, NOR RIGHT'

The Greens have unquestionably found it hard to compete from a Green 'autonomous' perspective within party systems that have historically based party competition along 'left–right' dimensions. Although initially placing themselves outside of this established dichotomy, the parties have often been unwillingly pulled into party competition along these lines. Again, however, the strength of the force pushing the Greens to align along traditional dimensions has varied.

In the UK, the marginalization of the Green party has largely removed any real pressure for it to place itself upon the left–right dimension. Although there is evidence to suggest closer links with the left than with the right, the Greens have predominantly continued to talk in terms of a 'neither left, nor right' strategy:

> *. . .the Green political space is there because we are the only people in it. The aim should be to expand and grow to fill our political space, and become credible and make our political space look more central to the political debate than it currently is* (Interview, 31 March 1996).

However, with New Labour moving towards the centre, many within the Green party now argue that space exists for the Green party to position itself clearly on the left. Former Party Speaker Peg Alexander argued that:

> *The Green party fits automatically into the space left by the new-look Labour party, a space which needs our commitment to economic and social equality and justice. . . . We must not be scared to place ourselves in this gap. The Green party is a natural home for such people* (Green Link, 1995, no 16, p6).

The Greens are not alone in recognizing the space available on the left, though. The Liberal Democrats followed a similar direction during the 2001 general election campaign. This raises the potential for further collaboration between the Greens and the Liberal Democrats to develop a new alternative to the centrist politics currently dominating the UK political landscape.

In Sweden, *Miljöpartiet* has placed itself towards the centre of the Swedish political system. Both the political nature of environmental protest in Sweden and the pattern of party distribution have encouraged the party towards this stance. As Bennulf notes:

> *For a Green party – if no position on the left–right spectrum is 'free' – the best strategy is to be perceived as having no position (or a position towards the middle) on the left–right dimension* (Bennulf, 1995, p140).

With distinct blocs on both left and right, the party has found little political room on either side. Any move from the position in the centre has, as in 1991, resulted in a loss of support for the party. Under such conditions, the party has found that it can maintain a 'neither left, nor right' strategy fairly successfully. Again, local experience has taught the party the value of this stance, with coalitions agreed between left and right parties.

By complete contrast, the French system clearly forced *Les Verts* into a more direct reassessment of the *'ni droite, ni gauche'* autonomous stance. *Les Verts* activist Catherine Gréze outlined the political realities:

> *Year after year, the electoral system was bound to give us the same results: whatever the scores, no Green members were to be sent to parliament, and election after election we were giving away our votes in the second round to the Socialist party with nothing in return (Vert Contact, 1997).*

Despite attempts by *Les Verts* to position themselves outside of the left–right dimensions, external pressures led to the party being placed within this dichotomy regardless of its own internal stance. For many activists within the party, the fact that *Les Verts* were perceived as 'on the left' regardless of actual party strategy was an important factor in shaping the decision to actively adopt this role.

Decisions to form alliances or coalitions are not only one way, however. In many cases the development of Green party strategy has often depended upon strategic initiatives and developments from within other political parties. Indeed, the changing attitudes of the established parties to the Greens have played a key role in shaping this aspect of Green party change. Undertaking a strategic policy of alliances and coalitions is necessarily dependent upon other parties being open to these agreements. The emergence of a Green challenge has resulted in a varied response from other political parties.

Posing no electoral threat and with no representation, the established political parties in the UK were able to virtually ignore the Green party, focusing instead upon incorporating environmental policies within their own political agendas. Instead, one can identify a broadening recognition of environmental movements, rather than any recognition of the Green party. Under such conditions, the Green party had few opportunities to work with other parties, even if they had wanted to. This virtual sidelining of the Green party within the political debate made it far easier for the UK Greens to maintain a commitment to an autonomous stance than was the case for other Green parties.

In Sweden, Green electoral success also provoked a response from the other political parties. Most especially, the response came from the two parties whose position within the party system was most threatened by the challenge of the Greens. Both the centre party and the Left Party worked hard to improve their image as environmental parties. Again, these moves left *Miljöpartiet* relatively isolated in terms of positioning within the party system. Both left and right blocs were able, to some degree, to claim environmental credentials. However, at a local level, established parties were keen to gain the support of the Greens in coalition, placing far greater pressure on them to reach some form of agreement. With other parties offering to discuss coalition terms, the Greens found that refusing to work with others gave the impression of an uncompromising, 'destructive' party.

In France, the more direct interest of other parties to work with *Les Verts*, and the potential rewards on offer, placed significantly more pressure upon the Greens to develop some form of coalition strategy. *Les Verts* faced similar difficulties in establishing themselves in the political arena. The rise of environmental concern resulted in the party facing the challenge of a second environmental party and the attention of the Socialists, who feared a loss of support to the Greens. In addition, environmental concerns were still placed within the traditional left–right divide dominating the French party system.

To summarize, electoral successes have undoubtedly created more opportunities for the Greens to consider changing their strategies towards working with other parties. While the strategy of 'autonomy' represented an effective way of distinguishing themselves from the established political parties, it has proved difficult to maintain when coalition opportunities provide the Greens with a chance to participate in government. The parties' strategic changes have been closely linked to the political opportunities confronting the Greens within their respective party systems. In each of the cases discussed here, the Greens have been forced to consider what can be gained from alliances and coalitions, and whether or not these gains are worth compromising Green party policy.

Chapter 5

Square Pegs in Round Holes: Organizational Reform

Any analysis of Green party change must undoubtedly seek to tackle the issue of party organization and the significant changes that have emerged in this respect. The issue of party organization has developed into a significant field of political research. Its implications stretch beyond merely providing an effective way for a party to organize, reflecting a party's ideological commitments, internal struggles and also its struggles within the party system within which it operates. Taggart, for example, suggests that:

> *Understanding how a party organizes itself allows us a glimpse into a party's true nature. It permits us to look beyond the persona deliberately cultivated and projected to the voters at election time. It also enables us to look beyond the activists' exalted claims of ideological commitment and purity to see how deep those claims run when faced with the ideology-sullying problems of political survival. The organization of the party is where the rhetoric meets the reality. It is the nexus between beliefs and action* (Taggart, 1996, p110).[1]

The organizational dimension has also been central to the analysis of European Green parties, where the specific and unusual nature of Green party organization has represented a distinguishing feature of the 'new politics'. These distinctive organizational characteristics have been a key aspect within many of the studies of *Die Grünen* in Germany. Theorists emphasized the Greens' close links with, and emergence from within, the new social movements – resulting in a commitment within the parties to accommodating new social movement ideals within the confines of a party political organization. These commitments were encompassed within the German Greens via the concept of *Basisdemokratie*. Poguntke summarizes this concept as follows:

> *. . .a new model of intra-party democracy characterized by a low degree of formalization, dominance of the grassroots over higher level functionaries or MPs, and politics with a strong emphasis on close linkages with the new social movements* (Poguntke, 1993, p388).

Transposed into party organization, these concepts were operationalized through numerous unconventional approaches to party structures. In particular, the Greens tried to counter the traditions of party politics, which they argued had led to the 'oligarchization, bureaucratization and professionalization' of politics (Frankland and Schoonmaker, 1992, p108). To achieve this, the party placed specific emphasis upon openness and participation in decision-making. Party meetings at all levels were open to all members and, where possible, the Greens sought consensus in decision-making after healthy and often vociferous debate. Outside sources were often sought for advice and opinion, and, on occasion, non-party members were actually nominated and elected as Green parliamentary candidates (Frankland and Schoonmaker, 1992, p108).

To avoid the 'professionalization' of Green politics, the party opted for a process of collective leadership and imposed strict controls over the holding of both party office and parliamentary seats. In addition, both offices and seats were rotated on a regular basis to reduce the possibility of activists viewing party politics as a career path. To further emphasize this, party workers received no, or minimal, salaries. The Greens also sought to challenge the male dominance of the political sphere by calling for the equal representation of men and women on party commissions and committees, and encouraging equal representation on parliamentary candidate lists.

As a final aspect in the process of democratic control, the party also stressed the importance of the concept of *Basisanbindung* (tied up with the grassroots – Poguntke, 1987a, p622). This concept stressed the importance of ensuring that members in senior offices within the federal party regularly maintained a direct link with those active at local and regional levels, whether this was through attending local party meetings or engaging in some other form of political activism.

The German Greens' emphasis upon the concept of *Basisdemokratie* in many ways became symbolic of the organizational distinctiveness of the newly emerging Green parties across Europe, reflecting what Kitschelt identified as their emergence as 'anti-party' parties and of the activists' disillusionment with traditional party politics (Kitschelt, 1988b, p131). It also represented an effective symbolic commitment that clearly distinguished their attitudes and approaches to party political activism from those of the long-standing, established political parties, further heightening the distinction between 'green' and 'grey'.

Given the significance attached to party organization, it is not surprising to find organizational changes cited as a key factor in many of the conflicts and debates within the Green parties during the early 1990s. Organizational reform is almost inevitably associated with a reappraisal of the Greens' commitment to new social movement principles and a supposed assimilation of 'new politics' parties within traditional party systems.

Many of these claims undoubtedly emerge from the experiences of the German Greens. As previously highlighted, the disastrous performance in the first all-German elections in December 1990 sparked a significant process of organizational reform, accompanied by intense internal party conflict. The reform process was identified as a recognition that the alternative organizational structures created by the Greens could not function effectively within the current structures of competitive European party systems. The federal party conference at Neumünster in April 1991 provided a focal point for the introduction of organizational reform.

At one level, it was claimed that the Greens' failure to adapt to the changing political environment within Germany during 1989 and 1990 was a reflection of the slow and cumbersome nature of the party organization. As Poguntke suggests:

> *The strict separation of party arenas stifles intra-party communication and induces polarized, public debate. As a result, swift adaptation to quickly changing political circumstances is hard to achieve* (Poguntke, 1993, p387).

The electoral failure was not the only reason for organizational change, however. Many of the weaknesses of the alternative organizational structures had begun to emerge during the party's four years of representation in the *Bundestag*. In particular, the party's commitment to the rotation of offices proved unwieldy given the limited political experience of many party activists. Just as the party's representatives were acclimatizing themselves to federal politics and its institutions, they were forced to give up their posts. In addition, the media focus upon the new parliamentary party caused friction between the parliamentary faction and the party faction.

Practical issues also made a continuation of the original structures problematic. Horizontal control and a restriction on party executives require a large active party membership. However, as Frankland describes:

> *Most reports during the late 1980s indicated that only 10–30 per cent of local members were active. After subtracting the numbers of active members engaged as local councillors and officials,* Landtag *deputies and staff assistants, one found that not many remained willing and able to 'control' the policy work of elected representatives* (Frankland, 1998, p5).

The separation of office and mandate that the party had stipulated also proved to be a divisive issue with regard to the role of the federal council. It was argued that because no parliamentarians were allowed to sit on the council, it had become largely removed from the actual political debates at federal and *Land* level. As a result, it appeared to concern itself with discussions that had little bearing on the issues and debates that confronted the elected party representatives at their respective levels.

To overcome these difficulties the party opted to abolish the federal council and loosen its commitment to the separation of office and mandate. A new *Land* council was created with two representatives from each *Land* party, one from the *Land* leadership one from the *Land* parliament. The *Land* council also included the federal executive, two members of the *Bundestag* representatives, and one Green member from the European parliament and two delegates from the federal working groups (Poguntke, 1993, p394). The Neumünster conference also saw the party vote to eliminate the rotation principle for members of the federal leadership, and an acceptance that some of the executive should be paid, 'professionalized' members. There was also an agreement to eliminate term limits on party leaders. Despite these changes, however, the party maintains a rigid commitment to the autonomy of local and regional parties to control programmes, finances and personnel, which has often been reflected in the debates over coalition strategies during the 1990s. This commitment continues to prevail within the Greens, with Jürgen Trittin still defining the party as 'no federal party, but rather a confederation of strong state associations' as recently as 1998 (Frankland, 1998, p7). Despite this, however, critics viewed the relaxation of organizational principles as a further reflection of the dominance of the 'realo' faction within the party and a continued acceptance of the institutional 'rules of the game', which the original 'anti-party' party had so clearly set out to challenge head on.

With the experiences of *Die Grünen* as a guide, this chapter examines organizational reform within the other three Green parties in order to identify the underlying pressures leading to organizational reform. In assessing the nature of organizational reform, the chapter questions whether these changes represent a significant transition away from Green party commitments to decentralization and direct democracy. Taking each case study in turn, the following section will place key periods of organizational change within the context of changes in dominant factions, change in party leadership and external 'stimuli/shocks'.

COMPARING THE EARLY ORGANIZATIONAL STRUCTURES OF THE GREEN PARTIES

We have already noted the characteristics that were identified within *Die Grünen* as reflecting 'new politics' principles. An initial examination of the early organizational structures of the three other Green parties highlights similar 'new politics' characteristics. Vedung's analysis of the Swedish Green party, for example, claims that 'decentralization, local influence, direct democracy, and diffusion of power are key words in their theory of political organization' (Vedung, 1989, p145).[2]

Table 5.1 outlines the Greens' organizational commitments to new social movement structures and ideals. It highlights aspects that broadly reflect the parties' concerns with, firstly, direct democratic organization and, secondly, anti-professionalism. Within these general categories, analysis of the executive bodies, speakers and regional bodies have been used to reflect the former theme, while categories on voting rights and rotation reflect the latter.

All three parties originally attempted to make the executive decision-making bodies open and democratic, with the central decision-making body being the parties' main convention. This open approach towards party assemblies has often been identified as a symbolic commitment towards openness and direct participation for members. Similarly, the parties' executive bodies were directly elected by party members. Another key commitment was decentralization and local party autonomy. The parties incorporated this within a three-tiered organizational framework, with a clear division of activities identifiable between national, regional and local parties. Enhancing this division was a commitment to the autonomy of local parties to organize and plan their actions with relatively little pressure from national party bodies. An emphasis upon the active participation of party members was also

Table 5.1 *A Comparison of the Early Organizational Structures of the Green Party, Miljöpartiet de Gröna and Les Verts*

Party	Executive body	Speakers	Regional bodies	Voting rights	Rotation rule
UK Green party	Party conference is main decision-making body. Party council is primarily regionally based. Council appoints national committees.	Large group of speakers from different policy groups. Three party chairs exist.	Local and regional groups have autonomy over their actions and strategies.	All members have the right to vote at local and regional levels. All can attend, vote and contribute to debate at party conference.	Can only serve on council for three years consecutively. Can't hold more than one post at the same time.
Les Verts	General assembly meets annually and debates policy. Conseil National Inter-Regional (CNIR) is the elected controlling body. Executive college is elected to control day-to-day organization.	There are four speakers (two women and two men).	Regional and local organizations have autonomy over their actions. They are responsible for choosing 75% of CNIR members.	All members vote for CNIR and local party representatives, as well as for the presidential candidate. Free access and voting rights at general assembly.	Strict rotation rule for posts. There is control over the number of positions held simultaneously.
Miljöpartiet de Gröna	Party congress consists of regional delegates. Council of representatives consists of one representative from each region. General organization is controlled by four committees. Parliamentary party is independent.	Two speakers (one man and one woman) are chosen from a political committee. There are also two parliamentary spokespersons.	Local- and regional-level activities exist. Both are autonomous in their actions. Central executive is made up of regional representatives.	Votes for regional and national representatives, as well as for delegates to congress. All members can participate at congress but can't vote.	Rotation is strictly enforced. Representatives are allowed no more than nine years in major positions.

apparent, emphasizing the parties' concerns to implement direct democracy and horizontal control. In each case, members were given direct access and influence over policy-making and party strategy at local, regional and national levels.

The Green parties' commitments to anti-professionalism can be identified as clearly as the commitment to decentralization and active participation. The parties all refused to let party members view activism as a career path. Although the parties have had to face the practicalities of needing both a public front for the media and a reference point for contact and dissemination of information, they shunned the notion of a single party leader, opting instead for elected party spokespersons. In addition, the parties adopted procedures for the rotation of offices. This was often applied to elected office, as well as internal party posts. By restricting the number of offices a person could hold simultaneously, no one could build up a power base within the party.

ORGANIZATIONAL REFORM WITHIN *MILJÖPARTIET DE GRÖNA*

During the latter part of the 1980s and the early 1990s, *Miljöpartiet de Gröna* faced increasing pressure to reassess its organizational approach. After losing parliamentary representation in 1991, *Miljöpartiet de Gröna* focused upon organizational reforms in the light of practical difficulties that had emerged during its first parliamentary term. *Miljöpartiet* had experienced severe difficulties when confronted by a curious media and a hostile party political environment. Coordination between the various party committees proved cumbersome, giving the party the image of an inefficient and amateurish organization – an image quickly seized upon by the media and political opponents alike.

One of the central organizational criticisms was that the established party organization proved to be insufficiently precise in detailing the role of the parliamentary representatives within the overall party framework. Conflict and confusion subsequently emerged regarding the level of autonomy and accountability between the parliamentary party and the national party organization. The greater media profile of the parliamentary representatives resulted in representatives being sought for comment rather than the official party spokespersons, who were not members of the parliamentary party. One party activist summarized the confusion as follows:

> *The people in the standing committee for politics, they had very little to say because all the political interest from the media was focused upon the parliamentary group. A lot of people from the standing committee were always complaining about this. In the end we had to start special groups to try and build bridges between the two groups and that took a lot of time. We lost the election because of all this* (Interview, 22 September 1995).

The first attempt to tackle this problem resulted in the introduction of two additional spokespersons from within the parliamentary group to represent the party in parliament. However, this failed to solve the problem that was further heightened by the regular rotation of the spokespersons.

The party's electoral success at regional and local level also created organizational problems. The party had always placed significant emphasis upon local party autonomy and the rotation of offices. However, success found the party stretched regarding the number of active members prepared to represent the party. In some districts there were simply not enough members to implement rotation; in others, members had to take on numerous posts.

For *Miljöpartiet*, organizational reform resulted in relatively little internal party conflict – not that the party was entirely unanimous in its support for organizational reform, or that the ideological implications of these changes were ignored during debates over party organization. There was, however, a general acceptance, among both supporters and opponents of the reforms, regarding the practical difficulties experienced when working within the original organizational structures, as one party activist explained:

> *In historical perspective, I must say that we over-emphasized organization and the cause has been hurt by this. If you look at our rules, they are pretty much the same as other parties, really. We have made a lot of fuss about being different, but we are all medieval in this respect. We cannot change the way humans are. We need a chairman and a secretary and everything. We have to function. We have to sit around a table and come to an agreement. With 300 people at a party congress, you cannot discuss in detail how you should design poster campaigns* (Interview, 21 September 1995).

Organizational reform didn't lead to any significant exodus of party members, either. As one opponent of the changes noted, nothing had really changed because it was still the same group of people running the party (Taggart, 1996, p134).

Figure 5.1 places the organizational reforms within *Miljöpartiet de Gröna* in relation to the key factors for change identified by Harmel and Janda.

Figure 5.1 highlights the importance of external stimuli along both the 'electoral' and 'challenges to party democracy' dimensions. In this case, electoral performance and systemic constraints are fundamental in explaining organizational reform. The key events that coincide with organizational change include the party's first parliamentary term between 1988 and 1991 and the electoral disappointment following this period. Electoral success in 1988 brought challenges to party democracy in terms of party activism and membership and an increase in media scrutiny of the party.

Parliamentary representation had a significant influence along both 'factional' and 'party democracy' dimensions. Figure 5.1 indicates that the rise of the parliamentary faction occurs shortly before the process of organizational reform. This transition into a parliamentary party was identified by party activists as a significant strain on the original organizational framework. Although the party sought to maintain an anti-professionalist stance, it could not stop the parlia-

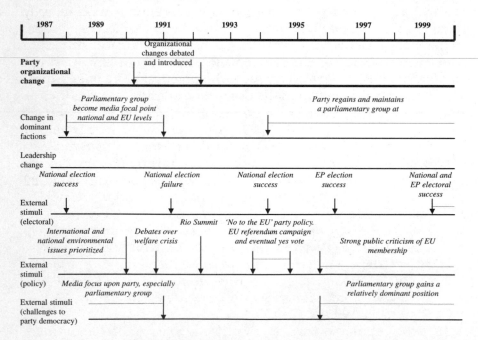

Figure 5.1 *Potential Sources of Organizational Change:*
Miljöpartiet de Gröna

mentary party from becoming the focal point for media interest and political comment. *Miljöpartiet* therefore clearly found itself faced with numerous contradictions between the type of organization that it wanted to develop and the organizational requirements of a party with parliamentary roles and responsibilities.

The need for reform was exacerbated by the party's loss of parliamentary representation in 1991. During its own internal post-mortem of events, organizational difficulties figured heavily in explaining the party's failure. It was claimed that the party had failed to portray itself or its policies clearly to the electorate. Organizational changes were seen as the most direct way in which the party could tackle these problems of coordination. The significance of these organizational issues to electoral performance can be seen in the activists' explanations of not only the 1991 defeat, but also the party's return to parliament in 1994. When asked to account for the factors enabling this success, organizational issues were identified as of primary significance. The electoral success of 1994, and subsequent strong electoral performances in 1999, have undoubtedly been influential factors in explaining the relative unanimity with which organizational reforms have been implemented and accepted within the party. The process of organizational reform cannot, however, be seen completely as a reaction to electoral defeat. Although the reforms were not implemented by *Miljöpartiet* until 1992, organizational change was already being outlined in 1990.

Virtually no change in leading personnel means that the 'leadership change' factor is largely insignificant in this case. The main split within the party was factional – between the parliamentary party and the rest of the party organization. Again, however, the party appears to have developed a pragmatic attitude towards this situation, which has eased the tensions between the groups despite increased media attention for the parliamentary representatives. As one activist suggested, 'we accept it, but not as a very important basis but as something that we have to adjust to because of the media world we live in' (Interview, 22 September 1995).

ORGANIZATIONAL REFORM WITHIN THE GREEN PARTY: GREEN 2000 AND BASIS FOR RENEWAL INITIATIVES

The 1990 Green 2000 initiative was the primary focus for organizational reform in the Green party. However, reaction to Green 2000 represented the build up of pressures within the party that had begun with an earlier attempt at organizational reform known as the Main-Green initiative. As with Green 2000, MainGreen sought to streamline the party organization into a more centralized party structure, its proponents arguing that the existing decentralized structures were 'not only premature but impractical' (*Econews*, 1986, no 31, p3). Although the MainGreen proposals were rejected, the debates themselves created underlying antagonism within the party. Conflict centred less upon the actual policy and organizational proposals, however, than around the manner in which these proposals were both instigated and challenged. So, while MainGreen didn't actually result in the implementation of organizational change, it did entrench conflicting positions within the party by the time of the Green 2000 initiative.

Green 2000 emerged at the start of the 1990s as an initiative designed to enable the party to capitalize effectively upon the relative success of the late 1980s. As one national party activist recalled:

> *There was a whole background as to whether the actual structures that we had could work and a feeling that the decision-making process was so labyrinthine and so lacking in responsibility that something needed to be done about that. But that was said in a context too of actually trying to set a direction for the party in terms of what the party wanted to achieve and where it actually saw itself politically* (Interview, 7 August 1995).

Given the huge barriers to electoral success in the UK, it was argued that the party needed to sacrifice some of the commitments to alternative organizational structures for the cause of parliamentary representation. The motion called for the creation of a party executive smaller than the existing party council, a more centralized structure and a change to the nature of party conferences. As the overriding aim, the objective of Green 2000 was for the party to gain parliamentary power by the year 2000 (*Green Activist*, October 1991, p1).[3] The motion was, however, far from unanimously supported and led to bitter internal conflict, which split the party.[4] Although passed at the 1991 party conference, debate ensued not only regarding the practical implications of the motion itself, but, more predominantly, regarding the manner in which the decision had taken place. It was suggested that the whole process had significant implications for the status of internal party democracy and the position of those party members who had opposed the motion. This concern was further enhanced when candidates who had supported the Green 2000 campaign gained 10 out of the 11 positions on the executive, with Sara Parkin being elected as party chair (Wall, 1994, p68).

The implementation of the new organizational framework did little to quell divisions within the party. The conflicts and factionalism continued way beyond the passing of the motion at the 1991 conference. In the year that followed, a number of key party figures resigned or were dismissed, leaving the party in a state of turmoil and organizational disarray. Green 2000 was perceived as a key factor in both the dramatic fall in party membership and the subsequent failure at the 1992 general election.

The 1993 Basis for Renewal programme, in contrast, signalled moves towards reconciliation within the party. One of the main initiators of the Basis for Renewal programme explains the context within which this motion emerged:

> *There was a general coming together of the two sides over a couple of years because it was a crisis. We were struggling to avoid bankruptcy and the general disappearance of the Green party. And at the end of that we had a situation where people like me, the decentralists, had accepted the need for leadership, had accepted the need for professionalism and that elections needed to be contested properly. And people like the Green 2000ers had accepted that local elections were most significant and that non-electoral campaigning had an important part to play* (Interview, 31 March 1996).

In attempting to breach the divisions, the programme recognized the value of organizational change, while maintaining a commitment to open democratic control. The reforms introduced within Green 2000, however, still form the basis for the party organization. Indeed, some of the most forthright opponents of the Green 2000 initiative now readily accept the need for a level of organizational reassessment. One such party activist stated:

> *I was concerned in principle that the organizational approach was wrong and was disempowering and unparticipatory. Now that I'm less certain about since I've actually worked within it. We are possibly better organized .... Looking back on the debates there were some respects in which they were right and some in which they were wrong. They were right about professionalism, though. There is no excuse for doing something badly and a lot of the time we were doing very badly. There was no particular reason for it and there was no great principle involved. It was simply that we could have done it better and we*

> *were doing it all in a rather amateurish fashion* (Interview, 9 August 1995).

This again implies that the conflicts over organization focused as much upon personal rivalries and concerns over power within the party as upon ideological commitments to decentralized party structures. The fact that the institutional changes introduced in Green 2000 remain today despite the majority of its supporters having left the party appears to support this assessment.

Figure 5.2 again places the organizational reforms within the Green party in relation to the key factors for change identified by Harmel and Janda.

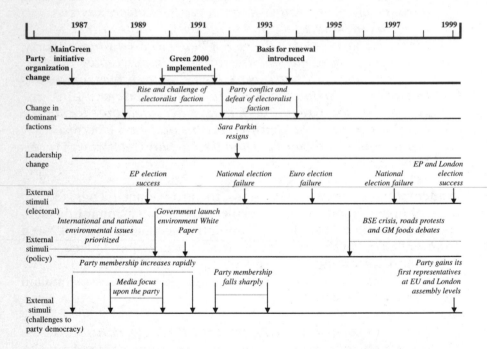

Figure 5.2 *Potential Sources of Organizational Change:*
The Green Party

Again, Figure 5.2 identifies a balance between internal and external pressures. As with *Miljöpartiet de Gröna*, many of the organizational changes and, in particular, the impetus for change, coincide with the changing electoral fortunes of the party. A key factor in this case was the 1989 European parliamentary elections. Harmel et al claim that:

A small party that was developed primarily to promote a message (more so than to govern) may not be shocked by electoral stagnation or even downturns, but an extraordinary electoral success could give fuel to those within the party who may be bent on a more organized, pragmatic vote-seeking approach (Harmel et al, 1995, p4).

This scenario reflects the experiences of the UK Green party, for whom the European election performance raised both the party's profile and expectations of a parliamentary breakthrough. The result, therefore, provided an important stimulus to those activists who identified 'vote-seeking' as the party's primary goal. Figure 5.2 also identifies external stimuli along the 'challenges to party democracy' dimension. Although functional while the party was small, the rise in membership and increased media attention highlighted numerous weaknesses within the organizational framework.[5]

While change was viewed as necessary by many within the party, it provided the focal point for internal factionalism. Reform represented a struggle over the party's future direction and ideological commitments. To opponents, organizational change implied the prioritizing of an electoral strategy and a factional take-over of the party. The dimension of 'leadership change' is again a less significant factor in promoting organizational change than factional division. This was largely due to the party's continued commitment to group leadership. The resignation of Sara Parkin is, however, included on this dimension in Figure 5.2. Although not involved with the original motion, Green 2000 became closely associated with Parkin's high-profile position within the party. Her subsequent departure was seen as influencing the collapse of the electoral faction around Green 2000 and prompted numerous further resignations.

Basis for Renewal coincides with a number of important stimuli in Figure 5.2. Externally, the electoral failure during 1992 raised questions concerning the prudence of prioritizing 'electoral' goals. Similarly, the rapid fall in party membership forced the party to reassess its future. Internally, Basis for Renewal appears to have been implemented following a change in the dominant faction within the party and a reduction of the factional conflict surrounding Green 2000. However, unlike Green 2000, these changes were not perceived as representing a radical challenge to the ideological basis of the party. Recent electoral successes may again place organizational strains on the party, with Green representatives in the European parliament and in the London assembly. However, these performances have not created the same public and media interest that accompanied the party's performances during the late 1980s.

ORGANIZATIONAL REFORMS WITHIN *LES VERTS*

Les Verts have consistently been preoccupied with party organization, with particular emphasis being placed upon the regional focus of the party organization and the level of autonomy and independence in decision-making that is maintained by these regional groups. Interestingly, organizational reform had only slight impact in terms of party division and conflict, reflecting an acceptance of the need for pragmatic organizational change. Although not without criticism, internal debates focused more upon strategic issues rather than structural ones. In addition, organizational reform occurred later than in Sweden and the UK, following the breakdown of the entente with *Génération Écologie* and the resignation of Antoine Waechter.

Organizational change received relatively little opposition from within the party – partly because changes were not as far reaching as those within the other parties, but also because most party members felt that there were more important and contentious issues (Faucher, 1997, p5). Organizational reforms were seen primarily as a practical reassessment of internal procedures that had previously resulted in heightened party factionalism and conflict. In particular, organizational reform focused upon removing the regular factionalism over alternative strategy papers at the party's annual conference. *Les Verts* were wary of the dangers of adopting too pragmatic an approach to organizational change. The new organizational structures were designed as a compromise to competing party goals. On the one hand, reform satisfied those party members who recognized the need for a more effective organization than the relatively ad hoc system that had evolved along with the party. On the other, it maintained a commitment to those supporters who felt that institutionalized changes might threaten the party's commitment to direct democracy, making it too similar to traditional parties. Although facing similar problems regarding open party conferences and collective leadership, the party was cautious of implementing a more hierarchical approach that focused around a core executive. These intermediary reforms appeared successful, however, with 74 per cent of party members voting to accept organizational change (Faucher, 1996, p7). This was a significant achievement for a party with a long history of internal conflict and turmoil.

Figure 5.3 places the organizational reforms within *Les Verts* in relation to the key factors for change identified by Harmel and Janda.

The pattern here is markedly different from the previous case studies. On this occasion, one can identify a weaker link to 'external stimuli' and a closer connection to internal pressures. Although

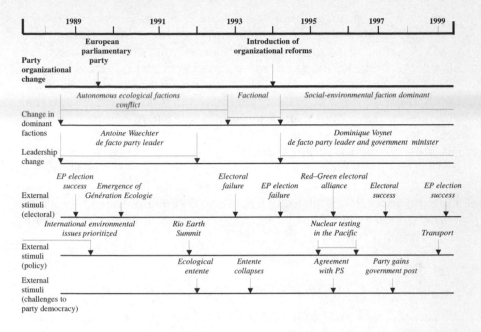

Figure 5.3 *Potential Sources of Organizational Change:* Les Verts

officially the party has no single leader, a more direct focus upon leadership exists within *Les Verts*, with the selection of a presidential candidate often producing a de facto party leader. In this context, organizational reform coincides with the rise to prominence of Dominique Voynet and the resignation of Antoine Waechter. Furthermore, these changes reflected more than merely a change of personality; they represented a change of direction within the party towards Voynet's 'social environmentalism' and away from Waechter's 'natural' ecological stance. Both leadership change and organizational reform are related to wider factional disputes. However, party factionalism focused more upon issues of electoral strategy and potential alliances, rather than on internal organizational structure. In addition, organizational change was instigated following factional conflict, in contrast to the UK case, where organizational change sparked party divisions.

The connection between electoral performance and organizational reform appears weaker in this case. Neither success during the 1989 European elections, nor national electoral disappointment in 1993, appears to have led directly to organizational reform. In this case, the 'external stimuli' that challenged the party's 'electoral' goal affected a different process of change, focusing upon electoral strategies and alliances rather than organizational reforms. Within the context of French party politics, these issues provide a more direct electoral stimulus. That is not to imply that there is no connection between external stimuli and organizational reform in this case. Harmel and Janda note that although external factors are important, it is often the internal reaction within parties to these events that induces organizational change. In Figure 5.3, it is evident that the party's electoral failure during 1993 would have heightened the move towards internal changes in factional dominance and leadership – both of which preceded the organizational reforms during 1994. *Les Verts'* sudden rise to a position within government has placed significant strains upon the utilization of an unconventional party organization. However, the major debates within the party have again focused more upon strategic rather than organizational issues. Potentially, the performance of the Greens in the next national election could be the catalyst for organizational reform.

A COMPARATIVE ASSESSMENT OF ORGANIZATIONAL CHANGE

The comparative analysis of organizational change presented in the previous section verifies the significance of the factors identified by Harmel and Janda. In particular, a significant interaction is evident between 'internal' and 'external' pressures in the process of change, and the influence that this has on both the nature and context of organizational reform. In assessing each of the three key variables, it is possible to see this changing balance between external stimuli, internal factional conflict and leadership change in the process of organizational change. This is significant in explaining both the different processes of change within the parties and the varying levels of conflict that accompanied these reforms – from intense internal division reflecting the 'realo–fundis' disputes within the German Greens, to a pragmatic acceptance of the weaknesses of initial organizational structures.

In common with the experiences of the German Greens, the analysis highlights the importance of external stimuli in prompting organizational change within the other three Green parties. This was most overt in the UK and Swedish cases, but was also evident within *Les Verts*. Organizational change was prioritized when external stimuli forced the parties to question their electoral goals or challenged their commitment to internal party democracy. In Sweden and the UK, there was a strong link between the initiation of organizational reform and heightened electoral support, although the extent of electoral success was markedly different. As in Germany, both parties used organizational reform as part of a process for improving the party's electoral status. As such, they identified the original organizational structures as a key obstacle in the parties' attempts to become influential political actors. In Sweden, changes were implemented following a period of national parliamentary representation. Here, the impetus for organizational reform emerged from the practical difficulties experienced in utilizing an unconventional party organization within a conventional party system. For the Green party, however, success involved an increased level of support and media attention, but no representation. The primary motivation, in this case, was merely a perceived opportunity for gaining national representation.

The practical difficulties of unconventional party organization also challenged commitments to openness and 'party democracy'. Both the Swedish and UK parties found it difficult to implement decentralized organizational frameworks for two main reasons. Firstly, they were attempting to implement organizational systems based upon regional and local activity within party systems that prioritized national, centralized party activism. Secondly, they faced practical problems regarding low levels of active membership – especially problematic given the parties' emphasis upon local control and the rotation of offices. With some regional and local parties based upon only a handful of activists, the autonomy of the local party and the enforcement of rotation rules became impossible. In contrast, *Les Verts* have been more successful in utilizing a decentralized organizational framework and identified less of a link between electoral success and organizational form. While, on occasion, similar problems existed regarding the level of local party activism, the party organization appeared better suited to the more regionally based, French political system. In this case, the status of the local and regional parties became more significant, as did the commitment to autonomy from the national organization.

How does one account for the differing responses to organizational change from within the Green parties? In Germany, intense factional conflict was identified between 'realos' and 'fundis'. Similarly, in both the UK and the French cases, factional conflict played a distinctive role. Within *Les Verts*, organizational change followed bitter internal factionalism regarding party strategy and direction. *Les Verts* also provide the one case where a clear issue of leadership change can be identified, with factionalism closely linked to the division between Waechter and Voynet. Although not the focal point for factional conflict, the organizational changes were strongly influenced by the impact of these internal disputes on the party. Rather than being the catalyst for factional divisions, organizational reform was identified as a means of reducing factional infighting. In the Green party, by contrast, organizational change provided the impetus for awakening internal factional divisions concerning the party's future direction and style. In this respect, the Swedish case appears noticeably different. Although 'realo–fundis' stances over organizational change were identified within *Miljöpartiet de Gröna*, they were not particularly forceful or divisive (Taggart, 1996, p135). A general acceptance existed among party activists regarding the need for some form of organizational reform.[6]

In Germany, organizational reform within *Die Grünen* has been closely connected to a reassessment of the party's primary goals and objectives. It is clear from this comparative study that, elsewhere, Green party goals have also been altered and reshaped as the parties have evolved within their respective party systems. Thus, one can identify not only a changing prioritization of party goals during periods of organizational reform, but also the impact of external stimuli in challenging these goals.

In both the Swedish and UK cases, important challenges to 'electoral' and 'party democracy' goals were identified. For *Miljöpartiet de Gröna*, the electoral goal focused upon maintaining national parliamentary representation. The political credibility and financial rewards connected with national representation were clearly important in focusing the party towards this goal. Loss of representation during 1991 forced the party to reduce its activities, and the threat of failure in 1994 had serious implications for its continuation as a national party. The pressures surrounding national representation were, therefore, undoubtedly an important factor in the party's acceptance of a more traditional party organization. Organizational reform was introduced in this context and appeared vindicated by the party's eventual success during 1994 and continued national representation since then. In addition, the relative weakness and conservative nature of the environmental movements in Sweden placed considerably less pressure upon the party to prioritize 'alternative' goals. Where 'party democracy' issues were raised, organizational reforms were seen as part of the solution rather than the problem.

In the case of the UK Green party, the party's apparent division over its 'primary goal' clearly contributed to the bitter conflicts surrounding party organization. Green 2000 was perceived as a development based upon electoral motives. However, the Green party's electoral chances remained weak during the 1990s. Given this weak electoral position and the more significant role played by the environmental movements in influencing national policy, many within the party placed greater emphasis upon goals relating to policy and party democracy, rather than electoral success. Green 2000 was identified by opponents as a challenge to these goals, rather than an enhancement. Within this context, it is easier to explain the differing responses to organizational reform experienced by the UK and Swedish parties. The opposition to Green 2000 was less about the actual structural changes themselves, than it was about the manner in which change was being introduced, and the implications this had for the future direction of the party.

By way of contrast, although *Les Verts* have arguably prioritized 'electoral' goals, resulting in a governmental role during 1997, party organization was not identified as a significant factor in influencing this goal. Given the context of French party politics, it is unsurprising to note that the central focus for debate surrounded issues of alliances and coalitions. External relationships rather than internal issues have been identified as the key factor in pursuing an electoral goal. In addition, the more regional nature of French politics has not provoked such a concern over the incompatibility of the more unconventional aspects of Green party organization. It will be important to assess, in time, what impact experience of national parliamentary representation and government responsibility has on the party organization. Given that it was not until *Miljöpartiet de Gröna* had experienced national representation that many of the organizational weaknesses and problems emerged, similar pressure may await *Les Verts* in the coming years.

To summarize, Green parties have undoubtedly reassessed their party goals, moving beyond the initial concerns with raising awareness of environmental issues and initiating a new political challenge, towards attaining a direct political impact through national parliamentary representation. In doing so, the Greens have been forced into closer contact with the competitive party political arena, which has put pressure on the alternative organizational structures initiated by the Green parties. Organizational reform, therefore, reflects the process of adaptation within the Green parties and a shifting pattern of Green party goals in pursuit of a solid role for Green politics. The different political opportunities available to the parties within their respective party systems have played a vital role in shaping the prioritization of Green party goals within each case. The extent to which there is a common perception of the primary party goal, and the depth of commitment to these goals, have been key factors in determining both the instigation of organizational reform as well as party activists' attitudes towards this reform process. It would appear, therefore, that the Green parties are reshaping in the light of pressures from the established European party systems. In the German case, this process has been closely linked with the increasing institutionalization and 'professionalization' of the party. However, has this pattern of organizational reform resulted in the process of institutionalization within all of the Green parties and a loss of 'new politics' organizational style for the sake of electoral success?

ORGANIZATIONAL REFORM: IDEOLOGICAL CHANGE OR ORGANIZATIONAL EVOLUTION?

While there is only scope within this chapter to provide a tentative examination of this question, it is possible to gain an initial perspective by examining the new organizational structures of the three parties, as presented in Table 5.2, within the categories outlined earlier in Table 5.1.

The organizational reforms are clearly distinguishable; however, Table 5.2 suggests that the parties have still attempted to reflect the commitments outlined earlier. Party conferences remain the central decision-making body of the three parties. Despite amendments on the part of *Les Verts* and the Green party, the general pattern remains one of decentralized decision-making. However, all parties have developed smaller, more efficient party executives, which might signal the transition towards a more centralized style of operation. Regional autonomy and influence is still encouraged, with both the Green party and *Les Verts* introducing new regional bodies. Similarly, regional delegates form the majority of the voting members at party conferences.

Table 5.2 also demonstrates the parties' continuing commitments towards participation, with all three parties providing local and regional members with influential voting rights. However, in both *Les Verts* and the Green party, there has been a change in policy regarding the right of all party members to vote at national conferences, with both parties adopting a system of delegate conferences. However, members maintain the right to vote for party candidates, regional and national representatives and conference delegates.

The implementation of office rotation is one area in which significant change is evident. In line with the German Greens, all three parties have reassessed the extent to which party organization can successfully and effectively encompass a commitment to 'anti-professionalism'. Some changes to rotation rules have been introduced out of practical necessity. This is especially true with regard to the low levels of party membership and, more significantly, the small proportion of active members who are available in regional and local parties. Implementation of strict rotation of posts became a direct problem when no new candidates stood for posts to which the previous occupants had completed their allotted term, or when there were no suitably experienced candidates to take over such posts.

To summarize, Green parties have clearly changed their organizational structures and, in some cases, have taken on board more 'traditional' approaches. As with the German Greens, all three parties have become more 'professionalized' in certain respects, such as those

Table 5.2 *A Comparison of the Reformed Organizational Structures of the Green Party, Miljöpartiet de Gröna and Les Verts*

Party	Executive body	Speakers	Regional bodies	Voting rights	Rotation rule
UK Green party	Party conference is still main decision-making body. Party council is replaced by regional council and small party executive.	There are two speakers (one man and one woman) who have seats on the executive but no voting rights.	Local and regional parties remain autonomous. Regional council gives a more coordinated approach to regional party activities and to arbitrate over regional issues.	Members vote for elected representatives, candidates, etc. Voting at party conference is restricted to local party delegates.	Rotation is maintained for all offices, although loosened slightly due to the shortage of active members.
Les Verts	General assembly is now two-tiered with a regionally based congress of representatives, as well as a national assembly. CNIR remains the central body. More centralized executive college.	There are four speakers (two women and two men) who are elected from within the executive college.	Local and regional parties remain relatively autonomous. Still elect 75% of the CNIR.	Members have the right to vote for candidates, CNIR representatives, etc. Voting at conference is restricted to regional representatives elected for two years.	Although maintained for some offices, rotation has been relaxed. Points system for multiple office holding remains in place.
Miljöpartiet de Gröna	Party executive board replaced the four committees. There are greater links between the parliamentary party and the party executive.	There are two spokes-persons (one man and one woman).	Local and regional parties are still relatively autonomous. However, parliamentary and national party has become the main focus of activity.	Members have the same voting rights as before.	Rotation rule has been relaxed, especially regarding members of the parliamentary party.

concerning spokespersons and the weakening of the rotation principle. However, the Green parties still maintain a distinctive approach to party organization, participation and democracy. Even within the German example, Poguntke argues that *Bundnis '90/Die Grünen* are the only German party to provide 'a pronouncedly participatory and elite-challenging internal political culture' (Poguntke, 1993, p395). Without doubt, some of the more challenging aspects of Green party organization have been removed as the parties have evolved. However, as Doherty suggests, the reforms represent an amendment to the more utopian aspects of Green party organization rather than concrete evidence for the assimilation of the Greens into established party frameworks (see Doherty, 1994).

All of the parties discussed here have, therefore, implemented significant organizational changes, reassessing some of the more distinctive aspects of Green party structure. Using Harmel and Janda's model of party change has again highlighted the multicausal nature of organizational reform. While the analysis has identified a broad range of different stimuli, influencing the processes of organizational change within the three parties, in all cases organizational reform is closely related to the systemic political context within which these changes took place.

The analysis demonstrates that not all organizational change is necessarily ideologically driven. Political experience and expediency has played a significant role in altering the prioritization of goals within the Greens, with the parties prioritizing electoral goals in an attempt to gain a firm foothold as established national political actors. The differences in both the pattern and timing of organizational change within the parties, and the level of conflict accompanying this change, are closely related to the degree to which this goal has been attainable, the level of agreement within the party regarding the prioritization of this goal over others, and the extent to which organizational reform has been identified as an influential factor in achieving it. Subsequently, internal conflict over organizational reform has focused upon debates concerning the prioritization of goals within the Greens and the perception of organizational reform as part of this process. As a result, the parties who experienced less internal division over the prioritization of electoral and parliamentary goals, *Les Verts* and *Miljöpartiet de Gröna*, displayed less internal division over the process of organizational reform.

All of the Green parties have clearly been forced to find a balance between the 'Green' commitment to the organizational style of the 'new politics' and the practicalities of operating within competitive party systems. Despite significant organizational reforms, the party organizations still attempt to incorporate the values and ideals of the 'new politics', such as decentralization, anti-professionalism and participation. However, rather than maintaining a common Green party organizational framework, arguably based around the pattern developed within *Die Grünen*, the parties have begun to adapt the organizational embodiment of these commitments to the systemic context within which they operate.

Chapter 6

Redefining the Environment: Changes in Green Party Policy

The public expects us to be environmental. We have to work out how to secure that, and then demonstrate that we are also concerned with social issues and economic issues. How do we fill it out from there, rather than saying we've been too environmental, now let's be social. It's about bringing things into your own identity and securing your own space (Interview with Green party activist, 7 August 1995).

It is one thing to identify the damaging environmental impact of modern industrial society, but it is quite another to provide a political programme that ensures a radical change in this process. When identifying the distinguishing characteristics of the European Greens, Poguntke and Müller-Rommel place the specific nature of the Greens' programmatic profile alongside organizational structure and electoral profile as 'the essential elements of new politics' (Müller-Rommel and Poguntke, 1989, p21). The policy dimension represents the attempt to develop abstract Green ideals into practical political change. As with party organization, it provides not only a critique of existing attitudes and approaches to political decision-making, but also offers a Green alternative reflection of the 'new politics' identity. This identity can largely be summarized as follows:

Ecological politics, opposition to nuclear power, individualism with a very strong focus on self-determination and self-actualization, participatory democracy with direct citizens' involvement with decision-making, a general left-

> *wing orientation, redistribution of global wealth in favour*
> *of the developing nations, and an unambiguous prefer-*
> *ence for unilateral disarmament* (Müller-Rommel and
> Poguntke, 1989, pp21–22).

As outlined in previous chapters, the manner in which Green parties
have portrayed this 'new politics' identity has changed as the parties
have developed and evolved. As the parties have sought more effective
ways in which to put across the Green message to the public, these
reforms have raised questions among party activists regarding the focus
and priorities of Green policy.

In Germany, the balance between different aspects of the ecological identity within the party's programmes often reflected the
diversity of influence of the various factions within the Greens. As
such, the focus of the Green party programme has been an issue for
debate since the party's formation in 1980. While the 'Greener'
elements within the party have favoured the prioritization of environmental concerns, the broad new social movement base provided
vociferous support for a much more diverse programmatic perspective, which presented a more radical systemic challenge.

The initial party programme in 1980 attempted to pull these
diverse strands together, arguing that Germany was faced with an
economic and environmental crisis. While this crisis was most clearly
reflected in an ongoing process of environmental destruction, the root
causes of this destruction lay in a capitalist system that placed excess-
ive emphasis upon economic growth and the pursuit of profit. Reflecting the ideological roots outlined in Chapter 1, the party argued that
change could only occur as the result of a changing process of interaction both in human relations and in human relationships with the
natural world. This meant not only a commitment to environmental
protection, but also greater emphasis upon direct democracy, participation and equality.

Frankland and Schoonmaker portray the Greens in their early
federal programmes as being 'champions of underdogs abroad and at
home,' claiming that:

> *The Greens advocate full equality for women. They pro-*
> *mote the rights of foreign workers, homosexuals, gypsies,*
> *the handicapped, prisoners and the aged. For all citizens*
> *they stress the right of free speech and assembly, the right*
> *of conscientious objection to military service and the right*
> *to be free of surveillance* (Frankland and Schoonmaker,
> 1992, p131).

Throughout the party's history, the balance between ecology and broader new social movement objectives has shifted within the parties' policy priorities. The increasing importance of environmental and anti-nuclear campaigns in Germany during the 1980s helped to concentrate greater attention upon the Green message. Not only did the German Greens improve their position electorally, but other parties started to recognize the electoral salience of Green issues. The Social Democrats (SPD) were particularly keen to accommodate the Green agenda within their programmes, claiming that the Greens raised important issues but failed to provide practical programmatic solutions. It was one thing to identify problems, but quite another to actually tackle the task of putting these problems right. As such, the Greens were often portrayed as an 'irresponsible' opposition party that lacked a concrete pro-gramme for reform.

Parliamentary representation added a new dimension to the policy debate. Rapidly expanding parliamentary success increased calls within the party for a more concrete programme. If the party was to seek coalition with the SPD, it was argued, it needed concrete policy proposals rather than vague ideological statements of intent. As such, debates within the party over policy direction focused upon whether the party should maintain a longer-term commitment to a radical overhaul of industrial capitalist society, or whether it should focus upon more short-term objectives that could be achieved through coalition activity at regional and federal level. During the 1980s, therefore, emphasis moved away from an ecological stance.

By 1990, however, the German Greens were again focusing upon environmental policies, ironically at a time when the agenda had shifted. Thus, in an election dominated by the implications of German unification, the Greens found themselves focusing upon the perils of climate change. While undoubtedly a significant issue to focus upon, it was far removed from the top of the political agenda of most of the voters. The campaign focus was identified as a key factor in the poor electoral performance during 1990, leading the Greens to another change of emphasis during the 1990s.

During the 1994 federal elections, the Greens, conscious of the potential for coalition with the SPD, focused their electoral campaign upon broader social issues, including the shortening of work time and the creation of more jobs. This clearly reflected the primary concerns of a large proportion of the German electorate.[1] Electoral success in 1994 and the strengthened political position of the party encouraged the Greens to continue this policy approach. Indeed, the Greens' social agenda was a vital dimension of the coalition agreement with the SPD after the 1998 federal elections. Unemployment again figured high on the party's agenda and was seen as a more vital indicator of the party's performance in government than other more directly 'environmental' concerns. When joining the coalition government in 1998, the Greens declared that their performance in government over the coming four years should be judged mainly by the contribution that they had made to combating unemployment.

As the brief outline above demonstrates, the German Greens have regularly experienced a fluctuation in the focus and prioritization of their policies, from 'social environmental' to 'natural environmental' issues. Overall, however, recent years have undoubtedly witnessed a focus upon the 'social' dimension. For some, this represents another dimension in the process of institutionalization of the 'new politics'. As the Greens have become an established part of the party political system, so they have been forced to focus upon expanding the Red–Green dimension of the party's identity at the expense of a more ecological 'deep Green' perspective in order to maintain strong links with the SPD.

The divisions over policy priorities within the German Greens, outlined above, have also often been used to identify divisions between different types of Green party. In particular, the choice of either a 'natural' or 'social' focus has been interpreted as reflecting the different heritages of the parties, the variation in activist base and also a distinction in the level of commitment to a 'deep Green ecological' ideological perspective.

These divisions are primarily focused upon the manner in which parties incorporate, represent and prioritize the different aspects of the 'new politics' identity outlined above. Müller-Rommel, for example, identifies a split in policy orientation between 'pure Green reformist parties' and 'alternative Green radical parties' (Müller-Rommel 1985, p491). He suggests that pure Green reformist parties prefer to 'select genuine ecology issues that do not bring them deeply into policy conflict with the established parties over the social welfare state and foreign policy' (Müller-Rommel, 1985, p491). By contrast, the 'alternative Green radical' parties are characterized by a commitment to 'fundamental changes in social and political institutions' and seek 'a new alternative, social–radical democratic paradigm' (Müller-Rommel, 1985, p491).

These alternative approaches to Green party policy are identified by Arne Naess as being reflective of a deeper ideological commitment within the Green parties to different levels of 'Greening' society. He claims that there is a difference in the style of Green thinking between the countries of central and Mediterranean Europe, such as Germany, France and Italy, and those of the 'marginal lands' – namely, Scandinavia and the UK. The latter represent the 'natural' Greens, whose primary policy focus rests with environmental protection issues, while the former, the 'social' Greens, place greater emphasis upon society in a wider context (Naess, 1988, p4).

Prendiville clarifies these classifications within an empirical study of policy priorities within *Les Verts*. He identifies 'social' issues as focusing upon 'socio-economic problems, solidarity, anti-racism, democracy, self-management and unemployment' (Prendiville, 1994, p109). He outlines the basis of 'natural' environmental priorities as 'environment, conservation, recycling, organic farming, animal protection, nuclear, pollution and energy' (Prendiville, 1994, p109).[2] These distinctions undoubtedly reflect the more philosophical binary divisions discussed in Chapter 1, and the implications associated with these strategies suggest a distinction between those parties with a 'pure ecological' identity, on the one hand, and those who have been more open to compromise, on the other. Shull (1999), for example, claims that these distinctions reflect an ongoing debate within the Greens regarding the prioritization of efficiency over identity. As the Greens become more enmeshed within the political system, it appears that the commitment to a pure 'ecological' perspective has been diluted in favour of a broader picture of 'environmental' politics.

This chapter examines the Greens' continuing attempts to represent the 'new politics' identity and assesses the changes that have occurred as the parties have evolved. In particular, it will question whether there are distinctive types of identity within the different Green parties, which is reflected within party policy, and whether the process of development and change has, in any way, altered this identity. Addressing these issues, the analysis will focus upon the following questions:

- To what extent do the divisions highlighted above provide an accurate portrayal of changes within Green party policies?
- Is there evidence to suggest that Green parties themselves see party policy within these contexts?
- Is it possible to identify the use of 'social' and 'natural' or 'fundamental' and 'moderate' distinctions within party policy debates and, if so, do they reflect the ideological divisions highlighted above?

Party analysis has often highlighted the complexities involved in identifying and analysing a party's policy commitments. Party policy is often multidimensional, and includes both day-to-day policy positions, which are responsive to changing political issues, and the more long-term core values upon which these policy stances are based. In presenting a comparative assessment of policy change, therefore, one is faced with a number of fundamental questions and potential obstacles. In particular, what exactly should an assessment of party policy examine; to what extent do policy changes alter the underlying values of a political party; and, subsequently, how can these changes be accurately measured? In tackling the first issue, one is faced with the analytical dilemma that party policy has traditionally been 'surrounded by considerable ambiguity' (Laver and Hunt, 1992, p3). This ambiguity especially concerns the identification of those policies that are representative of the core values and beliefs of a political party.

Party documents and, in particular, election manifestos provide the primary focus for identifying core policy ideas because they represent a clear statement of intent regarding a party's policy decisions and proposals. However, while manifestos may provide clarity on one dimension, they are, by definition, designed primarily with electoral considerations at heart and may not necessarily, therefore, portray a truly accurate representation of the 'core' values and policies of a party. Consequently, while analysts such as Hamilton (1989) accept the need to equate policy with the contents of party programmes and manifestos 'with all their ambiguity', analysis is conducted in the knowledge that what is presented is 'a range of policies within which interpretations fall' (Hamilton, 1989, p18). Understanding transformations in party policy is subsequently problematic, as change may merely reflect a change in focus within a broad range of core party policies, rather than a radical ideological shift.

Demker (1997) attempts to overcome this by distinguishing between a 'fundamental' and an 'operative' level within a party's ideology. The former is defined as the party's 'postulates', while the latter is defined as party 'doctrine':

> *The doctrine consists of concrete and dated wishes and claims in political life and includes verbal attitudes of the party about issues which have been raised in the political debate. This doctrine is founded on several postulates. Postulates are here understood as fundamental, core values and perceptions on an abstract level* (Demker, 1997, pp412–413).

While analysis of party documents provides an overall picture of the party doctrine, this provides the basis from which one is able to 'search for the deeper, underlying core values' (Demker, 1997, p413). Demker's approach recognizes that the process of policy development functions on more than one level and that, while the underlying 'core values' of a party may stay relatively stable over long periods of time, day-to-day policy proposals based upon these core values, and identifiable in party manifestos, are far more likely to fluctuate in line with the contemporary political agenda.

This chapter, therefore, provides a comparative picture of Green party policy at two different, but related, levels. Firstly, it considers the parties' attempts to portray their core values and priorities to the outside world, focusing, in particular, upon statements within party documents and websites that attempt to classify these central beliefs and commitments. While these documents, arguably, still may not provide a complete picture of the core values of the parties, they highlight how the parties wish to be perceived by the wider public and provide a relatively concise identification of core beliefs and values that have been sanctioned by the majority of party members. Analysis of party manifestos and programmes, despite its weaknesses, remains the most direct method for accessing party policy stances and for identifying change. The second aspect of this analysis will therefore concentrate upon changes within party manifestos, focusing particularly upon differences between issue priorities during the 1980s and those in evidence during campaigns in the late 1990s.[3] As with previous chapters, Harmel and Janda's model will be used to explain the factors influencing any policy changes. The chapter will then examine whether the changes identified may justifiably be viewed as reflecting a change in the parties' core values and in the ideological base of the Greens.

PRESENTING GREEN IDEAS[4]

How, then, do the Green parties themselves identify the core principles upon which their more detailed policy is constructed? As with the German Greens, it is possible to identify a set of core commitments within the party literature that have remained relatively uniform over time and that are presented as the underlying objectives of the Greens. Since these statements represent the primary summary of the parties' overall aims and objectives, they act as an important benchmark for assessing Green party values. *Les Verts*, for example, claim that these statements reflect the party's commitments to Green ideology and represent 'the values of ecology' (*Les Verts*, 1997). While aspects of policy prioritizing and policy issues have fluctuated over time, the description of these core commitments has remained a relatively stable part of the parties' presentation of its ideals and values to the public.

In defining the core commitments of the Green party in France, *Les Verts* focus upon an ideological commitment to three central themes of ecologism – namely, environmental protection, a critique of industrialism and greater participation and direct democracy. These commitments are placed under the banner of 'responsibility, solidarity and citizenship' (*Les Verts*, 1997).[5] 'Responsibility' focuses upon society's responsibility for the natural environment and the damage being caused by modern industrialism. The party argues that:

> *Humanity must take into account the effects of its activities on the planet, and must take action so that future generations may live in a preserved environment* (Les Verts, 1997).

In policy terms, 'responsibility' is epitomized by the party's commitment to the abolition of nuclear power, the reduction of pollution and the control of waste. 'Solidarity' focuses upon a critique of modern industrial society and provides the basis for the party's attack on the current economic system. *Les Verts* identify solidarity in terms of solidarity with the poor and socially excluded in both a national and international context. The party's primary policy focus within this dimension lies with a call for the redistribution of work, greater social protection and increased aid to developing nations. The final theme of 'citizenship' focuses upon the rights of the individual and includes a demand for greater democracy and participation in decision-making. *Les Verts* criticize both the undemocratic nature of the present French political system and also the inequality in the division of power within modern society, both in political and economic terms. To combat these problems, party policy focuses upon the need for greater regional control, less accumulation of office by politicians in France and a greater equality within these offices between men and women.

    Miljöpartiet de Gröna frames its core values within the concept of 'four solidarities' (*Miljöpartiet*, 1988; 1992; 1997), which reflect many of the same values and concerns identified by *Les Verts*.[6] However, *Miljöpartiet* focuses more directly upon issues of environmental protection in contrast to the more alternative left stance of *Les Verts*. The first two 'solidarities' reflect this central concern with environmental protection, emphasizing 'solidarity with nature and the global ecological system' and 'solidarity with future generations'. The former displays many similarities to *Les Verts'* commitment to 'responsibility for the planet', emphasizing the importance of understanding the impact of human actions upon the natural world. 'Solidarity', *Miljöpartiet* claims, implies:

> *...respect for all life and for nature of which we are a part. All human activity, all use of natural resources and all development must be based on that respect. This also means that economic activity must respect ecological reality* (Miljöpartiet, 1997, p1).

Commitments to this core principle are linked to the party's focus upon issues of waste and pollution control, an anti-nuclear disposition and an alternative transport policy. The party also develops a relatively ecocentric stance, arguing that 'all living beings should be protected regardless of their usefulness to mankind' (*Miljöpartiet*, 1997). Environmental protection also represents part of society's responsibilities towards future generations, given the long-term implications of continued environmental destruction and pollution. As well as issues of energy conservation, the party identifies child care and child protection as key policy issues within this sphere.

The remaining commitments focus upon issues of social exclusion and deprivation. 'Solidarity with all the world's people in need' highlights the unequal consumption of natural resources between the developed and developing nations, claiming that 'the Swedish level of consumption and production on a global scale would soon lead to collapse' (*Miljöpartiet*, 1997). The party calls for a reduction in consumption within the developed nations and fair trade and support for the developing world. 'Solidarity with the indigent citizens of our country' focuses upon inequality within Sweden, and is reflected in calls for shortening the working week, as well as a greater share of welfare benefits for 'low-income groups, the aged, the ill, the handicapped and people with drug and alcohol problems' (*Miljöpartiet*, 1997).

Interestingly, the Green party in the UK does not present its core values and commitments within classifications such as those identified in both France and Sweden. While the party recognizes the importance of commitments to many of the same values and concerns, the focus, in this case, rests upon an overall project – namely, the development of a 'sustainable society'.[7] This represents a commitment to:

> *. . .creating a society in which individuals, through their ability to satisfy their basic needs more fully, are then able better to contribute to future sustainability. This principle is reflected in the radical Green agenda both for changes in values and lifestyles, and for reformed social, economic and political structures* (Green Party MfSS PB403).

The Green party 'Manifesto for a Sustainable Society' (MfSS) identifies the main requirements of a sustainable society as:

> *. . .minimum disruption of ecological processes; maximum conservation of materials and energy...a population in which recruitment equals loss, a social system in which the individual can enjoy, rather than feel restricted by, the first*

> *three conditions; a social system where spirituality is
> recognized and respected* (Green Party MfSS PB310).

Again, the central policy dimensions that accompany these commitments focus upon both natural and social concerns. These include the reduction of pollution and waste, an anti-nuclear stance, support for equality at both national and international levels, and a critique of many of the features of modern industrial society.

Although the presentation of 'core values' varies between the three parties, common features are clearly identifiable. Within the concepts of 'responsibility, solidarity and citizenship', *Les Verts* attempt to combine both a focus on environmental protection with a critique of modern society, while also relating these concerns to national issues and perspectives. A similar model is evident both within the 'four solidarities' identified by *Miljöpartiet de Gröna*, and the 'Manifesto for a Sustainable Society' (MfSS) developed by the Green party. All three approaches emphasize an important balance between the protection of the natural environment and the need for societal change. A clearer picture of policy transition is evident, however, when examining the parties' changing policy priorities.

CHANGING POLICY ISSUES WITHIN *LES VERTS*

Party direction within *Les Verts* has often been reflective of the style and personal strategic priorities of the party's de facto leaders, and has regularly been defined in terms of either 'natural' or 'social' issues. This is partly a reflection of the party's emphasis upon annual strategic action plans. During the late 1980s, Antoine Waechter directed the party towards a distinctive 'autonomous' ecological perspective. A 1988 survey of party priorities found that 47 per cent of party activists supported a focus on the 'natural' environment, in contrast to 25 per cent who favoured the prioritization of 'social' concerns (Prendiville, 1994, p109). Support for Waechter within the party was strongly reflected in, and indicative of, the party's commitment to an ecological orientation.

This strategic orientation is evident within the policy issues prioritized by the party during the late 1980s. In the 1989 European election manifesto, *Les Verts* centred their campaign on environmental protection, alternative energy strategy and anti-nuclearism (*Les Verts*, 1989). Social issues were not completely neglected, with policies directed towards solidarity with the developing world, unemployment and 'quality of life' (Hainsworth, 1990, p101). As well as the wider environmental themes regarding the ozone layer and the Chernobyl disaster, *Les Verts* were also able to focus attention upon national environmental concerns. These included the construction of the Loire Dam, problems of acid rain in Alsace, port development in Brittany and the proposed construction of a number of new nuclear power stations (*Les Verts*, 1989). The focus upon environmental issues therefore reflected not merely the party's ideological priorities, and the wider global concerns for environmental protection, but also significant national environmental concerns apparent at this time. Indeed, the party recognized the importance of environmental concerns in raising their electoral profile. After the municipal elections of 1989, the party thanked not only their electors but also 'the Breton rivers, the ozone layer and the Amazonian forest, which were a great help' (cited in Prendiville, 1994, p47).

However, during the 1990s environmental protection issues had less impact, leading one activist to suggest that:

Concerns over pollution, atmospheric or otherwise, nuclear dumping and the conservation of the environment have failed to rouse the French to action (Greze, 1997).

Changes to *Les Verts*' policy priorities during the 1990s coincided with the rise to prominence of Dominique Voynet and the shift towards alliance with the left. These moves provoked a refocusing of the party's policies away from traditional environmental protection and towards key 'social' issues. This transition is most evident in the party's 1997 election campaign, which claimed to focus 'beyond environmental issues to tout a wider political revolution for a new planet, a new mode of development' (Greze, 1997). Although maintaining a commitment to environmental protection issues, the election manifesto focused predominantly upon the reduction in working hours to 35 hours per week, the introduction of men/women parity in the constitution, a better quality of life and defence of the public sector, and a more tolerant immigration policy (*Les Verts*, 1997).[8]

The mixture of emphasis upon social policies and environmental protection issues, and, more interestingly, the focus upon the necessity of improving the 'social' in order to enhance the 'natural', was the centrepiece of the campaign, as well as being the cornerstone of the agreement with the *Parti Socialiste* (PS). During the campaign, Voynet called for 'a society where the quality of life, of health and of the environment plays a bigger role than the markets' (cited in Greze, 1997). In line with this, environmental issues, such as the BSE scare and water pollution, were linked directly to the need for social change:

Queen Mary College Main Library
CheckOut Receipt

12/03/07
09:48 am

Item:The evolution of green politics :
development and change within European
Green Parties
231214253X

Due Date: 19/3/2007,23:59

Thank You for using
the 3M SelfCheck System!

> *The trend towards increased performance and the dehumanizing of our society are in opposition to the principles of precaution: before taking a decision, we must measure the consequences (Les Verts, 1997).*

Les Verts have therefore adopted a stance designed to reflect both the central priorities upon the French political agenda during the 1990s, and to demonstrate the diversity and breadth of policy developed by the party. The party has undoubtedly refocused its position towards social concerns, although where environmental protection issues emerge, such as with *Superphénix*, the party is at the forefront of these issues.

Figure 6.1 once again places the process of policy reform within *Les Verts* in relation to the key factors for change identified by Harmel and Janda's model.

Policy development within *Les Verts* is reflective of both internal factional pressures and external stimuli. Figure 6.1 highlights two distinct periods of policy development within *Les Verts,* with a brief transitional period in between. In relation to internal pressures, the transition from one policy stance to another is closely related to the internal changes surrounding the transition from Waechter to Voynet's de facto leadership, and the change in dominant faction accompanying this.

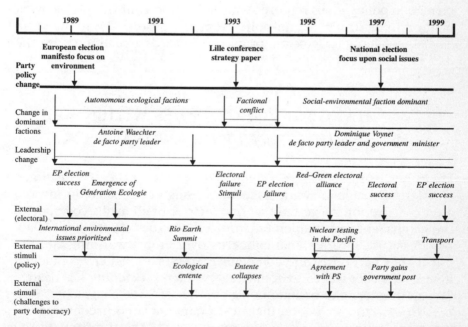

Figure 6.1 *Potential Sources of Policy Change:* Les Verts

Figure 6.1 also identifies the main external shocks surrounding both 'electoral' and 'policy' representation issues. Electorally, the failure of the ecological entente to make a breakthrough at national level again appears to be a significant factor in pushing the party towards a reassessment of its stance. This factor has already been identified as influential in instigating both organizational and strategic changes within the party. Focusing upon policy development, Figure 6.1 indicates that the failure to achieve national representation through a Green agenda was one of the main influences in directing party interest towards a more left-wing agenda, and the eventual electoral coalition with the Socialists.

Figure 6.1 also highlights the ability of long-standing political parties to adapt themselves to a Green agenda. With environmental issues given priority during the late 1980s, a focus upon environmental protection issues appeared to be effective both in terms of electoral- and policy-based party goals. However, during the 1990s, *Les Verts* found this position challenged on two fronts. Other political parties attempted to adopt a more environmental approach within their programmes and policies, while also attempting to portray *Les Verts* as a single-issue party. In addition, concern over environmental issues was quickly replaced by more immediate concerns regarding unemployment and welfare reform. These events represent external shocks to both 'policy'-focused and 'electorally'-focused party goals. The change in policy focus represents an attempt to confront problems of electoral performance and policy representation. The focus upon 'social' concerns reflects the transition towards a coalition with the left.

CHANGING POLICY ISSUES WITHIN *MILJÖPARTIET DE GRÖNA*

Environmental issues were a significant feature of the 1988 national election campaign in Sweden. Electoral studies conducted during and after the election suggested that one quarter of all media coverage of the campaign focused upon environmental issues (Michelletti, 1989, p172). Again, international concerns over global warming and the effects of Chernobyl were complemented by national environmental issues as Swedes faced environmental problems including seal deaths, radioactive deer and pollution on a number of Swedish beaches.

Miljöpartiet's election manifesto concentrated predominantly upon environmental protection measures. At the forefront of the programme was the complete shutdown of Swedish nuclear power by

1991, the introduction of tough anti-pollution laws, a reduction in road freight transport, a reduction in fossil fuels and chemical use, and a 1 per cent of gross national product (GNP) investment in the environment (Affigne, 1990, p124). Again, however, it would be wrong to suggest that *Miljöpartiet* focused purely upon issues of environmental protection. Protecting the natural environment was placed firmly within the context of broader societal change:

> *Underlying the ideology of the Green party is the aware-*
> *ness that life itself is threatened by modern civilization. A*
> *civilization that produces dead lakes and forests, soil*
> *erosion, air pollution, poisoned soil and groundwater,*
> *global warming and social collapse is not a life-supporting*
> *system (Miljöpartiet, 1988, p2).*

Of the three parties discussed in this book, *Miljöpartiet de Gröna* was arguably the most directly impeded by the changing nature of the national political agenda during the 1990s. In contrast to 1988, the 1991 election campaign was bereft of environmental considerations, focusing instead upon economic concerns. This was identified by analysts and activists alike as a primary factor in the party's failure to maintain national representation.[9] The party faced criticism that it was merely a 'single-issue' party based upon environmental protection. National and European elections during the mid 1990s, therefore, represented important tests of the party's ability to reach beyond the sphere of environmental protection.

The party emphasized a more encompassing policy portfolio, identifying the links between social policies and more traditional environmental concerns. One of the key examples of this was the claim that environmental protection can generate employment:

> *Today when unemployment is high there are great possi-*
> *bilities of investing in the environment. In parliament,*
> Miljöpartiet *wants to channel large funds to the develop-*
> *ment of environmentally friendly bioenergy, renewable*
> *energy sources and solar cells (Miljöpartiet, 1994).*

The party argued that new jobs could be created by shifting the balance of taxation from labour to taxes on energy and non-renewable resources, making it 'profitable for business to do away with environmental degradation and energy waste rather than with people' (*Miljöpartiet*, 1994).

As well as the focus upon employment issues, *Miljöpartiet* tackled issues such as health and welfare provision, the decentralization of government and improvements in public transport. Although environmental issues were largely neglected, concern over the construction of the Oresund bridge meant that they weren't totally sidelined. Two other campaigns proved to be the most influential for the party, however. The first was the claim that 'allergy is politics', which sought to demonstrate to the Swedish public the close connection between lifestyles, work, health and issues of environmental protection. The second campaign concerned Sweden's proposed membership of the European Union (EU). The EU issue has, as noted earlier, been a key factor in *Miljöpartiet*'s electoral recovery. While opposition to EU membership proved detrimental in 1991, the stance gained in popularity following Sweden's membership.

Figure 6.2 places the process of policy reform within *Miljöpartiet de Gröna* in relation to the key factors for change identified by Harmel and Janda's model.

The pattern of policy change here is somewhat similar to that identified for *Les Verts*. Figure 6.2 suggests that the two parties faced similar pressures influencing policy developments. *Miljöpartiet*'s predominant focus upon environmental protection issues coincides with both an increased concern for environmental issues and the party's first experiences of national electoral success. In addition, the

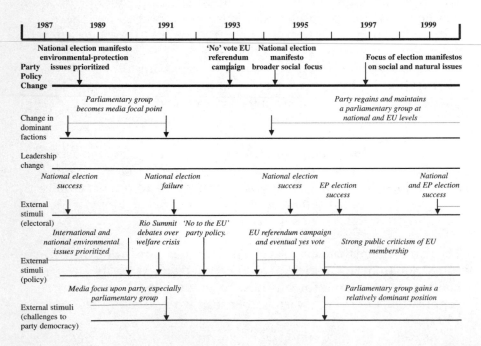

Figure 6.2 *Potential Sources of Policy Change:* Miljöpartiet de Gröna

significance of breaking the threshold to national representation, for both the reputation and funding of political parties in Sweden, has already been highlighted. As with *Les Verts*, *Miljöpartiet* experienced a backlash following this success, both in terms of a process of 'Greening' within the long-standing political parties and with regard to criticisms of the party being a 'single-issue' party. The combination of these factors, together with a growing concern for economic and social issues in Sweden, were influential in *Miljöpartiet*'s electoral failure during 1991.

Miljöpartiet de Gröna's move towards prioritizing social policy issues appears to have emanated from these experiences. However, in contrast to *Les Verts*, one issue – namely, opposition to membership of the EU – has dominated party policy in recent years. The EU issue demonstrates the manner in which an external stimulus relating to policy goals can play a significant role in refocusing a party's policy priorities. The party adopted an anti-EU stance during the 1991 national election campaign, against the general flow of public opinion at this time, and gained little response. In 1994, as debates over EU membership came to the fore, *Miljöpartiet* was seen as the only party united in opposition to membership and became the focal point of the 'no' campaign throughout the referendum period. The party's opposition to membership remained at the forefront of party policy and was enhanced by the increasing hostility of the Swedish electorate to EU membership following Sweden's formal entry into the union.

Figure 6.2 indicates that internal factional conflict played little or no role in influencing policy development. This contrasts with *Les Verts*, where internal conflicts were pivotal. The external pressures or stimuli, however, display a striking resemblance to those identified with *Les Verts*. Again, the main pressures focus upon electoral- and policy-oriented issues. Figure 6.2 highlights the relationship between the party's reassessment of policy priorities and the adoption of Green issues by other parties, the changing national political/policy agenda, and the impact of electoral defeat. The party's goals along 'electoral' and 'policy' dimensions were clearly challenged by these events. A changing policy focus represented a crucial factor, both in improving the party's electoral performance and in refocusing the party's policy agenda.

POLICY CHANGE WITHIN THE GREEN PARTY

The UK Green party has consistently prided itself on the detailed attention given to policy development, in comparison with other Green parties, and has often provided the theoretical basis for many Green party policies throughout Europe. The significance of the 1989 European elections for the UK Green party has already been highlighted, both in terms of Green electoral support and the impact of environmental concerns on the political agenda. Again, international environmental concern over global warming and the impact of the Chernobyl disaster were combined with nationally specific environmental issues. In the UK case, these issues included the death of seals off the British coast, conflict over the state of UK water systems, and concern regarding outbreaks of both the Listeria and Salmonella viruses.

Issues surrounding the state of the natural environment predominated during the election campaign. The Green party placed significant emphasis within their European election manifesto upon environmental protection issues such as waste and energy policies, conservation issues, and water and air quality. The party was also careful to link environmental concerns with wider issues of modern societal problems:

> *Because the biggest cash prizes are given to those who can produce and pollute the fastest, greed always seems to win out over need. That's why we have a world in which the rich minority is able to dictate the living standards of the poor majority. That's why the atmosphere is so polluted that we are now faced with potentially disastrous climatic change. That's why trees are dying from acid rain, and why our streams and rivers are so dirty* (Green Party, 1989, p4).

The significance of environmental concerns on the national political agenda served to heighten the need for environmental protection policies both at a national policy level and also at an internal party level. With such a clear emphasis, it is hardly surprising that Green party policy priorities were focused towards environmental protection.

As earlier chapters have highlighted, established parties in the UK were quick to seize upon the Green agenda and the Green party has consistently struggled to carve out an identity and to attract significant levels of support. Debates emerged during the 1990s concerning the deeply philosophical nature of party policy and its contribution within the wider context of national political debate. In particular, activists were concerned that the party was not capable of providing an accessible, short-term policy outside of the MfSS that could be used during election campaigns, or when specific issues arose. One Green party activist claimed:

> *The Green party in Britain probably has more policy*
> *documentation than any other Green party worldwide.*
> *The national policy is primarily philosophical, which has*
> *created a small cottage industry in local and sometimes*
> *regional manifesto production, to produce short-term*
> *policy. . . . A lot of this effort could be avoided if our*
> *national policy was policy and not the product of a desire*
> *for superior Green abstractions* (Steve Dawe, Green Link,
> 1994, p10).

This argument lies at the heart of the Green party's policy difficulties
and has been identified as a partial explanation for the public's general
perception of the Greens as a single-issue party, with few policies
outside of the sphere of environmental protection.

A second debate focused upon the realignment of policy priorities,
similar to those experienced by both *Les Verts* and *Miljöpartiet*. The
question of a 'social' agenda was at the heart of the policy concerns
within the Basis for Renewal programme, and was utilized as the
primary focus for the party during the 1997 general election. In the
consultative stages, the party's policy committee asked members
whether or not the party should have a detailed social agenda on issues
such as homelessness and unemployment, or whether the ecological
agenda was 'too urgent to be clouded by such issues' (*Green Link*,
March 1993, p10). Supporting the call for a broader social agenda a
former party speaker argued that:

> *We've got by far the most radical policies on rights at work,*
> *some of the best policies on the welfare state and public*
> *services and we're one of the few parties now, who gener-*
> *ally still talk about public ownership of things like rail-*
> *ways. . . . We can say we are the party of social rights,*
> *community control and you can have a better environ-*
> *ment thrown into the package. People say these things*
> *about divisions but they don't read the policy* (Interview,
> 30 March 1996).

Supporters argued that the change in the political and economic
climate surrounding issues of social policy, especially with regard to
the changing style of the Labour party, provided more space for the
Greens to be able to tackle and put forward issues of social policy. Also,
the emergence of the Real World coalition provided an opportunity to
develop broad support for a feasible alternative to the present environmental, economic and social policies advocated by the long-standing
political parties.

This change of direction is clearly evident within policy proposals following Basis for Renewal. The party states that:

> *A Green analysis recognizes that our social and ecological problems are inseparable. Having won recognition for its strong environmental policies, the Green party must now demonstrate the link between these and the Green social and economic agenda* (Green Party, 1994).

This approach provided the focus for the Greens' 1997 general election campaign. The party selected four main themes for the election campaign: a radical agenda for transforming the economy; the need to build strong, stable local communities; the links between poor health and environmental degradation; and Europe (Green party, 1997). Within these general themes the party raised questions regarding poverty, quality of life and the increase in respiratory diseases, such as asthma. This approach appears to mark a significant shift for the Green party and reflects the party's growing recognition of the competitive challenges that it faces.

Figure 6.3 provides a diagrammatic analysis of the process of policy reform within the Green party.

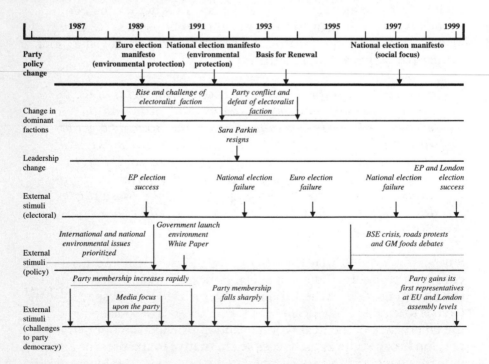

Figure 6.3 *Potential Sources of Policy Change: The Green Party*

In this case, clear connections between stimuli and policy change are not as evident as with the other two parties. However, some similarities are apparent. For example, the party's policy priorities during the late 1980s were again influenced by the predominance of environmental issues on the political agenda. Its performance in the 1989 European parliamentary elections was strongly connected to this environmental emphasis. Furthermore, similarities exist regarding other pressures, such as the backlash from other parties, the weakening of environmental issues and the increasing focus upon economic issues.

One important distinction is that the process of policy reassessment within the Basis for Renewal programme occurred during the period following internal party conflict. These changes were introduced at a time when the party was trying to rebuild itself in the face of electoral setbacks and a rapid decline in membership. This period represented a reassessment of the party's primary goals in the light of recent experiences and setbacks. The party's near disastrous flirtation with a national electoral strategy highlighted the limited role it could play electorally under the present electoral system. Under these circumstances, electoral failure during 1994 and 1997 were not seen as significant external shocks challenging the party's primary goal and, as such, have not had a dramatic impact upon policy reform. In contrast, policy development plays a significant role within the Green party.

The Green party's changing policy focus appears primarily as a reaction to external shocks along the policy dimension. In particular, it is partially a reaction to the criticisms of Green party policy as being too philosophical and of the party's inability to develop policy stances quickly on topical issues. These criticisms were not only related to issues surrounding electoral campaigning, but were also cited as explanations for the greater levels of media exposure gained by environmental movements such as Friends of the Earth and Greenpeace. Developments within the party along this dimension are supported by the strategic decision to focus upon specific policy areas or themes. The road traffic reduction policy can be seen as one such example, coinciding directly with the numerous anti-roads protests in the UK and a growing political interest in transport policy.

To summarize, there are similarities between the experiences of the UK Green party and those of *Les Verts* and *Miljöpartiet de Gröna*. However, the UK Green party's uniquely disadvantaged electoral position results in less of a focus upon electoral influences in policy reassessment than is the case with the other two parties. The main challenge has revolved around the party's ability to represent its policy goals successfully in the light of a competitive party-political environment in which it finds itself marginalized.

ACCOUNTING FOR POLICY CHANGE: A COMPARATIVE ASSESSMENT

Both internal and external pressures provide the fundamental explanations for changes to party-policy direction. In all three cases, external stimuli have influenced the process of change. As before, a key factor has been those stimuli that challenged the parties' electoral goals. This was most evident within *Les Verts* and *Miljöpartiet de Gröna*, where a reassessment of policy priorities was identified as a significant factor in the electoral successes of both parties. In the UK, although electoral failure encouraged the redirection of policy priorities, its impact was more limited.

External stimuli that challenged the parties' 'policy representation' goals were also influential in the process of change – in particular, the incorporation of environmental issues by long-standing parties in an attempt to recapture the emerging 'Green' vote. This process, combined with the weakening salience of environmental concerns, forced the Greens to reassess their policy priorities. In particular, the parties were challenged to demonstrate that they were not merely 'single-issue' environmental protection groups, and to show the importance of Green politics within a wider political agenda.

Internal pressures appear to have had more influence upon the French and UK cases than in Sweden. In France, internal factionalism centred specifically upon party strategy and direction and, as such, the direction of policy development lay at the heart of these divisions. The change in leadership, and the factional shift that accompanied it, played a vital role in the party's reprioritizing of policy issues. Factional conflicts played an influential role in the UK as well. Basis for Renewal marked an attempt to reshape and reconcile differences that had divided the party during the early 1990s, as well as reorientating party policy.

As in previous chapters, the pattern of policy change can help to understand the shifting prioritization of party goals. Burns (1997) identifies a direct link between the type of factors influencing policy change and the prioritization of goals within a political party. In particular, he distinguishes between policy changes that are sparked by external pressures and those that are the result of 'internal change in the ideas of party elites' (Burns, 1997, p514). He argues that:

> *If party policy changes only in response to external influences, reflecting mass attitudes and electoral behaviour, then it supports the theory that parties hold electoral and representative goals as central; it also indicates that parties*

> *require outside pressure before changing policy. Con-*
> *versely, if policy evolves in the absence of such external*
> *influences, it suggests that parties hold other goals more*
> *important than elections, such as policy development or*
> *public education* (Burns, 1997, p515).

Transposed onto the patterns of policy change within the Green parties, Burns' hypothesis appears to support the reprioritization of party goals suggested in previous chapters of this book. For *Miljö-partiet de Gröna,* party policy change has clearly been strongly influenced by external factors, in line with its increasing emphasis upon electoral goals. However, it would be wrong to presume that the Swedish Greens would be prepared to radically alter their policy base purely for electoral considerations. If this had been the case, rather than continuing with an anti-EU stance, the party would logically have adopted a more positive attitude given the support for membership identified during the early 1990s.

The other two case studies, however, prove to be more complex, displaying a balance between internal and external pressures. Again, this supports the claim, made throughout this book, that Green party development reflects a changing balance between party goals that depend upon national context and internal pressures. As discussed in previous chapters, the UK Green party's apparent confusion over exactly what its primary goal should be is reflected in the pattern of change and the diverse factors influencing this change.

GREEN PARTY POLICY REFORM: CHANGING PRIORITIES OR IDEOLOGICAL SHIFT?

Evidently, the German Greens have not been the only Green party to alter its policy focus in recent years. During the 1990s, Green parties concentrated upon refocusing policy towards 'social' issues rather than the traditional focus upon 'natural' environmental protection. However, the extent to which this change represents a significant ideological shift is debatable. Rather than representing two distinct approaches, it is clear from the discussion above that these positions largely repre-sent two sides of the same 'Green' coin. The natural and the social environment are inextricably linked: policy that focuses upon one aspect will undoubtedly have implications for the other. Measures designed for protecting the natural environment implicitly involve a change in social relations and social policy, and vice versa.

What the Green parties have chosen to emphasize within their policy stances in recent years is a distinct transformation in social relations. This necessarily involves not only a change in the way people relate to the natural environment, but also the manner in which they interact on a social level. To adopt an approach that distinguishes between the parties' focus on one aspect, rather than the other, is to misunderstand the wider implications of Green ideology and Green politics. This brings us back to the claim by Barry, outlined in Chapter 1 of this book, that:

> *The reconciliation of Green philosophy and politics depends on seeing that the normative basis of Green politics includes a concern with the human social world and its organization, as much as a moral concern with the non-human world* (Barry, 1994, p369).

The distinction between the 'natural' and the 'social' in this respect is clearly a misleading one, producing a division where one does not necessarily exist. Returning to Demker's approach to party policy, it is evident that all of the policy issues and stances adopted by the Greens remain within the framework of the core values of the parties identified earlier. Both the 'social' and 'natural' dimensions can be identified as two sets of Green doctrine based upon the same core values.

One must therefore seek an alternative interpretation of this change that does not necessarily imply a loss of ecological identity. Janda et al (1995) provide such an alternative by claiming that it is not only important to identify the 'substance' in a party programme – the key policy issues and party principles – but one must also consider the 'packaging'. In other words, one must consider the salience of policy issues and the intensity with which these issues are confronted (Janda et al, 1995, p178). While the practicalities of radically altering the substance of party policy represents a complex and detailed process, a party may alter the packaging of its ideas in the light of electoral performance or similar external pressures:

> *...a party hoping to do better in the next election could avoid some of the infighting and the ultimate risk involved in changing its basic positions on issues, but still strategically downplay some issues that were emphasized in the last manifesto, while playing up others. This could have the effect of altering one dimension of the party's profile (the packaging), while leaving another (the substance) intact* (Janda et al, 1995, p179).

The idea that a party can alter the packaging of its policies through a reprioritization of particular issues, in light of political saliency, without actually changing the substance of its commitments provides an alternative explanation for understanding the policy changes identified within the Greens from 'natural' to 'social' environmental issues.

If one returns to the pattern of policy change discussed in this chapter, the link between policy prioritization and issue saliency is strong. Table 6.1 summarizes the political context and the policy priorities of the three parties at the end of the 1980s.

This period undoubtedly marked a highpoint for environmental concern across Europe, with Green issues a key electoral priority. International environmental issues dominated, such as global warming, the

Table 6.1 *A Comparison of Policy Issues and Agendas within* Les Verts, Miljöpartiet de Gröna *and the Green Party, 1987–1990*[10]

Party	Election	Issues Highlighted During Election Campaigns	Green Party Manifesto Policy Priorities
Les Verts	1989 European elections	International environ- mental concerns Domestic issues Nuclear power development Acid rain in Alsace Dam development	Issues of environmental protection Alternative energy strategy Anti-nuclearism Unemployment Quality of life
Miljöpartiet de Gröna	1988 national elections	International environ- mental concerns Seal deaths Radioactivity Nuclear power Beach pollution	Shutdown nuclear power Tighter anti-pollution laws Reduction in road freight Reduction in fossil fuel consumption Social cohesion
UK Green party	1989 European elections	International environ- mental concerns Poll tax Health service European policy Seal deaths State of UK water systems Listeria and Salmonella viruses	Conservation issues Waste and energy policies Water and air quality Economic divide between rich and poor

depletion of the ozone layer and the rise in air-pollution levels. More immediately, however, environmental issues were placed firmly at the heart of the political agenda due to the explosion at the nuclear power facility in Chernobyl and the broad repercussions of this disaster. In each case, the Greens' strong electoral showing during this period was linked to the emphasis upon environmental concerns and a perceived lack of response by long-standing political parties to these new issues.

The late 1980s reflected a relative high point in the history of the development of European Green parties, both in terms of electoral success and the significance of environmental issues upon the political agenda. Within a climate of increased saliency for environmental issues, the Green parties were able to capitalize upon this, focusing upon a Green agenda that centred upon the protection of the natural environment. That is not to say that they excluded social questions and policy concerns. The parties made significant attempts within their manifestos to identify direct links between ecological problems and the wider social dimension. However, the political agenda and, in many cases, the electoral agenda were dominated by issues relating to the natural environment.

The political situation summarized in Table 6.2, however, shows a marked difference.

The 1990s clearly proved much more of a struggle for the 'new politics' parties. The Greens' electoral successes heightened the competition for 'Green' votes. Long-standing political parties, while not proving avid converts to the environmental cause, nevertheless proved successful in incorporating environmental policies within their own agendas. They challenged the political credentials of their new competitors, portraying them as disorganized, ineffective and, in particular, as 'single-issue' protest organizations rather than political parties with detailed policy agendas.

In all three countries election campaigns during this period were focused upon what could be considered more 'traditional' areas of concern, such as welfare, education, health and employment. With social issues taking prominence, the Green parties' programmatic priorities logically had to reflect this change. While initially this proved problematic for the Greens, the parties have all made increasingly effective attempts to demonstrate the interconnection between social concerns and natural environmental issues. The parties, therefore, have reversed the process in line with the key issues on the national political agenda. Although the Green parties have utilized the 'social' and 'natural' dimensions, it is clear from this discussion that they do not perceive these issues as separate from one another. Environmental reforms cannot be achieved without changes to social policies, and vice versa.

Table 6.2 *A Comparison of the Policies, Issues and Agendas within* Les Verts, Miljöpartiet de Gröna *and the Green Party, 1992–1997*[11]

Party	Election	Issues Highlighted During Election Campaigns	Green Party Manifesto Policy Priorities
Les Verts	1997 national election	Problems of cohabitation between president and government Social inequality Shorter working week Welfare reform Monetary union	Reduction in working hours Defence of the public sector More tolerant immigration policy Moratorium on nuclear power and the closure of the *Superphénix* programme
Miljöpartiet de Gröna	1994 national and 1995 European elections	Membership of the EU Economic concerns Welfare issues Resignation of Prime Minister Carlsson Oresund bridge	No to the EU Environment creates jobs Allergy is politics Health and welfare provision Taxation No to the Oresund bridge Decentralization of government
UK Green party	1997 national elections	Parliamentary sleaze Europe Education Economy Health	Transforming the economy Building strong local communities Tackling poor health Europe Road traffic reduction

In the face of increasing pressure from other political parties, and under conditions of a rapidly changing political agenda, all three parties have therefore sought to reassess and ultimately 'repackage' the Green message. The parties have attempted to emphasize the 'other side' of Green policy, prioritizing social policy issues and reflecting the central national political agenda at that time. In Sweden, therefore, *Miljöpartiet* has successfully capitalized upon anti-EU sentiment within the electorate; in the UK the Green party has attempted to reflect the growing concern over both transport policies and welfare reforms; and in France the Greens have focused upon employment and immigration policies.

Party policy continued to focus upon environmental protection issues when such issues became a key concern. In France, *Les Verts* maintained a focus upon nuclear power in the light of its continued expansion in France, and especially in relation to the *Superphénix* reactor. A similar focus could also become significant in Sweden. The country is rapidly heading towards the deadline for phasing out nuclear power agreed at the referendum. With many experts now claiming that it will be a practical impossibility for the country to achieve this deadline, nuclear power may again become a significant political issue in Sweden.

The combination between the process of repackaging and the recognition of the interrelationship between 'social' and 'natural' environmental concerns provides a much clearer picture of the under-lying process of policy change within the Green parties. While there has been a change and reprioritization of some aspects of the Green policy programmes, these have not necessarily challenged the funda-mental values upon which the Green parties have defined policy. The various policy stances identified within the Green parties' manifestos actually reflect different dimensions of the parties' central core values and commitments – whether in terms of a 'sustainable society' for the UK Green party, the 'four solidarities' for *Miljöpartiet de Gröna*, or in terms of 'responsibility, solidarity and citizenship' for *Les Verts*.

One can identify within the Greens, therefore, a process of repriori-tizing policies in the light of a changing political agenda and competit-ive environment. Such a role is central to the activities of any political party, and reflects not only the internal ideological beliefs of the party but also its attempts to represent this ideology within a specific national context. Papadikis, when analysing change within *Die Grünen*, suggests that:

> *. . .if we are to pursue the thesis that contemporary politics is characterized by flexibility of policy articulation and by the proximity and interchange of issues, we may find that the Greens, as much as any other party, seek to broaden their social bases and ideological appeal* (Papadikis, 1989, p62).

Faced with the sudden 'Greening' of traditional parties and the constant accusations of being merely single-issue protest organizations, Green parties during the 1990s have been forced to recognize that their positions have altered drastically from that of the late 1980s. Whether it be via external stimuli such as electoral defeats or the demise of environmental issues on the political agenda, or through internal conflicts such as those between Waechter and Voynet in France, or the realos and fundis in Germany, the Green parties have been forced to question how best to present and package the Green perspective. In his discussion of ideological change within European Green parties, Doherty suggests that one should view such change as a balance between 'context and learning process' (Doherty, 1994, p347). In many ways, the pattern of policy development that has emerged here would support a similar interpretation.

The pressures of the external political environment have again played an important role in forcing Green parties towards this process of reassessing policy priorities. The electoral results of the late 1980s reflected the success of the Greens in portraying the dangers facing the natural environment and the need to develop policies in order to address these concerns. Although party policies highlighted the interaction between environmental problems and the need for social change, the latter aspect was marginalized due to the international concern over environmental disasters. Under the pressures of party competition, however, the Green parties have faced challenges for the 'Green' vote as other parties have attempted to incorporate environmental policies within their party programmes. Within a changing political climate, in which economic and social concerns have been prioritized, the Green parties have been forced to demonstrate their commitment to wider political concerns. It is under these conditions that the parties have begun to highlight the social dimension of their core values and commitments.

These changes are clearly closely connected to the electoral goals of the Green parties. All of the parties experienced a drop in electoral support during the early 1990s, coinciding with the removal of the environment from the forefront of political debate. Therefore, the parties have recognized the importance of attracting voters on the basis of more than just environmental protection issues. As a party spokesperson for the UK Green party argued:

> *If someone is a member of Friends of the Earth, they are in Friends of the Earth because they are seriously concerned with the environment. Now, if they are not voting for an environmental party, then why aren't they? And to me this has got to be because they are worried about other key issues. If you want these people to start supporting you, even if they aren't now, then the other issues are the ones that you have to persuade them on. I'm sure that even the most Labour-oriented member of Friends of the Earth would have to admit that when it comes to environmental policies the Greens are doing better. But that is obviously not their most overriding concern when it comes to voting* (Interview, 31 March 1996).

The Green parties are undergoing a learning process as competitive political parties. Experience within the competitive party arena has demonstrated that, as with all political parties, they must compete on all aspects of party policy, rather than merely focusing upon environmental protection, if they are to gain continued electoral success. While other aspects of party ideology have always existed, the parties have struggled to portray these aspects as effectively as they have environmental protection issues – leading to claims by opponents that the Greens are merely 'single-issue' protest groups. However, the Greens are clearly beginning to tackle the challenge of providing a broad representation of the Green ideology upon a party political stage.

Chapter 7

Interpreting Transformation within European Green Parties: Evolving or Conforming?

The preceding chapters have traced the transformations within European Green parties as they have evolved from the radical new political actors of the 1980s into a recognized, although not always necessarily welcome, part of the contemporary party political environment. It is evident from the analysis that the Green parties who operate today are in many ways far removed from the style and format of the original 'anti-party party' concept that shaped Green party politics in its formative years and that led to the Greens being recognized as a fresh challenge to traditional politics. During their lifetimes, the Greens have at times faced crippling internal conflicts and debates over the process of reform and the implications of these changes to their ideological make-up. That they have survived these conflicts and often recovered from what could have been fatal electoral performances reflects a level of endurance which many individuals doubted the new parties would be capable of. However, it is important to consider the impact of these turbulent years of development and change. After all of these upheavals, what impact has the process of change had upon the Greens? Furthermore, what is left of the original 'new politics' parties that broke the political stranglehold of the established political parties during the 1980s?

Drawing upon the evidence of previous chapters, this final chapter will consider the process of transformation in two ways. Firstly, it will provide an overview of the pressures that have led to Green party change and the varying experiences of factional conflict that have accompanied it. Secondly, it will consider the implications of the reforms and the suggestion that this transformation represents the institutionalization of the Greens and, with it, the decline of the 'new politics'.

PARTY GOALS AND THE PROCESS OF CHANGE: FINDING A ROLE FOR THE GREENS

It is clear from the history of the emergence of Green parties that there was never a clear blueprint for what a Green party should seek to do or how its role should develop over time. In many cases, the creation of the Greens was largely due to frustration regarding the failure of established parties to deal with new issues and concerns, rather than a real desire to reshape party politics. Activists, therefore, came into Green party politics largely instilled with ideas from new social movement activism and organization, and with a general picture of what was wrong with established political parties. What exactly the role of the new party would be other than the 'voice of the new social movements', and how this role would evolve over time remained a relatively open question that the parties have been forced to tackle as they evolved under the public spotlight.

The different patterns of development and change identified within the Green parties in this book are all largely reflective of the parties' desire to develop a clear and effective role within their respective political systems. At times, this has involved not only developing a role as a new political party within a competitive, established party system, but it has also involved the Green parties in seeking a clear demarcation of their role within the wider environmental movement. The need to change has often been due to pressures on the Green party that have questioned its ability to fulfil its role. Factional conflict has often been reflective of uncertainties and disagreements within the party regarding what its role should be, its perceived success in fulfilling this role, and what aspect of the party needed reform in order to achieve this. As the comparative analysis in this book demonstrates, while all four parties have been faced with a similar dilemma, the responses have been quite diverse. Indeed, the manner in which this problem has been tackled has been intrinsically linked to the political context in which the different parties operate.

Divisions over these issues were undoubtedly at the heart of the factional disputes within the German Greens. While different perceptions of the role of the party were accommodated during its formative years, as it became more successful and more established, so these differences became harder to smooth over. Many argued that the

German Greens were not one party but had numerous different identities. As the party gained electoral success, there was increasing pressure from the different factions to control the role and the direction in which the party should develop. Under the glare of an interested and often hostile media, these factional differences expanded into deep internal conflict. In this case, political opportunities emerging from electoral successes forced the party to confront its roles and responsibilities head on. The realo–fundis factional splits within *Die Grünen*, as outlined earlier, represented a debate over the future direction and style of the party. Should it become parliamentary focused and seek to partake in coalitions, or should it prioritize its role as the radical party voice of the social movements and stand alone in the party system?

Interestingly, out of the three parties discussed in this book, the party who has experienced the least electoral success has experienced the most comparable levels of factional conflict with that of the German Greens. While the party has not been afforded similar political opportunities, the UK Green party has found itself similarly divided over what its role should be. In this case, it has been a lack of electoral success that has forced the UK Green party to confront what its main roles and responsibilities should be, and these questions have proven equally as divisive. As a political party, it faces severe barriers to gaining parliamentary representation and has achieved little in the way of significant electoral breakthrough. Attempts to change the party into a more 'professional' and 'electable' organization have faced direct criticism from those party activists who claim that, given the systemic constraints, the party's main aims and efforts should be focused in other directions. However, the party finds itself similarly marginalized as an environmental pressure group or movement. The environmental movements have developed an effective network that provides much greater access to decision-making and influence than the UK Green party can achieve. The Green party undoubtedly finds itself in an awkward dilemma, unsure as to its precise role within the UK political system. This lack of clear direction has obviously been a vital factor in accounting for the internal splits within the party.

By contrast, the Swedish Green party appears to have been more united in defining its role. The party has developed within a political system that prioritizes party politics and marginalizes movements, and faces an electoral system with relatively weak barriers to gaining representation at both local and national levels. In addition, the party has enjoyed relatively strong support from within the environmental movement, which was active in the formation of the party. The lack of conflict over development and change within *Miljöpartiet de Gröna* reflects the party's clarity in focusing upon a parliamentary role. In contrast to the deep divisions experienced in Germany and the

UK, the Swedish Greens have been relatively unified in seeking to improve the electoral and parliamentary strength of the party and to demonstrate its effectiveness as a national political actor.

The experiences within *Les Verts* exhibit aspects of all of the above examples. As in Sweden, the party has had to develop a role within a political system that marginalizes movement protest and emphasizes the importance of political parties. It therefore emerged as a development from within the environmental movements as an attempt to gain political recognition for environmental issues and concerns. As in the UK, however, the party has faced the challenge of competing within a system that gives political credibility to parties with parliamentary representation, but which marginalizes small parties. The only options available are, therefore, marginalization or coalition. Factional splits within the French Greens cannot be effectively explained by a division over the party's role, on this occasion, as the party was relatively unified in seeking to develop a parliamentary role. In this instance, it was not so much what the role should be, but what was the most effective strategy in order that the party could achieve this. The pattern of change within *Les Verts* represents a gradual evolution of the party's perception of how best to develop the role as the party voice of the environmental movement, given the restrictive external conditions.

For the Greens in Sweden, France and Germany, a key factor in defining the parties' contemporary role has been the development of a new relationship with the established parties of the left. In each case, Green party emergence in these countries was connected to the failure of these established parties to successfully champion the causes of the new social movements, leaving activists with little option but to form a new party to represent their views. While this failure was influential in shaping the Greens' 'neither left, nor right' strategy and their antipathy towards established parties, success for the Greens in each case was always likely to result in forcing some form of dialogue with these parties. In each case, while negotiations have often proved difficult and divisive for the Greens, the eventual outcome has been some form of working relationship or left coalition. Again, the acceptance of these agreements reflects the growing clarity among these parties regarding their desired role within the system and how best to achieve this. There is a level of pragmatism within the parties' attitudes towards these agreements. While activists are wary of developing a role as the 'environmental wing' of the left parties, they also recognize that these agreements are vital if the Greens are to gain political experience and solidify their expanding parliamentary roles.

A vital aspect in the process of developing and defining the role of any political party inevitably involves the prioritization of party goals. The Greens have been no exception to this and lessons from broader party literature – in particular, the work of Harmel and Janda – have provided significant insight into the complexities and pressures surrounding the link between party change and party goals. While the experiences of the German Greens have been extensively covered elsewhere, the analysis in the preceding chapters demonstrated the diversity among the Green parties regarding the prioritization of party goals and the impact of challenges to these goals on the process of party change. Once again, a balance between internal and external pressures on party goals helps to explain the variation in the patterns of change and the prioritization of party goals within the different Green parties.

This book focused upon three of Harmel and Janda's 'primary goals' – namely, 'winning votes', 'advocating interests/ideology' and 'implementing party democracy'. Each of these goals has played a role in influencing the pattern of development and change within the Greens, although the influence of these goals has varied over time and between the different parties. The parties' initial concerns focused predominantly upon challenging the established focus of party politics, and as such they concentrated upon raising awareness of environmental concerns and advocating a new form of party organization and party democracy. At a wider level, the Green parties also sought greater democracy and participation throughout the party systems. However, given that parties who fail to break the threshold of national parliamentary representation tend to face political marginalization and gain little or no influence, the Greens implicitly had to focus upon winning electoral support if they were to stand any chance of achieving any of their other initial objectives.

Regardless of the Greens' attitude to electoral competition, therefore, the electoral goal became a key dimension in the development of all of the Green parties. As a result, both electoral success and failure have been key stimuli in instigating transformation within the European Green parties. In addition, this book also highlights an alternative party goal, which is to gain an influential role within the party system. As demonstrated, this may not necessarily correspond with winning votes or seats. This alternative party goal is identified as a key factor in influencing party strategies towards relationships with other political parties, especially in the case of *Les Verts*. With the advent of government participation, the Greens are facing the pressures of an additional goal – namely, maintaining public office. Undoubtedly, this will be at the forefront of the Greens' future decisions regarding the maintenance of coalition agreements. Furthermore, party goals not only vary over time, but they may also vary between different areas of party activity. For example, while 'electoral' goals may shape changes to party strategy, organizational reforms may be introduced in line with the parties' goal of 'implementing party democracy'. As such, a more complex picture of party change emerges.

It is not only the prioritization of goals that has differed between parties, but also the perception of how these goals can best be achieved. The four parties have often identified different aspects of party development and reform as imperative to achieving the same primary goal. These differences again reflect not only the internal characteristics of the parties, but also the external environment in which they compete. Hence, while organizational reforms were perceived as the primary requirement for the UK and Swedish Greens to achieve their electoral goals, in France and Germany strategic relationships with other parties provided the primary focus for achieving the same goal.

As with party roles, factional conflict and debate are linked to a pattern of uncertainty. Given the constant fluctuation in party goals, conflict over change has primarily occurred when either there is debate over the primary party's goals, or when disagreement exists concerning how best to achieve these goals. In particular, parties have often become divided over the extent to which electoral goals should take precedence, reflecting the debates regarding what exactly the role of the Greens should be. Without doubt, this book has demonstrated that one of the main external driving forces to shape the transformation of the European Green parties has been the opportunities available for the parties to gain electoral success and, subsequently, parliamentary representation. As a consequence, external barriers to achieving these objectives, such as the electoral system, party funding and the attitudes of other competitors towards the Greens, have helped to shape the perception of how attainable electoral successes are. Where electoral barriers have been seen as a surpassable hurdle, the emphasis upon electoral goals in the process of party reform has predominated. However, where these objectives have remained marginal, the debates over the predominance of electoral over other party goals have been more diverse.

Electoral performances have also created challenges and pressures upon party goals other than those of gaining seats. Good or bad electoral performances have, on numerous occasions, created pressures upon other aspects of party activity. In particular, electoral performance has imposed pressures upon the party's organizational commitments to direct democracy and active participation. As the parties have expanded, both in terms of members but also with regard to the different roles and responsibilities that they have accumulated, organizational structures have been placed under increasing strain. As Chapter 5 highlighted, the Greens have had to face the challenge of balancing the desire for democratic organization with the demands of competitive party politics. At times, this has involved practical solutions overcoming ideological commitments. However, on other occasions the potential of electoral success has not been seen as worth this form of compromise. Often, where reform has been followed by a strong electoral performance, change has provoked little internal conflict and debate. However, where change has not produced the desired electoral successes, the response has usually been internal division and conflict.

Overall, the process of transformation within the Greens has reflected a balancing act between the ideological goals and commitments inherent within the Greens' historical roots, and the electoral opportunities and constraints facing the parties. Electoral goals and electoral experiences, as one might expect, have played a significant role in influencing the process of development and change within the European Green parties. Indeed, it could be argued that given the original rationale for the formation of the parties, the primary role of a Green party must be to translate support for environmental movements and Green issues into parliamentary representation and, where possible, influence over policy-making. However, does this mean that the Green parties of today have simply succumbed to the demands of the parliamentary process? Is the picture of Green party transformation simply a process of institutionalization within the established party political process of the European party systems?

LESSONS OF CHANGE: EVOLVING
OR CONFORMING?

Undoubtedly, at the heart of the process of transformation lies a pattern of pragmatic compromise within the Greens as they have grown into their roles as political parties. This book, however, raises some important questions regarding the extent of this 'compromise' and the potential impact that this has upon the future development of the Greens. While one would be foolish to suggest that the Greens are the same today as when they emerged on the political scene, it would also be wrong to suggest that the process of transformation has merely turned the Greens into 'part of the establishment'.

During their formative years, the parties focused primarily upon highlighting the 'Green challenge' to established party politics, and attempted to offer the electorate a distinctly 'new' form of politics, both in terms of ideology and in terms of active participation within the party. Success, however, brings with it a new set of challenges. As the Greens have grown in stature, they have faced the more difficult task of marrying the desire to represent the ecological, new social movement identity at the heart of the 'new politics' with the challenge of becoming effective and influential political actors within the national party systems of which they are a part. Having gained support from the electorate for the concept of a new form of politics, it was now up to the Greens to actually demonstrate that this new form of politics was possible, that change could be implemented and was not just an ideological concept, and that a Green vote was not a 'wasted' one.

This transformation from radical opposition to the implementers of Green politics has been at the centre of the explanations for both the reform processes and the conflicts that have marked Green party development at the end of the 20th century. A leading Green party activist in the UK summarized the difficulties facing the Greens as follows:

> *Part of it is the problems which come with any new political party trying to work within a particular form of system. What you really are, I think, is a transitional phase anyway. You're trying to marry two sets of things. One is what works for the situation in which you find yourself and the other is where you want to be at the end of the day. And a lot of the problems revolve around this tension of time scales* (Interview, 7 August 1995).

The changes witnessed within the Greens have largely reflected an attempt to fit the notion of Green politics to the political systems within which they operate – finding a method for gaining the initial foothold for the development of Green politics. The analysis in this book focused upon three major aspects of the Green identity that were at the heart of the distinctiveness of the 'new politics' parties. The emergence of the Greens represented a challenge to the establishment not only in terms of the environmental issues that they espoused, but also by challenging the very credibility of the established parties as representatives of the people and highlighting the democratic and participatory deficits within these parties' organizational structures. However, to become an established player on the political scene, the Greens had to go beyond merely raising environmental consciousness and providing a critique of the establishment (both of which could, arguably, be provided by the environmental movements without the need of a party format). They had to demonstrate that they could actually change things by developing an active role in governmental decision-making.

In doing this, the Greens have readjusted some of the more unconventional or alternative aspects of the 'new politics' identity that have proved to be damaging or, at times, simply inoperable within a party political context. As this book has demonstrated, the different national political challenges facing the four Green parties resulted in different aspects of party activity being identified as the primary focal point for pragmatic reform. The differing focus for the reform process, and the significance attached to these reforms, are reflective of the internal characteristics of the parties and the prioritization of different ideological commitments and party goals, as well as the manner in which these internal features interact with external systemic pressures and constraints. In some instances, therefore, it would be fair to say that the process of change has not always been completely of the Greens' own choosing.

If one considers the transformations in party strategy, increased electoral success while giving the Green parties greater political recognition on the one hand, also brought the parties directly into contact and competition with the established political parties, on the other. While the Greens initially maintained a critical distance from the established parties, seeing them as part of the problem, not part of the solution, the pressure on the parties to 'get their hands dirty' and participate in government (not only from within the Greens themselves, but also from the other parties) has, on a number of occasions, brought this ideological stance into question.

Under these conditions, both the German and the French Greens have moved from a 'neither left, nor right' autonomous strategy, reflective of the Greens' 'anti-party' sentiments, towards direct working relationships with established left parties. To a slightly lesser extent, in Sweden the Greens have committed themselves to coalition at both local and municipal level, but have stopped short of a full coalition at national level. The UK Green party remains the only one of the four case studies to maintain its autonomous stance; but one may question whether this is through ideological choice or restricted opportunity. The party's almost complete marginalization within the party system leaves it with little opportunity for strategic links with other parties and, to all intents and purposes, actively encourages the UK Green party to define itself separately from the traditional parties.

This strategic transformation has been strongly influenced by the parties' attempts to achieve a stable basis within their respective party systems, raise environmental awareness, and be perceived as effective national political actors who can influence policy rather than act as marginalized, 'single-issue' protest groups. Party strategy has, therefore, been closely linked to the political opportunities confronting the Greens within their respective party systems. In the cases of the four parties discussed here, the Greens have had to decide whether there is more to be gained from participation than lost.

Les Verts' strategic options were strongly influenced by the pressures of working within a system that encourages the development of alliances and coalitions and that gauges political credibility on the basis of parliamentary representation and political influence. Whatever the party's own strategic statements, it has largely been perceived by the public, the media and other political parties as a party of the left. This stance was further enhanced by the willingness of both *Génération Écologie* and, later, the *Parti Socialiste* to view the Greens as acceptable coalition partners. Thus, a willing coalition partner, combined with the pressures of a party system that rewards small parties who are open to electoral alliances and marginalizes those that are not, provided the main impetus for the Greens to develop an active coalition strategy.

Both the Swedish and German Greens found that electoral success at local and regional levels forced this strategic issue onto the parties' agendas as they became pivotal 'hinge' parties. Again, the willingness of other parties to see the Greens as coalition partners was a vital factor in changing party strategy. The experiences of working in coalition and, often, the electoral gains that resulted from active participation have played a crucial role in encouraging party members to accept these agreements and to subsequently consider similar relationships at national level. In Sweden, the party's wariness of the Social Democrats and its experiences of the perils of full coalition has resulted in a limited toleration agreement at national level. However, one must also recognize that the party does not yet have the parliamentary strength to be a full coalition partner.

The Green parties have therefore found their strategic position challenged by electoral success. While the parties initially distinguished themselves from the other political parties by maintaining a distance from them, this has been harder to do as they have gained increasing numbers of parliamentary seats. Maintaining this distance also limited what the Green parties could achieve at a practical level and, in many ways, this has been a paradox for the Greens. Green party politics was designed to be different from conventional party politics, and setting themselves apart from the other parties was symbolic of this difference. The increase in Green support, in many ways, implied that a proportion of the electorate wanted to see the type of change outlined by the Greens. However, the nature of party competition meant that the Greens were unable to attempt any of these changes unless they changed their stance. If the Greens wanted to progress as parties, they had to not only compete against the others, but to negotiate with the other political parties in the party system. Failure to adapt to this role often resulted in the Greens being portrayed as a negative, destructive political force that called for change but was not prepared to actively participate in order to achieve it. This was used to strong effect by the established political parties who sought to weaken support for the Greens.

While this change of strategy may be seen as 'bowing to the inevitable', Green participation in alliances and coalitions has often represented the best method for the Green parties to answer their critics. The only way in which the Greens could overcome the claims of political inexperience and naivety and the arguments that Green politics was impractical, was to gain greater experience through active participation in government and by taking responsibility for policy-making. Participation has given further credibility to the Greens and to their claims that Green politics can play an active and effective role in government.

One must also be wary of seeing the change entirely as a one-way process involving just Green party compromise. While the Green parties were keen to disassociate themselves from other political parties in their formative years, so the other parties disassociated themselves from the Greens. A great deal of time was devoted to presenting the Greens as damaging to the stability of contemporary party systems and as a short-term phenomenon with a limited life span. However, as the Greens have evolved, so the established political parties, especially on the left, have often had to accept that the Greens may be the most suitable coalition partners. In many ways, this recognition of Green politics by the established left parties is a significant achievement when one considers that, for many of the Green parties, the failure of these parties to represent Green issues effectively was a primary motivating force behind the formation of the Greens in the first place.

Strategic issues will clearly have a continued influence upon the future development of the Greens. In particular, the parties will have to decide how far they are prepared to compromise for the sake of maintaining a coalition. As both the German and French Greens have found, as with any small party active within a coalition, while these agreements may have many advantages, they also have the disadvantage of associating the parties with policies with which they don't necessarily agree and that challenge their ideological principles. While the Swedish Greens have been able to avoid this nationally through the limited toleration agreement, it is questionable how successful this will be in the long term.

These experiences also raise the question of how far the Greens' future development relies upon the continuation of these forms of alliances and coalitions. In France, the Greens rely upon the continuation of the left coalition so that the party can maintain national parliamentary representation. Their parliamentary future is therefore intricately linked to the performance of the left government and the maintenance of the coalition. By contrast, the Greens in both Germany and Sweden have managed to break the parliamentary threshold independently. While this arguably gives these two parties an additional level of independence from their coalition partners, neither has yet managed to develop a sustainable electoral base that ensures that they will always break the parliamentary threshold. They must, therefore, balance the demands of coalition with the need to maintain support among their own electorate. This has been difficult due to the often unrealistic perception of what a junior coalition partner can actually achieve. As small parties operating in highly competitive environments, the Greens' strategic options are definitely limited.

Increasing support and electoral success were also at the core of the transformation in the organizational structures within the Greens. Again, the parties' alternative organizational structures reflected the Greens' desire to conduct party politics in a different way. As Chapter 5 demonstrated, the model of Green party organization that was adopted reflected an attempt to bring into the party realm many of the ideas and structures that the activists had experienced within the social movements. The notion of being an 'anti-party' party meant not only challenging the politics of the establishment, but also challenging the way in which those political decisions were to be made. The party's organizational structures were clearly designed to demonstrate the significance of participation and direct horizontal democratic control to the 'Green way' of conducting politics. As such, they were not designed to fit neatly with the party political systems within which they were competing.

However, the Green parties have found that structures that were effective for a social movement have not always been as applicable to the more rigid and structured realm of party politics. As with strategic change, it is easy to view the organizational reforms within the Greens as evidence of a process of institutionalization of the new politics' ideals and the increasing professionalization of the Greens. Undoubtedly, all four of the Green parties examined here have found themselves forced to compromise on some aspects of their alternative organizational model as their roles and responsibilities increased and as their membership expanded.

In particular, the parties had to accept that while they did not want to create careerist Green politicians, they also had to gain an understanding of how the party process works if they were to change it. Many of the organizational concepts did not take into account the impact that parliamentary representation and responsibility would have on the parties. In particular, the Greens failed to consider the lack of experience within the party. The rotation principle, for example, failed to recognize that some positions required experienced actors. As the parties have grown, so has this experienced activist base.

The pragmatic response of the Swedish Greens to this problem was to accept that an alternative form of organization is only effective if that alternative leads to a better way of conducting politics. The organizational transformation within the Greens represents an acceptance that, while it is important to conduct politics in a more democratic manner, this should not necessarily equate to doing things badly – and, in many cases, the Greens were doing things badly. When put into practice within the party arena, some of the original organizational principles actually restricted democracy and participation in practice as they became slow, unresponsive to issues and debates and led, at times, to crippling internal stalemate between party factions. There was little point in showing the electorate an alternative organizational framework if that framework was perceived to be more inefficient than the established format that it sought to challenge. While there is no question that the original organizational structures gave greater openness to the Greens, they also provided substantial ammunition to their critics and competitors, and raised question marks over their political credibility.

Given this, it is not surprising that organizational change was closely linked to the Greens' increased experience of active participation in party politics and a number of electoral disappointments, following campaigns in which the Greens were portrayed as chaotic and disorganized. Organizational reform was often seen as an important aspect of maintaining the Greens' electoral support. For example, in Sweden, *Miljöpartiet's* relatively unanimous adoption of a new organizational framework was linked to both the party's experiences during its first term in parliament and its subsequent electoral failure in 1991. Organizational change was viewed as a result of practical experience and represented a vital factor in the party regaining national representation.

However, in the case of Germany and the UK, organizational change took on a much broader role since it was tied to debates over the future style and ideological direction of the party. Organizational reform in the UK Greens was instigated as part of the development of a more efficient and election-oriented organization. However, organizational change heightened factional divisions, with the reforms being seen as an attempt to alter the actual nature of the party and to shape its future direction and style. Debates surrounding organizational reform were as much about goal priorities within the UK Green party as they were about the specific reforms themselves.

It is also evident from the comparative analysis presented here that where organizational reform has played a pivotal role within party change, it has often been a response to the practicalities of attempting to utilize a decentralized framework within a relatively centralized party system. Hence, reform played a vital role in the UK and Sweden, while *Les Verts* found that the decentralized organizational framework proved more applicable within a French party system based upon a regional structure. All parties, however, have found that it has become increasingly difficult to remove personality from party politics. While the Greens continually refused to adopt party leaders, the media has often chosen figureheads, regardless of this. The parties are beginning to accept this as part of the media world in which they operate, but continue to ensure that control over the party by any individual is restricted. Despite these changes, however, Chapter 5 demonstrated that the Greens remain distinctly more democratic and participatory than their competitors and have worked hard to find a way in which they can still reflect their commitments to anti-professionalization, decentralization and active participation, while also competing effectively.

That the Greens are learning to cope and react to the challenge that the competitive party-political environment poses is evident, not only in the way in which they work internally and with others, but also with regard to the way in which they have presented the Green message. As Chapter 6 demonstrated, a greater emphasis has recently been placed upon 'social' concerns by the Greens. This has primarily been the result of changing national political agendas and an altered competitive environment, in which issues of environmental protection have been superseded by a more traditional economic and welfare focus. While the electoral results of the 1980s reflected the success of the Greens in portraying the dangers facing the natural environment and the need to develop policies to address these concerns, during the 1990s the Green parties have been forced to demonstrate their commitment to wider political concerns. Due to the changing political climate of the 1990s, the Greens have been forced to reprioritize these policies in line with a changing political agenda.

The manner in which Green policy has evolved reflects attempts to represent Green ideology within a specific national context and a competitive party political environment. It also marks a concerted attempt by the Greens to get beyond the image of a 'single-issue' party that is only effective when dealing with issues of environmental damage. The Greens have faced a relatively rapid learning curve as political actors, and during this process have been challenged to compete on all aspects of party policy, rather than merely focusing upon environmental issues as a conservation movement may be able to.

As the early 1990s demonstrated, the Greens cannot afford to rely upon the prioritization of environmental concerns for their political survival. Not only do these issues fluctuate upon the political agenda, established parties have also proven relatively successful in adopting the rhetoric, if not the realities, of Green discourse. For the Greens in Germany, France and Sweden, the reassessment of policy priorities was a significant factor in the parties' electoral successes during the 1990s, and placed a direct challenge to those who claimed that the Greens could only do well when environmental issues were at the top of the political agenda. In the UK, by contrast, the weak electoral position made the reprioritizing of party policy a less immediate concern. The UK Greens have faced less pressure to justify and substantiate their policies and have only infrequently been viewed as a threat by the established parties. This position has resulted in both a greater emphasis upon detailed policy development within the UK Green party and greater debate and discussion over the repackaging of Green party policy.

Once again, however, this process of transformation provides relatively little evidence to support the claim that the Greens are losing their identity and falling into the mainstream. It is, primarily, evidence that the Greens have recognized the grounds upon which they need to compete, and have found that it is not necessarily dominated by traditional Green issues. Having the most complete and detailed environmental policies has not automatically led to continual electoral success for the Greens. Where the Greens performed well during the late 1980s, the environment played a crucial role at the top of the political agenda. However, the Greens found themselves in a much weaker position when other issues took priority. When the electorate prioritized 'non-Green' issues, the Greens were not necessarily seen as an effective political choice.

The challenge for the Greens has, therefore, been to remove the reliance upon the prioritization of environmental issues in order to achieve strong electoral performances. In order to do this, the Green parties have had to fight harder on 'non-Green' social issues. This does not mean that the Greens have de-prioritized the protection of the natural environment; but that they have recognized that there is little point in winning the environmental argument time and time again if the primary political debates lie elsewhere. What the Greens have attempted, in recent years, has been to show the diversity and interconnection between the different aspects of Green politics. In particular, they have attempted to demonstrate that Green politics is as much about social concerns as it is about the natural environment and reflects the problems of the inner-city environment as much as it does the countryside. If anything, therefore, recent developments have forced the Greens to present and develop a fuller picture of Green politics than in their formative years.

Presenting this broader picture may be one thing, but trying to transform the public's perception of the Greens has proved much harder. Green parties are still strongly connected to environmental protection policies, and support still tends to fluctuate in line with the significance of 'traditional' environmental issues. Government participation, in this respect, has often proved to be a double-edged sword. While, on the one hand, it has given the Greens the opportunity to demonstrate the effectiveness of Green policies in practice, it has also often further entrenched the public's perception of the Greens. This is primarily due to Green coalition roles often focusing upon environmental portfolios, which – while, in some ways, representing the obvious focal point for the Greens to instigate policy – continues to pigeon hole the parties. In addition, the Greens have often found that while these portfolios give them responsibility for dealing with environmental issues when they occur, it gives them little opportunity to impact upon the actual causes of these problems. Again, the Greens need to change this position if they are to change the perception of the electorate.

Overall then, it would appear that the Green parties have, without doubt, become more aware of the restrictions and constraints that functioning within competitive party systems place upon them. In addition, electoral successes have also made the parties more aware of the importance of this dimension. However, the changes that have accompanied this learning process do not automatically imply a significant ideological dilution in the parties' attempts to represent and reflect both the ecological ideals and distinctive organizational characteristics of the 'new politics'. Green party development and change has been a transitionary process in which the Greens have sought to develop a more complex interpretation of how to successfully mould these commitments within the confines of a party political environment. Again, this reflects back upon earlier interpretations of parties as being based upon the internal characteristics of the particular party family, and the external pressures of the political environment within which they function.

The pattern of change has also demonstrated that the Green parties cannot function in isolation and, as such, are subject to strong pressures from the external political environment of which they are a part. In many cases, Green parties have faced many of the same pressures, barriers and constraints facing all other small parties who seek to gain a foothold within long-established European party systems. These include electoral barriers, issues of party funding and the adaptation to new issues by the long-standing political parties. These differing circumstances have been reflected in the specific characteristics and responses to party development and change that have been identified in this comparative analysis. Green parties may have similar aims, but they are far from homogeneous in nature. The disparity within the process of change among the European Greens represents their attempts to translate ecological objectives within markedly different national political environments.

The emergence of different types of Green party throughout Europe during this period also reflects a realization within the parties themselves that they should interpret their role not only through a Green party structure based largely upon the German model provided by *Die Grünen*, but also through the national political context and the respective pressures that are exerted upon them. As the Green parties have matured, many of them have discovered that the party model that had been initially instigated was not necessarily suited to both the national political context within which they were operating, or the levels of party activism within the party itself.

The resulting pattern, therefore, represents a broader interpretation of these parties' commitments to Green ideals based upon ideological frameworks, as well as a significant period of Green party experience. Although the Green parties have undoubtedly reassessed the requirements of a political party, as this book demonstrates, it remains inaccurate to claim that they no longer represent a distinctive party family with a 'new politics' focus. Although more pragmatic in their overall approach, the Greens continue to act in ways that are different from conventional political parties and continue to seek alternative approaches to the political process. The Green parties have been faced with the challenge of developing an effective political role through which to represent Green politics, within the competitive European party systems. In doing so, Green party evolution has centred upon a process of adaptation, based upon balancing the specific characteristics of what it means to be 'Green' with the pressures faced by all small political parties who function within a competitive party-political environment. How they continue to develop this balance will shape the impact of the Greens in years to come.

References

Affigne, A D (1990) 'Environmental Crisis, Green Party Power: Chernobyl and the Swedish Greens' in W Rüdig (ed) *Green Politics One*. Edinburgh, Edinburgh University Press, pp115–152

Affigne, A D (1992) 'Ecology Parties in Crisis: Swedish Greens and the Fall from Parliament 1991'. Paper presented at the 1992 Annual Meeting of the Political Science Association, September

Arter, D (1994) 'The War of the Roses: Conflict and Cohesion in the Swedish Social Democratic Party' in D S Bell & E Shaw (eds) *Conflict and Cohesion in Western European Social Democratic Parties*. London, Pinter, pp70–95

Barry, J (1994) 'The Limits of the Shallow and the Deep: Green Politics, Philosophy, and Praxis', *Environmental Politics*, vol 3, no 3 (Autumn), pp369–394

Bell, D S & E Shaw (eds) (1994) *Conflict and Cohesion in Western European Social Democratic Parties*. London, Pinter

Bennie, L et al (1995) 'Green Dimensions: The Ideology of the British Greens' in W Rudig (ed) *Green Politics Three*. Edinburgh, Edinburgh University Press, pp217–239

Bennulf, M (1995a) 'Sweden: The Rise and Fall of Miljöpartiet de Gröna' in C Rootes & D Richardson (eds) *The Green Challenge: The Development of Green Parties in Europe*. London, Routledge, pp128–145

Bennulf, M (1995b) 'The 1994 Election in Sweden: Green or Grey?' *Environmental Politics*, vol 4, no 1, pp114–119

Bennulf, M & S Holmberg (1990) 'The Green Breakthrough in Sweden', *Scandinavian Political Studies*, vol 13, no 2, pp165–184

Berger, S (1972) *Peasants Against Politics*. Cambridge, Harvard University Press

Blondel, J (1968) 'Party Systems and Patterns of Government in Western Democracies', *Canadian Journal of Political Science*, vol 1, pp180–203

Blondel J (1969) *An Introduction to Comparative Government*. London, Weidenfeld and Nicolson

Blondel, J (1990) 'Types of Party System' in P Mair (ed) *The West European Party System*. New York, Oxford University Press, pp302–310

Boy, D (2001) 'An Interim Assessment of the Green Party in Government in France'. Paper presented at ECPR Joint Session of Workshops, Grenoble, April

Budge, I, D Robertson, & D Hearl (1987) *Ideology, Strategy and Party Change: Spatial Analyses of Post-War Election Programmes in 19 Democracies*. Cambridge, Cambridge University Press

Burchell, J (1996) 'No to the European Union: Miljöpartiet's Success in the 1995 European Parliament Elections in Sweden', *Environmental Politics*, vol 5, no 2, pp332–338

Burchell, J (2000) 'Here Come The Greens (Again): The Green Party in Britain During the 1990s', *Environmental Politics*, vol 9, no 3 (Autumn), pp145–150

Burns, J W (1997) 'Party Policy Change: The Case of the Democrats and Taxes, 1956–1968', *Party Politics*, vol 3, no 3, pp513–532

Byrne, T (1994) *Local Government in Britain: Everyone's Guide to How it All Works*, sixth edition. London, Penguin

Carson, R (1962) *Silent Spring*. Harmondsworth, Penguin

Cohen, J L (1985) 'Strategy or Identity: New Theoretical Paradigms and Contemporary Social Movements', *Social Research*, vol 52, no 4, pp663–716

Cole, A (1994) 'La Descente aux Enfers? The French Greens' General Assembly in Lille, 11–13 November 1993', *Environmental Politics*, vol 3, no 2 (Summer), pp318–325

Cole, A & B Doherty (1995) 'France: Pas Comme Les Autres – The French Greens at the Crossroads' in C Rootes & D Richardson (eds) *The Green Challenge: The Development of Green Parties in Europe*. London, Routledge, pp145–165

Dalton, R J (1994) *The Green Rainbow: Environmental Groups in Western Europe*. New Haven and London, Yale University Press

Demker, M (1997) 'Changing Party Ideology: Gaullist Parties Facing Voters, Leaders and Competitors', *Party Politics*, vol 3, no 3, pp407–426

Dobson, A (1990) *Green Political Thought*. London, Unwin Hyman

Doherty, B (1992a) 'The Fundi-Realo Controversy: An Analysis of Four European Green Parties', *Environmental Politics*, vol 1, no 1 (Spring), pp95–120

Doherty, B (1992b) 'The Autumn 1991 Conference of the UK Green Party', *Environmental Politics*, vol 1, no 2, pp292–297

Doherty, B (1994) *Ideology and the Green Parties of Western Europe: A Thematic Analysis with Reference to the Green Parties of Britain,*

France and Germany, 1973–1993. Unpublished PhD thesis. Manchester, University of Manchester

Duverger, M (1954) *Political Parties: Their Organisation and Activity in the Modern State.* Translated by B North & R North. London, Methuen

Eckersley, R (1992) *Environmentalism and Political Theory: Towards an Ecocentric Approach.* London, UCL Press

Einhorn, E S & J Logue (1988) 'Continuity and Change in the Scandinavian Party Systems' in S B Wolinetz (ed) *Parties and Party Systems in Liberal Democracies.* London, Routledge, pp159–202

Evans, G (1993) 'Hard Times for the British Green Party', *Environmental Politics,* vol 2, no 2, pp327–333

Eyerman, R & A Jamison (1991) *Social Movements: A Cognitive Approach.* Oxford, Polity Press

Faucher, F (1996) 'Crisis in the French Ecology Movement'. Paper presented at ECPR Joint Sessions of Workshops, 29 March–3 April

Faucher, F (1997) 'Strategies in Les Verts and the Green Party'. Paper presented at PSA Annual Conference, Belfast, 8–10 April

Frankland, E, G (1995) 'Germany: The Rise, Fall and Recovery of Die Grünen' in C Rootes & D Richardson (eds) *The Green Challenge: The Development of Green Parties in Europe.* London, Routledge, pp23–44

Frankland, E, G (1996) 'The Greens' Comeback in 1994: The Third Party of Germany' in R J Dalton (ed) *Germans Divided.* Oxford, Berg, pp85–108

Frankland, E, G (1998) 'From Protest to Power: The German Greens' Transformation in Germany'. Paper presented at ECPR Joint Sessions of Workshops, Warwick, 23–28 March

Frankland, E, G & D Schoonmaker (1992) *Between Protest and Power: The Green Party in Germany.* Boulder, Westview Press

Gaiter, P J (1991) *The Swedish Green Party: Responses to the Parliamentary Challenge 1988–1990.* Stockholm, International Graduate School

Gladwin, M (1994) 'The Theory and Politics of Contemporary Social Movements', *Politics,* vol 14, no 2, pp59–65

Greze, C (1997) 'Revolution Within the French Greens', EuroGreen Federation, Update@conf.igc.apc.org

Grove-White, R (1991) *The UK's Environmental Movement and UK Political Culture.* Report to EURES, Lancaster, November

Habermas, J (1981) 'New Social Movements.' *Telos* (Autumn)

Hainsworth, P (1990) 'Breaking the Mould: The Greens in the French Party System' in A Cole (ed) *French Political Parties in Transition.* Aldershot, Dartmouth Publishing Co Ltd, pp91–105

Hamilton, M B (1989) *Democratic Socialism in Britain and Sweden.* London, Macmillan

Harmel, R & K Janda (1994) 'An Integrated Theory of Party Goals and Party Change', *Journal of Theoretical Politics*, vol 6, no 3, pp259–287

Harmel, R, U Heo, A Tan & K Janda (1995) 'Performance, Leadership, Factions and Party Change: An Empirical Analysis', *West European Politics*, vol 18, no 1, pp1–33

Harrop, M (1997) 'The Pendulum Swings: The British Election of 1997', *Government and Opposition*, vol 32, no 3 (Summer), pp303–319

HMSO (1990) *This Common Inheritance: Britain's Environmental Strategy.* London, HMSO, CM1200

Hoffman, J (1999) 'From a Party of Young Voters to an Ageing Generation Party? Alliance '90/The Greens After the 1998 Federal Elections', *Environmental Politics,* vol 8, no 3, pp140–146

Holliday, I (1994) 'Dealing in Green Votes: France 1993', *Government and Opposition*, vol 29, no 4, (Winter), pp64–79

Hulsberg, W (1988) *The German Greens: A Social and Political Profile.* London, Verso

Inglehart, R (1979) 'Value Priorities and Socioeconomic Change' in S H Barnes & M Kaase (eds) *Political Action: Mass Participation in Five Western Democracies.* Beverly Hills, Sage

Inglehart, R (1990) 'Values, Ideology and Cognitive Mobilization in New Social Movements' in M Keuchler & R J Dalton (eds) *Challenging the Political Order: New Social and Political Movements in Western Democracies.* Oxford, Polity Press, pp43–66

Jamison, A, R Eyerman & J Cramer (1990) *The Making of the New Environmental Consciousness: A Comparative Study of Environmental Movements in Sweden, Denmark and The Netherlands.* Edinburgh, Edinburgh University Press

Janda, K, R Harmel, C Edens & P Goff (1995) 'Changes in Party Identity: Evidence from Party Manifestos', *Party Politics*, vol 1, no 2, pp171–196

Katz, R S & P Mair (eds) (1994) *How Parties Organize: Change and Adaptation in Party Organizations in Western Democracies.* London, Sage

Kemp, P & D Wall (1990) *A Green Manifesto for the 1990s.* London, Penguin, pp1–36

Kenny, M (1994) 'Ecologism' in R Eccleshall et al (eds) *Political Ideologies: An Introduction*, second edition. London, Routledge, pp218–251

Keuchler, M & R J Dalton (eds) (1990) *Challenging the Political Order: New Social and Political Movements in Western Democracies.* Oxford, Polity Press

Kingdom, J (1991) *Local Government and Politics in Britain*. Hemel Hempstead, Philip Allan

Kitschelt, H (1986) 'Political Opportunity Structures and Political Protest: Anti-Nuclear Movements in Four Democracies', *British Journal of Political Science*, vol 16, no 1, pp57–85

Kitschelt, H (1988a) 'Left Libertarian Parties: Explaining Innovation in Competitive Party Systems', *World Politics*, vol 40, no 2, (January), pp194–234

Kitschelt, H (1988b) 'Organisation and Strategy of Belgian and West German Ecology Parties: A New Dynamic of Party Politics in Western Europe?' *Comparative Politics*, vol 20, pp127–154

Kitschelt, H (1990) 'New Social Movements and the Decline of Party Organisation' in M Keuchler & R J Dalton (eds) *Challenging the Political Order: New Social and Political Movements in Western Democracies*. New York, Oxford University Press, pp179–207

Kitschelt, H (1993) 'The Green Phenomenon in Western Party Systems' in S Kamieniecki (ed) *Environmental Politics in the International Arena: Movements, Parties, Organisations and Policy*. New York, State University of New York Press, pp93–112

Kriesi, H, R Koopmans, J W Dyvendak & M G Giugni (1992) 'New Social Movements and Political Opportunities in Western Europe', *European Journal of Political Research*, vol 22, pp219–244

Kriesi, H, R Koopmans, J W Dyvendak & M G Giugni (1995) *New Social Movements in Western Europe: A Comparative Analysis*. London, UCL Press

Laver, M & W B Hunt (1992) *Policy and Party Competition*. London & New York, Routledge

Lawson, K & P Merkl (eds) (1988) *When Parties Fail: Emerging Alternative Organisations*. Princeton, Princeton University Press

Lindstrom, U (1986) 'The Swedish Elections of 1985', *Electoral Studies*, vol 5, no 1, pp76–78

Lucardie, P (1998) 'Green Parties: A New Type of Party Organisation? Some Preliminary Remarks'. Paper presented at ECPR Joint Sessions of Workshops, University of Warwick, 23–28 March

Mair, P (ed) (1990) *The West European Party System*. New York, Oxford University Press

Mair, P (1991) 'The Electoral Universe of Small Parties in Postwar Western Europe' in G Pridham & F Müller-Rommel (eds) *Small Parties in Western Europe*. London, Sage

Mair, P (1994) 'Party Organizations: From Civil Society to the State' in R S Katz & P Mair (eds) *How Parties Organize: Change and Adaptation in Party Organizations in Western Democracies*. London, Sage, pp1–22

Marcuse, H (1969) *An Essay on Liberation*. London, Penguin

Margetts, H (1997) 'The 1997 British General Election: New Labour, New Britain?' *West European Politics*, vol 20, no 4, pp180–191

Markovits A & P Gorski (1993) *The German Left: Red, Green and Beyond*. New York, Oxford University Press

Meadows, DH, DL Meadows, J Randers & W Behrens III (1972) *The Limits to Growth. A Report for the Club of Rome's Project on the Predicament of Mankind*. New York, Universe

Melucci, A (1985) 'The Symbolic Challenge of Contemporary Movements', *Social Research*, vol 52, no 4, (Winter), pp789–816

Melucci, A (1989) *Nomads of the Present: Social Movements and Individual Needs in Contemporary Society*. London, Hutchinson Radius

Merchant, C (1992) *Radical Ecology: The Search for a Livable World*. New York and London, Routledge

Micheletti, M (1989) 'The Swedish Elections of 1988', *Electoral Studies*, vol 8, no 2, pp169–174

Micheletti, M (1991) 'Swedish Corporatism at a Crossroads: The Impact of New Politics and New Social Movements', *West European Politics*, vol 14, no 3, pp144–165

Müller, W C (1997) 'Inside the Black Box: A Confrontation of Party Executive Behaviour and Theories of Party Organizational Change', *Party Politics*, vol 3, no 3, pp293–314

Müller-Rommel, F (1985) 'The Greens in Western Europe: Similar But Different', *International Political Science Review*, vol 6, no 4, (October), pp483–499

Müller-Rommel, F (ed) (1989) *New Politics in Western Europe: The Rise and Success of Green Parties and Alternative Lists*. Boulder, Colorado and London, Westview Press

Müller-Rommel, F (1990) 'New Political Movements and "New Politics" Parties in Western Europe' in M Keuchler & R J Dalton (eds) *Challenging the Political Order: New Social and Political Movements in Western Democracies*. Oxford, Polity Press, pp209–231

Müller-Rommel, F (1991) 'Small Parties in Comparative Perspective: The State of the Art' in G Pridham & F Müller-Rommel (eds) *Small Parties in Western Europe*. London, Sage, pp1–22

Müller-Rommel, F & T Poguntke (1989) 'The Unharmonious Family: Green Parties in Western Europe' in E Kolinsky (ed) *The Greens in Germany*. Oxford, Berg, pp11–29

Naess, A (1973) 'The Shallow and the Deep, Long Range Ecology Movement: A Summary', *Inquiry*, vol 16, pp265–270

Naess, A (1988) *Ecology, Community and Lifestyle*. Cambridge, Cambridge University Press

Neumann, S (1963) 'Toward a Comparative Study of Political Parties' in H Eckstein & D Apter (eds) *Comparative Politics: A Reader*. New York, Free Press

Norris, P (1997) 'Are We All Green Now? Public Opinion on the Environment in Britain', *Government and Opposition*, vol 32, no 3, (Summer), pp320–339

O'Neill, M (1997) *Green Parties and Political Change in Contemporary Europe: New Politics, Old Predicaments.* Aldershot, Ashgate

Panebianco, A (1988) *Political Parties: Organization and Power.* Cambridge, Cambridge University Press

Papadikis, E (1989) 'Green Issues and Other Parties: Themenklan or New Flexibility' in E Kolinsky (ed) *The Greens in West Germany: Organisation and Policy-Making.* Oxford, Berg, pp61–82

Parkin, S (1996) *A Survey of Power-Sharing by Green Parties in Europe.* Report compiled for Tasmanian Green Party, London

Pierre, J & A Widfeldt (1994) 'Party Organizations in Sweden: Colossus with Feet of Clay or Flexible Pillars of Government' in R S Katz & P Mair (eds) *How Parties Organize: Change and Adaptation in Party Organizations in Western Democracies.* London, Sage, pp332–356

Poguntke, T (1987) 'New Politics and Party Systems: The Emergence of a New Type of Party?' *West European Politics*, vol 10, no 1, (January), pp76–88

Poguntke, T (1989) 'The "New Politics Dimension" in European Green Parties' in F Müller-Rommel (ed) *New Politics in Western Europe: The Rise and Success of Green Parties and Alternative Lists.* Boulder, Colorado and London, Westview Press, pp175–194

Poguntke, T (1993) 'Goodbye to Movement Politics? Organisational Adaptation of the German Green Party', *Environmental Politics*, vol 2, no 3, (Autumn), pp379–403

Poguntke, T (1994) 'Parties in a Legalistic Culture: The Case of Germany' in R S Katz & P Mair (eds) *How Parties Organize: Change and Adaptation in Party Organizations in Western Democracies.* London, Sage, pp185–216

Porritt, J (1984) Interview in *Marxism Today*, March

Prendiville, B (1989) 'France: "Les Verts"' in F Müller-Rommel (ed) *New Politics in Western Europe: The Rise and Success of Green Parties and Alternative Lists.* Boulder, Colorado and London, Westview Press, pp87–100

Prendiville, B (1994) *Environmental Politics in France.* Colorado, Westview Press

Pridham, G & F Müller-Rommel (eds) (1991) *Small Parties in Western Europe.* London, Sage

Ragin, C C (1987) *The Comparative Method: Moving Beyond Qualitative and Quantitative Strategies.* Berkeley, University of California Press

Rhodes, M (1995) 'Italy: Greens in an Overcrowded Political System' in C Rootes & D Richardson (eds) *The Green Challenge: The Development of Green Parties in Europe.* London, Routledge, pp168–192

Richardson, D (1995) 'The Green Challenge: Philosophical, Programmatic and Electoral Considerations' in C Rootes & D Richardson (eds) *The Green Challenge: The Development of Green Parties in Europe.* London, Routledge, pp4–22

Rihoux, B (1998) 'Does Success Imply Organisational Rationalisation? An Empirical Exploration of Green Parties in Established Liberal Democracies, 1972–1997'. Paper presented at ECPR Joint Sessions of Workshops, University of Warwick, 23–28 March

Roberts, G K (1995) 'Developments in the German Green Party: 1992–1995', *Environmental Politics*, vol 4, no 4, (Winter), pp247–252

Roberts, G K (1999) 'Developments in the German Green Party: 1995–1999', *Environmental Politics,* vol 8, no 3, pp147–152

Robinson, M (1992) *The Greening of British Party Politics.* Manchester, Manchester University Press

Rootes, C A (1995) 'Environmental Consciousness, Institutional Structures and Political Competition in the Formation and Development of Green Parties' in C Rootes & D Richardson (eds) *The Green Challenge: The Development of Green Parties in Europe.* London, Routledge, pp232–252

Rootes, C A (1997) 'Shaping Collective Action: Structure, Contingency and Knowledge' in R Edmondson (ed) *The Political Context of Collective Action.* London and New York, Routledge

Rootes, C A & D Richardson (eds) (1995) *The Green Challenge: The Development of Green Parties in Europe.* London, Routledge

Rose, R & T T Mackie (1988) 'Do Parties Persist or Fail? The Big Trade-Off Facing Organizations' in K Lawson & P H Merkl (eds) *When Parties Fail: Emerging Alternative Organizations.* Princeton, Princeton University Press, pp533–558

Rüdig, W (1990) 'Explaining Green Party Development', *Strathclyde Papers on Government and Politics*, no 71

Ruin, O (1983) 'The 1982 Swedish Election: The Re-Emergence of an Old Pattern in a New Situation', *Electoral Studies,* vol 2, no 2, pp166–171

Sartori, G (1976) *Parties and Party Systems: A Framework for Analysis.* Cambridge, Cambridge University Press

Schonfeld, W R (1983) 'Political Parties: The Functional Approach and the Structural Alternative', *Comparative Politics*, vol 15, no 4, pp477–500

Schoonmaker, D (1989) 'The Challenge of the Greens to the West German Party System' in E Kolinsky (ed) *The Greens in West Germany: Organization and Policy Making.* Oxford, Berg

Shaw, E (1994) 'Conflict and Cohesion in the British Labour Party' in D S Bell & E Shaw (eds) *Conflict and Cohesion in Western European Social Democratic Parties.* London, Pinter, pp151–167

Shull, T (1999) *Redefining Red and Green: Ideology and Strategy in European Political Ecology.* New York, State University of New York Press

Smith, G (1990) 'Stages of European Development: Electoral Change and System Adaptation' in D Urwin & W E Paterson (eds) *Politics in Western Europe Today: Perspectives, Policies and Problems Since 1980.* New York, Longman, pp251–269

Smith, G (1991) 'In Search of Small Parties: Problems of Definition, Classification and Significance' in G Pridham & F Müller-Rommel (eds) *Small Parties in Western Europe.* London, Sage

Szarka, J (1997) 'Snatching Defeat from the Jaws of Victory: The French Parliamentary Elections of 25 May and 1 June 1997', *West European Politics*, vol 20, no 4, (October), pp192–199

Taggart, P (1996) *The New Populism and the New Politics: New Protest Parties in Sweden in a Comparative Perspective.* Basingstoke, Macmillan

Tarrow, S (1991) 'Comparing Social Movement Participation in Western Europe and the United States: Problems, Uses and a Proposal for Synthesis' in D Rucht (ed) *Research on Social Movements: The State of the Art in Western Europe and the USA.* Boulder, Colorado, Westview Press, pp392–420

Tarrow, S (1995) 'States and Opportunities: The Political Structuring of Social Movements' in J McCarthy, D McAdam & M N Zald (eds) *Opportunities, Mobilizing Structures and Framing: Comparative Applications of Contemporary Movement Theory.* London, Cambridge University Press

Touraine, A (1985) 'An Introduction to the Study of Social Movements', *Social Research*, vol 52, no 4, (Winter), pp749–787

Vedung, E (1988) 'The Swedish Five-Party Syndrome and the Environmentalists' in K Lawson, & P Merkl (eds) *When Parties Fail: Emerging Alternative Organisations.* Princeton, Princeton University Press, pp76–109

Vedung, E (1989) 'Sweden: The Miljöpartiet de Gröna' in F Müller-Rommel (ed) *New Politics in Western Europe: The Rise and Success of Green Parties and Alternative Lists.* London, Westview Press, pp139–153

Vedung, E (1991) 'The Formation of Green Parties: Environmentalism, State Response, and Political Entrepreneurship' in J Hansen (ed) *Environmental Concerns: An Inter-disciplinary Exercise.* London, Elsevier Science Publishers Ltd, pp257–274

Vincent, A (1992) *Modern Political Ideologies.* Oxford, Blackwell

Vincent, A (1993) 'The Character of Ecology', *Environmental Politics*, vol 2, no 2, (Summer), pp248–276

Wall, D (1994) *Weaving a Bower Against Endless Night: An Illustrated History of the Green Party.* Dyfed, Green Party Publications

Waller, M & M Fennema (eds) (1988) *Communist Parties in Western Europe: Decline or Adaptation?* Oxford, Blackwell

Webb, P D (1994) 'Party Organizational Change in Britain: The Iron Law of Centralization?' in R S Katz & P Mair (eds) *How Parties Organize: Change and Adaptation in Party Organizations in Western Democracies.* London, Sage, pp109–133

Westlake, M (1994) *A Modern Guide to the European Parliament.* London, Pinter

Widfeldt, A (1995) 'The Swedish Parliamentary Elections of 1994', *Electoral Studies*, vol 14, no2, pp206–212

Widfeldt, A (1996) 'The Swedish European Election of 1995', *Electoral Studies*, vol 15, no 1, pp116–119

Wilson, F L (1988) 'When Parties Refuse to Fail: The Case of France' in K Lawson & P H Merkl (eds) *When Parties Fail: Emerging Alternative Organisations.* Princeton, Princeton University Press, pp503–532

Wolinetz, S B (ed) (1988) *Parties and Party Systems in Liberal Democracies.* London, Routledge

Young, S (1992) 'The Different Dimensions of Green Politics', *Environmental Politics,* vol 1, no 1, (Spring), pp9–44

GREEN PARTY PUBLICATIONS

UK

Party Newsletters
EcoNews, 1987–1989
Green Activist, 1990–1993
Green Link, 1993–1998
Green World, 1994–1998

Other Publications
The Green Party (1987) 'General Election Manifesto', London
The Green Party (1989) 'Don't Let Your World Turn Grey: Green Party European Election Manifesto', London
The Green Party (1992) 'New Directions: The Path to a Green Britain Now. General Election Campaign Manifesto', London
The Green Party (1994) 'Manifesto for a Sustainable Society' (updated after 1994 autumn conference), London
The Green Party (1995) 'Constitution of the Green Party', London

The Green Party (1995) 'General Election Strategy', London
The Green Party (1995) Strategy Papers as Passed by GPRC, London, 1993–1995
The Green Party (1997) 'Green Party General Election Manifesto 1997', London
The Green Party (undated) 'The Green Party: A Brief History', London
The Green Party (undated) 'A Green Vision for the 21st Century', London

A selection of party documentation can be found on the Green party website at www.gn.apc.org/greenparty.

Sweden

Publications

Miljöpartiet de Gröna (1989) 'The Green Party of Sweden Party Programme', Stockholm
Miljöpartiet de Gröna (1990) 'The Green Party of Sweden', Stockholm
Miljöpartiet de Gröna (1991) 'Miljöpartiet (the Green party) in the Swedish Parliament', Stockholm
Miljöpartiet de Gröna (1991) 'The Green Party of Sweden: A New Political Dimension', Stockholm
Miljöpartiet de Gröna (1994) 'Green Party of Sweden: Information in English', Stockholm
Miljöpartiet de Gröna (Undated) *'Frågor och svar om EU'*, Stockholm
The *Miljöpartiet de Gröna* website is found at www.mp.se.

France

Party Newsletters

Vert Contact, 1994–1998
Tribune des Verts, *1994–1998*

Other Publications

Les Verts (1993) 'Le Choix de la Vie', Paris
Les Verts (1993) 'Une Europe d'avance: 1989–1994. La Première Législative Verte Française au Parlement Européen', Paris
Les Verts (1994) 'Les Verts à Votre Service', Paris
Les Verts (1994) 'Statuts des Verts: Adoptés par Reférendum le 17 Octobre 1994', Paris
Les Verts (1995) 'Dominique Voynet: "Oser, ca change tout!"', Paris
Les Verts (1995) 'Nucléair – Sortons-en!: Arrêtons définitivement les essais nucléaires', Paris

Les Verts (1996) 'Historique des Verts', Paris
Les Verts (1997) 'Les Verts: Defend the Values of Ecology', Paris
Les Verts (undated) 'Historique de l'Écologie', Paris
Les Verts (undated) 'Écologie: Solidarite Partage', Paris

The *Les Verts* website is found at www.verts.imaginet.fr.

Notes

INTRODUCTION

1 Within the UK there are three distinctive Green parties – namely, the Green party of England and Wales, the Green party of Northern Ireland and the Scottish Green party. The analysis within this study is focused exclusively upon the Green party of England and Wales, and the definition of British Green party is used for simplicity.

2 In the Swedish case, however, translation problems restricted the extent to which this material was easily accessible, although English translations were available for a number of key documents.

CHAPTER 1

1 See, for example, Kitschelt (1988a) and Vedung (1991).

2 The concept of 'resources' in this context extends beyond the traditional notion of land, labour and capital, and includes the mobilization of authority, social status and personal initiative (Eyerman and Jamison, 1991, p25).

3 Marcuse claimed that new social movement activism represented a reaction to consistent attempts by those controlling society to repress and contain libertarian ideals. Protest is focused specifically against capitalist industrial society, and against what is seen as 'the imposition of false values and a false morality' (Marcuse, 1969, p51).

4 It is this change that Inglehart argues can explain why political protest has moved away from protest based on the working class, to protest by the young and relatively affluent (Inglehart, 1979, p311).

5 Melucci claimed that although previous theories aid an understanding of new social movements, they present them as 'subjects endowed with being and purpose' (Melucci, 1989, p25).

6 Of particular note are Rachel Carson's *Silent Spring* (1962) and the *Limits to Growth* report published by the Club of Rome (Meadows et al, 1972).

7 As well as changing attitudes towards continuous economic growth, this policy is identified as having an additional function in that 'sustainability places a more just distribution of resources firmly on the political agenda' (Kenny, 1994, p231).

8 This gives them worth beyond that which is applied to them by humans.

9 Deep Green philosophy contains a close connection with the concept of holism. This perspective maintains an interconnection between all life on Earth. Within such a system, it is impossible to remove or alter one aspect without it having an effect on the overall dynamics of the system itself. The whole, in this case the ecosphere, is seen as greater than the sum of its individual parts. This holistic perspective has a long spiritual tradition running through many cultures.

10 For a more detailed discussion, see Kenny (1994), Vincent (1992) and Eckersley (1992).

11 See, for example, Naess (1973), Eckersley (1992) and Vincent (1993).

12 In particular, Kitschelt's analysis seeks to identify the specific form that new social movement representation has taken within modern electoral systems.

13 The existence of an established and successful left is also identified as a significant factor in enhancing the conditions for new party formation. Left party governments increase the 'rigidity and unresponsiveness of political systems to left-libertarian policy demands' (Kitschelt, 1988a, p234).

14 As an example of this process, Kitschelt cites the experience of the anti-nuclear activists. He claims that initial developments saw these groups attempting to work through the established traditional political parties. However, this policy proved unsuccessful as the anti-nuclear campaigners found that neither Conservative nor Socialist parties would support and represent them. The increasing sense of alienation from the established political institutions, he argues, 'encouraged left-libertarians to resort to the mobilization of anti-nuclear movements in order to advance their agenda' (Kitschelt, 1988a, p219).

15 Kitschelt claims that both have found themselves in conflict with the consequences of economic growth, and respond to tendencies

    in post-industrial society that risk the environment or human life,
    restrain citizen autonomy or undercut a democratic governance
    of social change (Kitschelt, 1988a, p204).

16 Kitschelt defines these parties as 'left' because they oppose
    modern society's emphasis on the market, and seek solidarity and
    equality. They are viewed as 'libertarian' due to their rejection of
    centralized bureaucracies and 'call for individual autonomy,
    participation and the self-governance of centralized communities'
    (Kitschelt, 1988a, p197).

17 He described this ideological stance as 'a general left-wing egali-
    tarian disposition' (Müller-Rommel, 1990, p217).

18 To incorporate these commitments, Poguntke claimed the party
    should be anti-hierarchical, involve the rank-and-file members
    directly in policy decisions, give open access to party meetings
    at all levels, control accumulation of office, and should be pre-
    pared to engage in extra-parliamentary, unconventional forms of
    political action.

19 To this effect he argues that all bar two of the West European
    Green parties can be classified as having a 'new politics' back-
    ground and orientation.

20 See also Kitschelt and Hellemans (1990), who expand upon these
    divisions but focus purely on the Belgian Green parties.

21 Kitschelt focused on only three Green parties in two European
    countries.

22 Fundis are, in this context, described as 'envisioning the Green
    party to offer an overhauled, ecologized Marxism as its strategic
    and ideological base' (Markovits and Gorski 1993, p216).

23 See, for example, O'Neill (1998).

24 As will be outlined in greater detail in later chapters, both Antoine
    Waechter and Dominique Voynet have been perceived as de facto
    leaders of *Les Verts* during the period under investigation here.

25 This is reflected in its seemingly paradoxical position of main-
    taining local party autonomy while pursuing a national electoral
    strategy.

26 Vincent also makes a similar point, claiming that there is 'no
    obvious overlap between the philosophical and political cate-
    gories' (Vincent, 1993, p270).

CHAPTER 2

1   Panebianco also suggests that the development of the party through
    the latter two stages is often directly related to its historical
    origins.

2   Although he suggests that these arenas may vary over time, in nature and quantity, he does identify two arenas which are always relevant – namely, the 'electoral' and 'parliamentary' arenas.

3   Panebianco identifies some important connections between a political party's level of institutionalization and its relationship with its environment, suggesting that the more institutionalized parties can expect to gain greater control over external forces.

4   This 'trade-off' facing parties is identified by Rose and Mackie as a key factor in determining whether they will 'persist' or 'fail'.

5   He claimed that within such systems, although a duality of parties was not always clearly evident, there was almost always 'a duality of tendencies' (cited in Mair (ed), 1990, p288).

6   In a slight expansion of this basic dualism, Duverger also suggests that the division into a number of different types of party can be understood as the result of the 'overlapping' of a number of different dualisms of opinion.

7   Dahl identifies the UK as an example of a two-party system with a high degree of internal party unity, and the US as one with low internal party unity. Within the multiparty classification, Sweden, Norway and The Netherlands are classified as having high internal party unity, while Italy and France provide the examples of low internal party unity (cited in Mair, 1990, p299).

8   Blondel places Germany, Canada, Belgium and Ireland within this classification.

9   Within these 'multiparty dominant' systems, two patterns were evident. A number of countries contained a large Socialist party competing against a divided right. In contrast, the remaining countries contained a strong right-wing party competing against a divided left group. He cites the 'presence of a substantial Communist party' as the explanation for this style of division (Mair, 1990, p310).

10 Although other theorists have taken this numerical analysis still further, for the purposes of this present discussion we can identify Blondel's six-group classification as an adequate example of numerical party systems classification. The six classifications are described as follows:

1   two-party system;
2   two-and-a-half-party system with a small left party;
3   two-and-a-half-party system with a small centre party;
4   multiparty system with a dominant right party;
5   multiparty system with a dominant left party;
6   multiparty system.

11 The other three categorizations focus upon countries with a single relevant party within the party system, and as such have little relevance for this current analysis.

12 The power of the president has also personalized the political arena and increased the influence of the media during campaigning.

13 He cites three key areas that have aided this convergence – namely, the federal structure of government; the independence of parliamentary parties from their extra-parliamentary organization, legally guaranteed within the constitution; and the limitation of public money for political parties (Poguntke, 1994, p187).

14 For voters, he claimed, habit suggests that it is easier to fight for changes within the party or vote for the opposition, rather than vote for a third party.

15 Merkl also tentatively suggested that this pattern is also likely within bipolar systems, although other alternative courses of action are available in this situation.

16 In both of these examples, however, the major parties have often managed to avoid this scenario, at times using it as a weapon to persuade voters to make a clear decision.

17 Bell claims that the influence of factions is related to how endangered the party feels, the nature of party leadership, and the nature of the competitive national environment (Bell and Shaw, 1994, p169).

18 Of particular interest in this respect was the impact of Eurocommunism within the movement during the 1970s and the attempted incorporation of new social movement activists during the latter part of that decade.

19 Mair includes Germany, Austria and the UK within the category of 'large party system'; Sweden and Denmark represent 'small party systems'. The Netherlands and Italy represent 'intermediate systems' and Belgium and France represent examples of 'transitionary systems'.

20 Although mentioned, Green parties do not figure heavily within this study. At the time of analysis, they were a relatively new and developing feature of modern party systems. As many of the classifications identifying 'relevant' small parties focused upon parties that had competed in elections over a stipulated minimum period, Green parties were often eliminated from the analysis.

21 In defining 'high environmental consciousness', Rootes focuses upon the levels of consciousness about environmental deterioration and the consistent ranking of the environment as a salient political issue (Rootes, 1995, p232).

22 In addition, new left parties developed during the 1960s have survived, and fill the political space that might otherwise be available to Green parties.

23 Müller-Rommel does provide a few brief generalizations at the end of the introduction concerning possible roles and functions (Müller-Rommel, 1991, p13).

24 Harmel and Janda define party change in this context as that which 'comes directly from a group decision or from action taken by a person authorized to act for the party in that sphere' (Harmel and Janda, 1994, p275).

25 Ragin (1987), for example, argues that it is possible that apparently different features can have similar effects depending upon the other factors with which they are associated.

26 This approach also reflects Harmel and Janda's argument that while it is impossible to claim that the existence of stimuli will automatically produce change, one can demonstrate that where change occurs within a party, the key factors for change are present.

CHAPTER 3

1 For more details, see Hoffman (1999) and Roberts (1999).
2 See also Tarrow (1991; 1995).
3 Identifying the 'openness' of political input structures is based upon four categories:

- the number of parties, factions and groups articulating demands;
- the balance of power between the executive and legislature;
- the patterns of intermediation between interest groups and the executive; and
- the ability to aggregate demands and build effective policy coalitions.

The capacity to implement policies is based upon three dimensions:

- the centralization of the state apparatus;
- government control over market participants; and
- independence and authority of judiciary in the resolution of political conflict.

4 To reiterate, Sartori defines 'coalition potential' as existing when parties are needed or are put to use in a feasible coalition majority. 'Blackmail potential' is defined as when a party's existence or appearance affects the tactics of party competition and, particularly, when it alters the direction of the competition of the govern-

ing-oriented parties by determining a switch from centripetal to centrifugal competition, either leftward, rightward or in both directions (cited in Mair, 1990, p321).

5   To reiterate, Mair identified four types of party systems within which small parties function:

- 'large party systems', where small parties have no relevant impact;
- 'small party systems', where small parties have an important influence and where the vote for a 'small parties block' is more than 50 per cent;
- 'intermediate systems', where the small parties' vote amounts to around 35 per cent, but where small parties have slightly less influence within the system; and
- 'transitionary systems', where there has been a change from a large to a small party system or vice versa (Mair, 1991, p47).

6   This is a dramatic change from the Fourth Republic, where centre parties dominated the political arena. Under the new system, however, these parties have been completely marginalized.

7   To progress to the second round of voting, a candidate requires at least 12.5 per cent of the vote in the first round, a significant barrier in itself. To actually gain parliamentary representation, however, relies upon other parties advising their supporters on how to vote in the second round of voting.

8   Although there is a role for local government within the system, recent governmental policy has greatly restricted the influence of this level. For more details regarding the changing nature of local government in the UK, see Byrne (1994) and Kingdom (1991).

9   At the forefront of the environmental movement during this early period was the French branch of Friends of the Earth, *Les Amis de la Terre*.

10   Dumont received 1.3 per cent of the vote in the presidential elections.

11   During the 1978 legislative elections a unified environmental movement campaigned as *Collectif 78*. The use of proportional representation for the European elections encouraged environmentalists to continue this process and campaign around one national list. As *Europe–Écologie*, the environmentalists narrowly missed out, gaining 4.5 per cent against a threshold of 5 per cent.

12   Brice Lalonde was among those who criticized the move towards a formal party structure, running a separate environmental list in the 1984 European elections.

13   Antoine Waechter was a doctor in ecology from Alsace who focused upon what he defined as 'organic politics'. The successes in 1986 helped to provide Waechter with a leading role within the party, resulting in his selection as the 1988 presidential candidate. His strategic emphasis upon autonomy and a *'ni gauche, ni droite'* strategy was adopted as party policy and became a cornerstone of *Les Verts'* political approach during the late 1980s.

14   The party achieved 10.6 per cent of the vote, gaining nine MEPs, which constituted the largest environmental group in the European parliament.

15   Lalonde had left the environmental movement after criticizing the process of party formation in 1984, and had proceeded to accept a government post from the PS. With the Socialist's position weakening throughout the 1980s and the success of the environmentalists in 1989, Lalonde decided to create his own environmental party.

16   In 9 of the 21 metropolitan regions, they defeated the Socialists, and in some of these held the balance of power.

17   Competition over environmental issues was not only from traditional parties. The electoral potential of environmental issues encouraged a proliferation of 'Green' candidates. Holliday estimates that in the 577 French constituencies, nearly 1500 candidates claimed some form of ecological affiliation (Holliday, 1994, p72).

18   Only two candidates made it into the second round of voting and both were defeated (Holliday, 1994, p66).

19   Waechter resigned and subsequently created a new organization, *Confédération des Verts Indépendants*.

20   A change of name to the Ecology party in 1975 did little to alter this situation.

21   John Davenport became the first Green councillor in 1976, gaining a seat near Worcester (Wall, 1994, p26). Local elections were also seen as important opportunities to encourage the growth of new local parties.

22   Jonathon Porritt was a leading activist within the Green party during the 1970s and 1980s, before becoming director of Friends of the Earth and cofounder of Forum for the Future.

23   Poor electoral performances served to heighten the demands for this change of approach, where it was argued resources and commitment could be utilized more effectively.

24   The Conservative government was facing mid-term hostility, and the Liberal Democrats and the Labour party were both still in the process of transition after internal changes within both camps.

25   This result represented the highest national vote for any Green party in Europe at that time.

26   Membership figures reached 20,000 in 1990.
27   The party also chose to avoid placing candidates in marginal constituencies where support was likely to be squeezed out by the competition between the major parties. Candidates stood in 84 constituencies out of a total of 651. The total national vote was negligible at 54,912 votes. Only in Stroud did a party candidate achieve more than 5 per cent of the constituency vote (O'Neill, 1997, p312).
28   For example, Sweden created an Environmental Protection Board in 1967 and hosted the first world-wide Environmental Protection Conference in 1972 (Vedung, 1991, p265).
29   The defeat for the anti-nuclear option had much to do with the fact that there were two 'yes' options on the referendum forms. It was claimed that the Social Democrats added an extra section concerning state control onto their 'yes' option, realizing that it would force the Conservatives to write their own 'yes' option and create an unfair contest (see Vedung, 1989). The results appeared to confirm this claim.
30   In addition, a court ruling in 1986 decided that the party had been discriminated against in the 1985 national elections. The outcome was that *Miljöpartiet* were to gain their own listing in public opinion polls.
31   Analysis (see Gaiter, 1991) suggests that *Miljöpartiet* representatives were more active and conscientious than the representatives of other parties. However, this was not translated into tangible policy gains.
32   In 20 cases the party even achieved representation without having campaigned for office (Micheletti, 1989, p170).
33   The final result meant that the Social Democrats could maintain a working majority with the support of the Left Party.
34   For more details on the European election campaign, see Burchell (1996).

CHAPTER 4

1   See, for example, Müller-Rommel (1989; 1990), Doherty (1994), Frankland and Schoonmaker (1992).
2   See, for example, Rihoux (1998) and Poguntke (1993).
3   See Doherty (1992).
4   For more details, see Wall (1994).
5   Merkl (1988) defines a 'hinge' position as one in which a party is able to gain an influential role between parties on the left and right. This situation relies on the two blocs being evenly matched

and not able to control a parliamentary majority without the support of the hinge party.

6   For more details, see Parkin (1996).

7   The Conservative party was not alone in developing an environmental agenda. In 1990 the Labour party unveiled its proposals within a document entitled *An Earthly Chance*. Similarly, the Liberal Democrats unveiled the party's proposals in 1990 with an agenda for environmental action entitled *What Price Our Planet?*

8   In 1992 the Green party had actively campaigned for Cynog Dafis in 1992, but did not do so in 1997. However, it chose not to field any candidate in opposition to Dafis in that constituency.

9   The bill passed in a much diluted format, with most of the credit going to Friends of the Earth and the Liberal Democrats.

10   It is important to note that these figures identify the public declaration of changes to party strategy. While utilizing this as a guide, one must recognize that the process of change may have been developed for significant periods before any public declaration. The positioning on the time lines, therefore, represents a focal point around which to identify factors that might have influenced these processes, rather than a definitive moment at which change took place.

11   The Social Democrat government attempted to introduce a set of 'economic austerity' proposals, but found that it could no longer rely upon the support of the Left Party to pass these measures through the Riksdag.

12   The alternative measures were passed with the support of their traditional allies, the Left Party, again leaving the Greens outside of the two dominant blocs.

13   It has been suggested that the party lost support from Green voters on the centre-right, but was unable to gain any new voters from within either of the parties on the left (see Bennulf, 1995).

14   With opinion polls placing the entente's support at around 15–20 per cent, the impetus to accept this situation was clearly strong.

15   This position had been further enhanced during the election campaign by Rocard's policy of claiming that the Socialist candidates would stand down in favour of better placed Green candidates in the second round of voting, despite no agreement between the two groups that the Socialists should do so.

16   Approximately 61 per cent voted to support the change in strategy direction. In contrast, only 12 per cent voted in support of an alternative strategy paper, which argued that the party should continue to maintain a position of Green autonomy and seek to work predominantly with independent ecologist groups (*Les Verts*, 1993).

17   The accord also consisted of an agreement on specific policy
     proposals and commitments between the two parties, a detailed
     discussion of which will be conducted in Chapter 6.
18   For a more detailed discussion of the coalition experience see Boy
     (2001).

CHAPTER 5

1   See, also, Katz and Mair (1994) and Panebianco (1988).
2   A similar pattern is also evident within research on the Green
    party in the UK and France. See Kemp and Wall (1990) and
    Hainsworth (1990).
3   The initial attempt to pass the motion was in itself an example of
    the discontinuity and animosity which existed within the Green
    party during this time. While the motion was initially passed at the
    conference, it was invalidated due to inquoracy (Wall, 1994, p68).
4   For more details, see Evans (1993) and Wall (1994).
5   For example, the system of speakers proved too confusing for the
    media, and the party's original open conferences were simply
    impractical with a party membership of around 20,000.
6   Activists also suggested that the traditionally consensual nature of
    Swedish politics encourages negotiation to reach an agreed con-
    clusion, rather than relying upon votes that can divide a party.

CHAPTER 6

1   Polls indicated that 62 per cent of West Germans and 81 per cent
    of East Germans identified unemployment as the number one
    political issue (Frankland, 1996, p89).
2   A similar picture emerges within Bennie et al's (1995) analysis of
    the UK Green party. The study identifies two major dimensions
    to Green policy, focused predominantly around the 'social–natural'
    distinction. The first factor is defined as the more traditional
    ecological perspective, 'in which the ecological problematique is
    absolutely paramount and where social concerns play no or a
    marginal role' (Bennie et al, 1995, p228). In contrast, the 'left-
    radical' position focuses less upon the traditional environmental
    issues and concerns, and more upon social and economic con-
    cerns and issues of social justice (Bennie et al, 1995, p228).
3   In attempting to compare changes within the policy sphere over
    time, the analysis must focus upon party manifestos produced

during approximately the same time period. To achieve this, the research must include both national and European election manifestos. While it may be argued that the style and focus of a manifesto for a European parliamentary election may differ significantly from a national election manifesto, these documents provide the most appropriate comparative tools for analysis.

4 Both the Green party and *Miljöpartiet de Gröna* present policy in two main ways, via a detailed party programme and within election manifestos. In the UK, Green party policy is outlined within the 'Manifesto for a Sustainable Society' (MfSS). *Miljöpartiet*'s 'Basic Ideas Programme' represents a similar document, although not as detailed as its UK counterpart, and is revised every two to three years. In both cases these programmes provide an extensive examination of the parties' ideological commitments and policy proposals. There is no prioritizing of concerns or issues within these documents, resulting in very little significant change to either content or style over time. These programmes are far from representative of the style or content of what is presented to the public during elections or other party campaigns. Within *Les Verts,* party policy is based upon election manifestos and the strategic *motion d'orientation* voted upon at the party assembly. The *motion d'orientation* represents the direction of party strategy and policy for the coming year. As such, these documents are more open to fluctuation, depending on the factional balance within the party, and this can sometimes make direct comparisons problematic.

5 The description summarized in this section is outlined in a number of party documents published by *Les Verts*. For more details, see, for example, '*Les Verts – Le Choix de la Vie*' (1993). For an English translation of these values, see the party web page '*Les Verts* – Defend the Values of Ecology' (www.verts.imaginet.fr/ anglais.html).

6 For a more detailed representation of these commitments, see *Miljöpartiet de Gröna* (1988) 'Party Programme' (English translation); *Miljöpartiet* (1992) 'The Green Party of Sweden: a New Political Dimension'. See also the party web page (www.mp.se).

7 For a more detailed presentation of these commitments see the Green party (1995) 'Manifesto for a Sustainable Society'; Green party (1994) 'Welcome to the Green Party'. See also the Green party website (www.gn.apc.org/Greenparty).

8 This is most clearly reflected in the call for a moratorium on nuclear power, and the immediate closure of the *Superphénix* reactor.

9 For more details on the election campaign, see Bennulf (1995).

10 Sources are:

- France: Hainsworth (1990); Prendiville (1994); Westlake (1994); *Les Verts* (1989);
- Sweden: Affigne (1990); Bennulf and Holmberg (1988); Michelletti (1989); *Miljöpartiet de Gröna* (1989);
- the UK: Rootes (1995); the Green party (1989); Westlake (1994).

11 Sources are:

- France: Szarka (1997); Greze (1997); *Les Verts* (1997);
- Sweden: Bennulf (1995); Widfeldt (1995; 1996); *Miljöpartiet de Gröna* (1994);
- the UK: Harrop (1997); Norris (1997); Margetts (1997); the Green party (1997).

Index